The Ernst & Young LLP
Guide to the
IPO Value Journey

The Ernst & Young LLP Guide to the IPO Value Journey

Stephen C. Blowers
Peter H. Griffith
Thomas L. Milan

John Wiley & Sons, Inc.

New York • Chichester • Weinheim • Brisbane • Singapore • Toronto

Published by John Wiley & Sons, Inc.

Published simultaneously in Canada.

Library of Congress Cataloging-in-Publication Data:

The Ernst & Young guide to the IPO value journey / Ernst & Young LLP.
    p.   cm.
  Includes index.
  ISBN 0-471-35233-0 (cloth : alk. paper)
    1. Going public (Securities)—United States.   I. Ernst & Young.
  II. Title: Ernst and Young guide to the IPO value journey.
  III. Title: Guide to the IPO value journey.
  HG4028.S7E76   1999
  658.15'224—dc21   99-26337

Printed in the United States of America.

10 9 8 7 6 5 4 3 2 1

ACKNOWLEDGMENTS

The wealth of experience reflected in this book is the result of contributions from numerous professionals and practices at Ernst & Young. In particular we would like to thank Jeff Blankenship in the SEC practice for his unflagging diligence, as well as Edmund Coulson, Director of the SEC practice, Kevin Virostek at The Center for Strategic Transactions, and Gregory K. Ericksen of the Entrepreneurial Services group for their support. Martin Nissenbaum of Personal Financial Counseling and Susan Mariolle of Tax Human Resource Consulting practice also deserve credit for their efforts. In addition to our internal resources, we would like to extend our gratitude to the NYSE and Nasdaq/Amex for their important contributions. We are also especially appreciative of Tammy Mitchell's writing talents and Diane Mota's and Andrea Mackiewicz's diligence in bringing this project to fruition. Thank you all.

STEPHEN C. BLOWERS, Cincinatti, OH
PETER H. GRIFFITH, Los Angeles, CA
THOMAS L. MILAN, Washington DC

CONTENTS

INTRODUCTION

The number of initial public offerings (IPOs) has exploded from just over 200 in 1990 to more than 600 in 1997, peaking at nearly 900 in 1996. Of the approximately $340 billion raised on Nasdaq through IPOs since 1970, more than 58 percent was raised between 1993 and 1998 (see Exhibit I.1). Despite the initial performance of IPOs, many companies fizzle during the first three years after going public, significantly underperforming the market in both profits and share price (see Exhibit I.2).

Bucking this trend is a fair number of highly successful companies, including such legendary performers as Yahoo!, Lucent Technologies, and Amazon.com. The contrast between the winners and the losers inspired Ernst & Young to undertake an ambitious research project called "Managing the Success of the IPO Transformation Process," which was aimed at identifying the keys to successful IPOs. The results of our study were so illuminating that we decided to incorporate the findings into this book, *The Ernst & Young Guide to the IPO Value Journey*.

As the title suggests, we are looking at the IPO in a broader context—not as an end in itself, but as a milestone in a larger process we call "the IPO journey" or "the value journey." Approaching the IPO as part of a larger transformation process called the Value Journey has been the basis for the work of our Center for Strategic Transactions, an Ernst & Young business advisory resource for CEOs (chief executive officers). Our research clearly shows that highly successful companies tend to treat their IPO as a process, while those that were unsuccessful often treat it as a financing transaction.

This book is a management guide for going public. It contains discussion about how to decide whether an IPO is right for your company and what to expect from the various participants in the IPO process: the Securities and Exchange Commission (SEC), the financial community, the press, and various stakeholders. The IPO process itself is described in detail, together with information about how to work with underwriters, attorneys, auditors, and other advisors.

The reference sections are enriched with our experience and research. We have woven in an explicit discussion of the elements that have proven to be conducive to an outstanding performance, both from the short-term perspective of the market and from the long-term perspective of the company. For the CEO, who is, after all, the spearhead of any IPO venture, we have provided a CEO Overview, which contains an executive sum-

EXHIBIT I.1.   Total dollars raised through initial public offerings, 1969–1998.

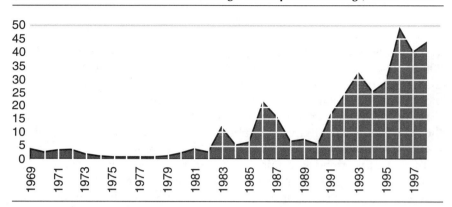

Source: Going Public: The IPO Reporter, based on information supplied by Securities Data Co.

EXHIBIT I.2.   IPO performance relative to overall market performance (NASDAQ).

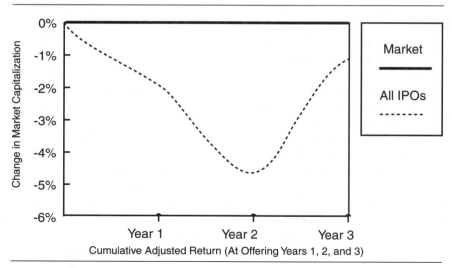

EXHIBIT I.3.   The Value Journey.

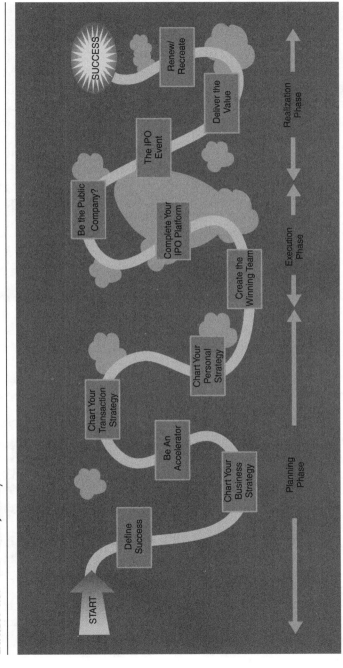

Source: Ernst & Young.

mary of the research results and of the major components of the IPO Value
Journey.

The book is organized according to the major "leadership challenges"
that face the CEO as the company embarks on an IPO Value Journey (see
Exhibit I.3). These leadership challenges arise on every front and have
to be addressed as the CEO navigates the company throughout this exciting
period of growth. Updated technical information is interwoven with this
structure. The chapter-by-chapter outline is as follows:

1. *The CEO's Overview* contains the results of our recent study entitled
   "Managing the Success of the IPO Transformation Process," along
   with an executive summary of the IPO journey. It includes a brief
   discussion of the CEO's role and the factors that separate the highly
   successful from the unsuccessful companies.
2. *The Journey's Early, Vital Steps* describes the planning stage of the
   IPO journey—defining success, charting your business strategy (including basic instructions for preparing a business plan, and becoming an accelerator.
3. *Chart Your Transaction Strategy* considers the need to implement one
   or more strategic transactions, such as acquisitions, alliances, and
   recapitalization. This chapter also discusses the pros and cons of
   becoming a public company, as well as alternative sources of financing.
4. *Chart Your Personal Strategy* outlines the unique personal financial
   opportunities that an IPO event can offer the CEO and other senior
   executives.
5. *Create the Winning Team* describes the various participants in an IPO
   process, with a special discussion of how to elicit better performance
   from your board. This chapter also contains information on compensation strategies, as well as a section on underwriting and working
   with underwriters.
6. *Complete Your IPO Platform* summarizes the steps you should take
   before embarking on an IPO.
7. *Be the Public Company* stresses the importance of acting like a public
   company well before the IPO and describes some of the key legal,
   accounting, and reporting issues you will face during and after the
   IPO event.
8. *The IPO Event* includes the road show, investor relations, the registration process, simplified registration, exemptions, and the compliance issues associated with being a public company after the
   offering.

9. *Deliver the Value* focuses on initiatives that take place after the IPO. These important initiatives follow through on the promises made in the road show and other communications. This chapter also makes suggestions about how to fulfill the critical need to continuously innovate and renew your company.

The book's appendices are: A. Outline for a Business Plan, B. Selecting a Stock Market, C. Registration Exemptions and Resale Restrictions, D. Overview of the SEC and SEC Rules and Regulations, and E. Simplified Registration under the Small Business Disclosure System.

Readers need to be aware that this book is not meant as a substitute for business advisors, accountants, lawyers, or investment bankers.

1

THE CEO'S OVERVIEW

People tend to think of going public as a goal in and of itself—as the end of the process. It isn't. It's the beginning of a long-term relationship with the public and institutional investors.

Sunhil Wadhwani, CEO, Mastech Corporation

An IPO (initial public offering) can mark a turning point in the life of a company. With this one event, the company can accelerate its growth, launch new products, enter new markets, and attract valuable employees.

Those who consider the IPO as just a short-term financial transaction underestimate its far-reaching impact. Ernst & Young views the IPO as part of the Value Journey, a journey of transformation from a successful private company to a successful public company that continually delivers value to its stakeholders (shareholders, employees, customers, vendors, etc.). The IPO event itself is only one component of this journey. The IPO event generally lasts 90 to 120 days, whereas the Value Journey begins at least a year or two before the IPO and continues well beyond it.

It is up to the CEO (chief executive officer) to anticipate the leadership challenges along the Value Journey and to lead the management team through the major operational, transactional, and people milestones. An IPO places CEOs in an odd position: they are being called on to be the quarterback in a game they may never have played, which means they will need all the leadership qualities they can muster. They will have to be visionary and architect, quarterback and cheerleader, spokesperson and manager.

Above all, they will have to become an evangelist whose fervent vision can motivate a variety of stakeholders and can steer the company toward competitive advantage. Much of the success of an IPO depends on the credibility and trust that the CEO can build—the employees' trust that the CEO will lead them in a beneficial direction and the market's trust that the CEO will deliver on his or her strategic plan.

The Value Journey is littered with land mines. Why do some companies succeed dramatically while others fail? What critical success factors set the CEOs of highly successful companies apart from their peers?

ANATOMY OF A WINNER: THE RESULTS OF THE ERNST & YOUNG STUDY

To identify the keys to a successful IPO, Ernst & Young and researchers at the Harvard University Graduate School of Business launched "Managing the Success of the IPO Transformation Process," the second in a series of *Measures That Matter* research projects. The survey population included senior executives of some 2,500 companies that launched IPOs between January 1, 1986 and August 31, 1996.[1] The response rate exceeded 20 percent (517 responses). Participants were asked to rate the long-term results of their IPO as highly successful, successful, or unsuccessful. These and other survey responses were matched to objective data describing each company's market performance (sales, net earnings, and market capitalization) for three years after the IPO.

The study yielded some strong indicators of the characteristics and practices that are associated with a successful public company. The following description of the survey results is meant to serve as a benchmark for CEOs who are considering a public offering. How does your company measure up?

• *Highly successful companies outperformed the competition before, during, and after the IPO.* Competitive position at the time of the offering was particularly critical. The stronger the firm was before the IPO, the more successful it tended to be after the IPO. Conversely, the risks of going public were higher for those that were less competitive at the start.

The highly successful companies were significantly stronger than their public competitors according to all financial and nonfinancial criteria. As a result, highly successful companies went public with share prices that averaged 20 percent higher than those of unsuccessful companies. In their

[1]Failed and untraceable companies were weeded out. Real estate investment trusts, warrant and unit offerings, non-U.S.-based companies, and penny stocks were not included.

IPOs, highly successful companies had an average market value that was $59 million greater than the market value of unsuccessful companies; three years later, the gap widened to more than $205 million (see Exhibit 1.1).

The average value of highly successful companies doubled during the first three years after the IPO; unsuccessful companies lost an average of 10 percent of their value during the same period.

• *Highly successful companies began to transform themselves into public companies months or years in advance of the IPO.* These companies viewed the IPO as a process rather than as an event. As part of the process, they introduced new approaches and/or system enhancements, executed strategic transactions, and implemented strong communication programs. Fifty-seven percent of the respondents made improvements in their employee incentive programs; these changes were believed to have had a greater impact on the company's subsequent performance than any of the other 17 policies and practices that were cited. Highly successful respondents also tended to be distinguished by improvements in strategic planning, internal controls, financial accounting and reporting, executive compensation, and investor relations policies.

Of the executives who reported successful offerings, 66 percent also revamped their plans for such transactions as acquisitions, recapitalizations, and other financings immediately before or after the IPO.

It is especially important to note that the earlier the change initiatives were put in place, the more likely was the success of the IPO. Those who

EXHIBIT 1.1. The value of success—difference in market value between unsuccessful, successful, and highly successful companies.

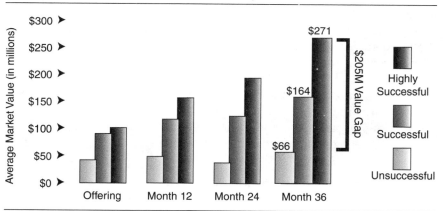

launched such programs a year or more before the offering were much
more likely to achieve success.

• *Nonfinancial success factors are critical.*   The most successful companies ranked high on such nonfinancial measures as the credibility and
the quality of management, retention of employees, customer service, and
the strength of their corporate culture. They tended to be ahead of
competitors in building a winning team, developing an information-based
infrastructure, and drawing on the advice of experienced and objective
business advisors. These efforts won them the attention of the most
successful venture capitalists and underwriters, which further supported
their higher offering prices and a stronger reception from investors (see
Exhibit 1.2).

AN EXECUTIVE SUMMARY OF
THE IPO VALUE JOURNEY

Our study, Managing the Success of the IPO Transformation Process,
strongly corroborates our experience as business advisors: For successful

EXHIBIT 1.2.   Success factors.

Financial Performance	Nonfinancial Performance
Sales	Quality of Management
Profitability	Quality of Products and Services
Return on Assets	Level of Customer Satisfaction
Cash Flow	Strength of Corporate Culture
Sales Growth	Quality of Investor Communication
Income Growth	Effectiveness of Executive Compensation
Market Share	New Product Development Capability
Cost Control	Innovativeness/Research Capability
	Research Productivity
	Strategic Planning
	Strategy Execution
	Management Credibility
	Ability to Attract and Retain Employees
	Quality of Major Processes
	Market Position/Leadership

Superior performance along every one of the eight financial and fifteen nonfinancial
criterial is strongly associated with long-term financial and nonfinancial success.

companies, the IPO was merely a highlight in a value-creating journey that spanned at least three or four years and presented a series of leadership challenges to the CEO.

The following is a brief account of the Value Journey and the leadership challenges that arise at each stage of that journey. Although many of the challenges may not present themselves in any particular order, they should be approached systematically. The challenge "Define Success" is logically first because it becomes the framework for every challenge that follows. The first five leadership challenges typically occur in the planning phase of the Value Journey; the next four occur in the execution phase; and the last two occur in the realization phase that follows the IPO event.

The Value Journey is meant to be used as a scorecard. On some items, you will score high and will not need to implement any changes; other items may indicate gaps you need to fill. It is up to the CEO to meet each leadership challenge with action steps that move the company toward the goal of becoming a successful public company.

Define Success

Your definition of *success* is like a compass that can guide you. Your path will be much clearer because you can align it with what is truly important to you personally and to your company.

Your definition of success should include personal as well as corporate goals, nonfinancial along with financial goals. It is particularly important to define what is important to you as well as what is important to your other important stakeholders. The time frames of various stakeholders will be different (see Exhibit 1.3); for instance, the investment community will define success primarily as short-term returns, whereas employees and customers will be concerned with long-term performance. Such differences may point to decisions that you need to make.

Chart Your Business Strategy

Designing and executing a compelling business strategy are probably the key responsibilities of the CEO. Two parts of this exercise are important: a clear snapshot of your company as it is today and a moving picture of where your company is heading.

EXHIBIT 1.3. Different views of success.

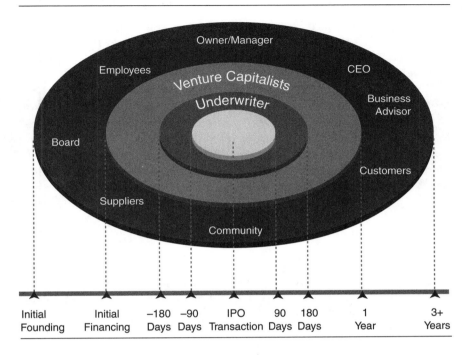

This is the time to prepare a thorough business plan that can serve as your own road map and that can communicate your vision to potential investors and other stakeholders. It is also the time to set priorities and, perhaps, to consider alternatives to a public offering. A natural law of value creation is that all companies are in the process of either growing or dying. Which parts of your company are creating value? Which parts are destroying value? How much time do you have?

It is helpful to think about priorities in terms of (1) the value they create and (2) the ease with which they are implemented. For initiatives that are difficult but create the highest value, you need to have the right resources. At the same time, it makes good sense to pick the low-hanging fruit. A compensation plan is an example of a relatively simple initiative that creates considerable long-term value. The point is to achieve a balance and to stay aligned with the goals you have defined for yourself and your company.

Be An Accelerator

In today's marketplace, speed is a critical differentiator of successful companies. The new economy says that value is driven by being first to market. It's no longer just "big companies beat small ones"; it's also—and more important—fast companies beat slow ones.

Consequently, a CEO needs to find ways to take the business as it is today and accelerate it to a different level. Looking back at your definition of success, which of your goals can you accelerate in the next 12 months? You may want to move faster in developing a new product, penetrating a new market, completing an acquisition, or preparing a compensation plan. What are the factors that enable or that inhibit your acceleration plan? What resources are needed?

Chart Your Transaction Strategy

Internal growth takes a company to a certain level; a transaction can take you to another level. You may want to implement one or more of a number of strategic transactions: acquisition, alliance, divestiture, recapitalization, private financing, and so forth.

Your challenge is to design transaction strategies that will accelerate your goals. Transactions are fraught with risk. We define the *successful transaction* as the right transaction undertaken at the right time in the right way. Many companies initiate an acquisition or an alliance to build critical mass, or they initiate a recapitalization to obtain liquidity. Yet many deals fail because management was not able to realize the value after the deal. For example, although the market generally rewards acquisitions, a full 77 percent of all acquisitions fail to equal or exceed the cost of capital (see Exhibit 1.4).

Chart Your Own Personal Strategy

Oddly enough, many business owners and CEOs are so busy focusing on creating wealth for the company that they neglect their own personal wealth and estate planning. Our research shows that 75 percent of respondents failed to institute a personal financial plan before the IPO.

Timing is everything. After the IPO, the company's assets will have greater value; thus, it behooves executives to plan ahead. You have an

EXHIBIT 1.4. **Company mergers and acquisitions that failed to equal cost of capital.**

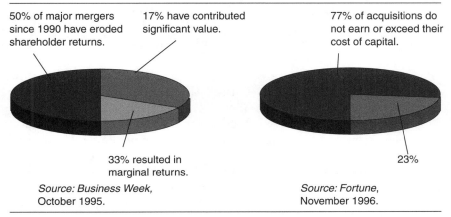

50% of major mergers since 1990 have eroded shareholder returns.

17% have contributed significant value.

77% of acquisitions do not earn or exceed their cost of capital.

33% resulted in marginal returns.

23%

Source: Business Week,
October 1995.

Source: Fortune,
November 1996.

opportunity to create and to transfer wealth, and this opportunity will be diminished substantially by waiting until the eve of a transaction. Neglecting your own financial planning can and does become a source of difficulty in the future. In federal estate taxes alone, the cost of waiting can amount to 55 cents on a dollar.

Create the Winning Team

A public company requires the strongest internal and external teams that it can assemble. Research clearly shows that market analysts and portfolio managers devote considerable attention to the quality of management. Does your present team have the breadth and depth to offer you the support you will need? This is the time to implement performance-measurement systems and to align them with the criteria of analysts who follow your industry. It is also the time to review your compensation plans for key employees so that they are rewarded for achieving your corporate performance goals, profiting from the company's success.

The sooner you choose an underwriter, the better. This person is your major link with the financial community, and it is vital that he or she become an advocate for your company. Remember, however, that the underwriter also represents the interests of investors.

It is also important to choose professional business advisors, including accountants and attorneys with substantial experience in the public capital markets, as well as at least two outside directors. If your outside directors

know you and your company well, they can give you advice that is likely
to strengthen your position.

Complete Your IPO Platform

As a company begins to move out of the planning phase and into the
execution phase of the Value Journey, CEOs often make the common
mistake of beginning to execute their IPO before their company is ready.
This is a time to determine whether all the building blocks are in place.
Particularly important is considering the improvement agenda that you
charted in your business strategy: What are you going to do with the
funds you raise in the IPO and how can you communicate this purpose
to your institutional investors? The best IPOs are made because of a
compelling need for the capital. (At this point, many companies decide
that they can meet their definition of success by a sale—or by some other
transaction—rather than an IPO.)

Be the Public Company

The time to learn how to act like a public company is before the IPO.
Otherwise, your good intentions may last for only one quarter. Acting
like a public company involves managing the expectations of investors,
which, in turn, depends on the accuracy of the forecasts in your business
plan. The ability to forecast earnings accurately every quarter is critical
to a successful public company. The public market is not the place to
learn this process. You also have to learn to communicate regularly and
strategically with all key stakeholders.

Let a research analyst from your investment bank help you find out
which companies the market will regard as comparable to yours so you
can use them as benchmarks. Finally, during the period just before the
public offering, make sure your capital structure can withstand the
inevitable surprises that occur in the public markets.

The IPO Event

A major challenge to the CEO is the 90-to-120-day period when you
tell your story to the world in your IPO prospectus and road show.

Prospective investors and potential members of the underwriting syndicate will be looking directly to you and your senior management team for the company's story. There will be many internal and external demands. You will need to control the process, managing whatever conflicts might arise—and manage your business at the same time.

It is particularly important that all your senior executives articulate a consistent story. The market will consider any internal inconsistencies as a strike against management. Communication skills are key because this is the time to build credibility. It will be helpful to establish a structure for clearing all communications through a central source.

Deliver the Value

The IPO event is only the beginning. You have made promises to many different stakeholders, including investors, analysts, employees, customers, and the board. Now is the time to meet those expectations, and preferably to exceed them—quarter after quarter. Keep in mind that many investors have a very short attention span. It is not easy to recover if you miss your forecast even for one quarter.

Your challenge is to continue to execute your business plan, just as you did when you were a private company. At the same time, you have to manage investors, whose definition of *long-term* is, "What are you going to do in the next quarter?"

Renew and Re-create

Mike Bigham, CEO of Coulter Pharmaceuticals, has compared this leadership challenge to reaching the summit of a steep hill and then finding Mount Everest on the other side. Not only must you maintain the momentum you have achieved and continue to exceed market expectations, you also must update your vision, create a new set of milestones, and remain innovative and fast growing. Consider yourself to be back at the beginning of the Value Journey, updating your goals and strategic plan and continuing to accelerate, while also building the infrastructure and management practices that a mature public company requires.

NEXT STEPS

In this chapter, we outlined the key findings of our research concerning the characteristics that distinguish highly successful companies. The results clearly show that the most successful companies regard their IPO as part of a long-term process. Accordingly, this book takes as its starting point the perspective of the IPO as a critical event in a larger process that we call the Value Journey.

We have briefly described the major leadership challenges that CEOs face when they embark on an IPO journey. In the next chapter, The Journey's Early, Vital Steps, we will consider in greater detail some of the leadership challenges that typically occur in the planning stage of the Value Journey.

2

THE JOURNEY'S EARLY, VITAL STEPS

It takes twenty years to make an overnight success.

Eddie Cantor, comedian

Success generally depends upon knowing how long it takes to succeed.

Montesquieu, Eighteenth century French philosopher

Our research indicates that the most common mistake of new public companies is to rush into their IPO (initial public offering) Value Journey just 90 or 120 days before the event. These are too often the companies whose results fizzle soon after the IPO. No wonder. It would be dangerous to attempt to climb a mountain without the proper equipment, a support team, and physical training. Like mountain climbing, an IPO is an arduous journey that requires extensive preparation.

We cannot overemphasize the importance of preparation. In the wake of an IPO, the CEO (chief executive officer) and other key executives experience dramatic changes in their daily lives. They face an escalation of responsibility, visibility, and legal requirements. New stakeholders will clamor for the CEO's time and attention. Almost half of the CEOs in our survey (47 percent) considered themselves ill prepared for the IPO. As might be expected, a larger proportion of the CEOs of the unsuccessful companies considered themselves ill prepared (62 percent); nevertheless, a full 34 percent of the highly successful CEOs rated themselves ill prepared.

Our research also shows that companies reporting highly successful

IPOs typically started behaving like public companies more than a year in advance. These companies put in place a variety of programs, policies, and strategic transactions to support their objectives. For example, they often upgraded their financial reporting and budgeting systems, installed or augmented their board of directors, crafted and executed communication strategies, and/or acquired a company to achieve critical mass.

It is important to place the planning phase of the IPO Value Journey in perspective: You are planning not just for a successful event or transaction, but for a continuously successful company. The first steps in the journey are to define success, to chart your business strategy in a formal business plan, and to be an accelerator.

DEFINE SUCCESS

The first step in an IPO Value Journey should be a careful exercise in defining *success*. Your definition of success can become your road map for the IPO Value Journey, reminding you of the right direction when you are uncertain or when you are veering off track.

Though defining success sounds like a very obvious thing to do, it is not. Many CEOs have reported to us in retrospect that they did not spend nearly enough time defining success for themselves. A definition of success is personal. Nobody else's definition is likely to coincide exactly with yours. Some CEOs care most about leaving a legacy. Others value the relationship between work and family goals, or their role in the community or the marketplace. One CEO focused on the personal financial planning issues of individual members of the management team. Another looked forward to a positive response from investors about the company to which he had devoted his life's work.

Taking the time to define success can save you from expensive detours. At one point, Tom Waite, CEO of Gateway 2000, wasted time and money exploring the sale of his company to Compaq, only to realize that autonomy and the perpetuation of the corporate culture he had built were more important to him than a sale. Similarly, the CEO of a major airline considered taking the company private so that he could earn himself an enormous profit before he came to realize that the well-being of his employees was an even higher priority in his definition of success.

So step back and take a look. What are you trying to do with this business? Why are you considering the option of going to the public markets? What is really important to *you*?

We suggest that your definition be multidimensional—embracing financial, nonfinancial, corporate, and personal goals (see Exhibit 2.1). When we ask CEOs to define success, they frequently do not mention money first. They will stress such nonfinancial accomplishments as creating a new market or providing security for the family. You may find it relatively easy to think about success in the context of the company. Just as important, however, are your own personal success factors: Why are you doing this? What makes you get up in the morning? Many CEOs nurture personal objectives such as spending more time with their families, playing golf, or having more fun.

The process of defining success does not stop with the CEO. Once you have defined success for yourself, it will be very useful to compare your definition with those of your most important stakeholders. You will find that the board, the venture capitalists, new investors, employees, and customers all have differing definitions. As you increase the number of stakeholders by going public, it becomes important to think about what is motivating these other groups as well. Such an exercise can help you align all the relevant interests more closely with your own.

CHART YOUR BUSINESS STRATEGY

Designing and executing a compelling strategic plan is widely regarded as the central responsibility of the CEO. There are three logical parts to your strategic plan: (1) where you are today, (2) where you are going with your business, and (3) how you will get there.

EXHIBIT 2.1.   A sample success grid.

	Nonfinancial	Financial
Corporate	• A risk-positive culture • Good citizenship • Opportunities for advancement for employees	• $600 million in sales by 2000 • 25% annual growth • Maintain cash flow • 10% return on investment (ROI)
Personal	• Passion for excellence • Having fun • Credibility • Life balance	• Long-term wealth accumulation • Funding for future tuition bills • Estate planning

A strategic plan should also contain your operating and strategic priorities. Setting your priorities is particularly important, and it must be viewed in the context of creating value. As mentioned previously, it is a natural law of value creation that all businesses are in the process of either growing or dying. You might want to start setting priorities by asking yourself the following questions: Which parts of your business are growing? Which are dying? How fast is each business growing or dying, and what should you do to move the process along?

Your ultimate goal of creating value can be viewed on several levels. Value can be measured as the value of your assets, including fixed assets, intangible assets, working capital, and intellectual capital. It can be measured by the value of your business design or by how you choose to organize those assets. Are you adding value with an innovative business design like that of a Starbucks or an Amazon.com?

The value of a public company is also measured according to the perceptions of stockholders and analysts. Being a public company involves managing those perceptions by maintaining the stockholders' and analysts' trust and your credibility. Part of that process is being sure that all your key executives agree about your priorities. Inconsistent communication can damage the value of your stock.

One way of organizing your priorities is to chart them in two ways: (1) along a continuum from low-value potential to high-value potential and (2) along a continuum from easy implementation to more difficult implementation. You should always try to take full advantage of any high-value efforts that are easier to implement, such as a compensation plan. If you want to tackle any difficult initiatives that create high value, you must dedicate considerable resources to these initiatives.

Finally, a strategic plan is a living document. Particularly in these fast-changing times, you will surely have to redefine the plan from time to time. A world-class leader is one who is able to adapt, which implies an ability to remove any barriers to change.

The Many Uses of a Business Plan

Whether you decide to go public or to pursue alternative financing, you cannot succeed without a sound and fully developed formal business plan. If you decide to go public, you can use your business plan as an invaluable tool to help tell your story to investment bankers and potential investors. A thoroughly prepared business plan can save you time and money by helping you jump-start the preparation of your IPO registration statement.

If you ultimately decide not to go public, your business plan remains a valuable tool. With only slight modifications, you can use the same business plan for the following purposes:

- Setting goals and objectives for the company's performance.
- Evaluating and controlling the company's performance.
- Communicating your message to middle managers, outside directors, suppliers, lenders, and potential investors.

Setting Performance Goals and Objectives.   Many entrepreneurs say that the pressures of the day-to-day management of a company leave them little time for planning. That is unfortunate, because without a formal plan, an owner is like a ship steering through stormy waters without a compass; you run the risk of proceeding blindly through the rapidly changing business environment. Writing a business plan guarantees neither a favorable business environment nor a life without problems. Yet a thoroughly thought-out plan can help a business owner anticipate a crisis situation and deal with it up front. It may even help avoid certain problems altogether.

On the whole, business planning is probably more important to the survival of a small and growing company than it is to a larger, more mature one. In many ways, the business plan for an early-stage company is a first attempt at strategic planning. An entrepreneur can use a business plan as a tool for setting the direction of a company for the next several years, along with the action steps and processes that will move the company toward its goals.

Evaluating Your Performance.   In the heat of daily operations, you may find that taking an objective look at the performance of your business is difficult. Often, the trees you encounter each day obscure your view of the forest in which your company operates. A business plan can be used to develop and document milestones along your path to success. It can provide you and your management team with an objective basis for determining whether the business is heading in the direction of meeting the goals and objectives you have set.

Communicating Your Message.   Your company's story must be told and retold many times to prospective investors, potential and new employees, outside advisors, and potential customers. The climax of your story is the part about the future. The vehicle for telling this story can be your business plan.

Your business plan can communicate your company's distinctive competence to these interested parties. It can show how all the pieces of your company fit together to create a vibrant organization that is capable of meeting its goals and objectives.

A Step-by-Step Guide to Preparing Your Business Plan

Whether you are writing your business plan for the first time or rewriting it for the twentieth time, the following is a tried-and-true process to guide you:

1. *Identify your objectives.* Before you can write a successful business plan, you must determine who will read the plan, what they already know about your company, what they want to know about your company, and how they intend to use the information in the plan. The needs of your target audience must be combined with *your* communication objectives—what you want the reader to know. Once you have identified and resolved any conflicts between what your target audience wants to know and what you want them to know, you are ready to begin preparing a useful business plan.

2. *Outline your business plan.* Once you have identified the objectives for your business plan and you know the areas that you want to emphasize, prepare an outline. The outline can be as general or as detailed as you wish. Typically a detailed outline will be more useful to you as you write your plan.

3. *Review your outline.* Review your outline to identify which areas—depending on your readers and objectives—should be presented in detail and which should be in summary form. Keep in mind that your business plan should describe your company at a fairly high level. You should avoid extremely detailed descriptions in most cases. However, you may be asked to provide detailed support—separately from your business plan—for your statements and assumptions.

4. *Research and write your plan.* It is not necessary to write the plan in the order of the outline. It is often more expedient to start with the easier parts. (While preparing your plan, you can refer to the detailed outline in Appendix A to be certain that you have covered each area thoroughly.)

You will probably find it necessary to research many areas before you have enough information to write about them. Most people begin by collecting historical financial information about their company and/or industry and completing their market research before beginning to write any part of their plan. Even though you may do extensive research before you begin to develop your plan, you may find that additional research is required before you can complete it. You should take the time to complete the required research because many of the assumptions and strategies described in the plan will be based on your findings and analysis.

After you complete the basic financial and market research and analysis, you can prepare initial drafts of prospective financial statements. Your research and analysis will give you a good idea of which strategies will work from a financial perspective before you invest many hours in writing detailed descriptions. As you develop your prospective statements, be certain to keep detailed notes on the assumptions you make. These notes will facilitate preparation of both the footnotes that must accompany the statements and other sections of your business plan.

The *last* element of a business plan, and possibly the most important, is the executive summary. Because it is a summary of the plan, its contents are contingent on the rest of the document, and it cannot be properly written until the other components of the plan are essentially complete.

5. *Have your plan reviewed.* Once you have completed and and looked over a draft of your plan, have someone with business management and strategic planning experience review it for completeness, objectivity, logic, presentation, and effectiveness as a communications tool. Then modify your plan as appropriate based on the reviewer's comments.

6. *Update your plan.* Business plans are living documents and must be periodically updated, or they become useless. As your environment and objectives—and those of your readers—change, update your plan to reflect these changes.

Key Components of a Business Plan

The following are the main components of a business plan. (For a detailed outline, see Appendix A.)

Executive summary. A brief summary (two or three pages) that explains your company's story and why a potential investor should make an investment in your business.

Market analysis. A description of your industry, target markets, competitors, and outlook for the future.

Company description. An overview of your business and the key competencies that differentiate you from your competition.

Marketing and sales strategies. A thorough analysis of your strategies for business growth and for achievement of the sales targets in your forecasts.

Products and services. A description of your products and services from a customer's perspective, highlighting competitive advantages, key information about your product life cycle, and product research and development activities that are key to maintaining your competitive advantage.

Operating techniques and strategies. An overview of your production and service delivery capabilities, describing current advantages and future opportunities for improvement and telling how your delivery of products and services to your customers compares to your competition.

Management and ownership. An overview of your key managers, plans for adding new members to your management team, current ownership and structure, and board of directors.

Financing requirements and expected uses. A summary of your current capital structure, your short- and long-term financing needs, your plan for using the proceeds from new financing sources.

Financial information. Historical financial statements for the past three to five years and forecasts for the next three to five years. (This is the place where all the other components of the business plan come together to show the bottom line: What kind of return can a prospective lender or equity investor expect? What are the key assumptions that drive those expectations, and what are the risks?)

Appendices/Exhibits. An addendum that includes any additional detailed or confidential information that might be useful to readers (e.g., resumes of key managers, product and service marketing brochures, recent articles, material contracts).

BE AN ACCELERATOR

Speed is a critical success factor in today's competitive environment. Fast companies tend to beat slower companies. Our research shows that to be highly successful, a company must enter the IPO ranking ahead of the competition. One invaluable way to do this is to accelerate your business initiatives. When you deliver faster, you eliminate some of the competition while reaping the present value rather than future value.

The CEO of an Internet company created and implemented a very detailed action plan for executing the company's business plan during the year that preceded the IPO as well as the year that followed it. The plan contained specific initiatives and milestones for the company's technical research and development, the integration of a recently merged company (including implementation of new information systems), and a work plan for the IPO itself. This company greatly impressed the investment banking community with its ability to execute the plan, actually meeting many of the technical and integration goals ahead of schedule.

One role the CEO can play is to be the company's accelerator. CEOs of successful companies believe acceleration is both a leadership attribute and a core competency. One benefit of acceleration is an ability to mitigate risks. The risks of a start-up are high in relation to its value. As a company matures, the risk falls and the monetary value rises, creating what is sometimes known as a "comfort zone." If the value flattens and risk increases, the CEO loses sleep and may contemplate selling the company.

For a public company, acceleration is particularly important. Institutional investors and research analysts have a low tolerance for uncertainty. Thus, if you accelerate your strategic plan, you will achieve greater credibility, which typically results in higher multiples. Your credibility is based on how the quality of your company's management is perceived. Before an IPO, a company has limited resources such as time, capital, and people. How you manage those limited resources can make a big difference in the perceived value of the company.

One element that can be well worth accelerating is the release of a new product. Being first to market is often a critical success factor. If you can get there first, you will have a competitive advantage because it is much easier to succeed by filling a customer's need with a new product than by trying to improve on an existing product. More important, perhaps, if you are first to market, investors will perceive you as a winner.

Your business strategy will probably contain many different initiatives, among them the elements that need to be in place to enable the company to go public—revenue and sales systems, compensation plan, employee incentives, internal and external communication plans, and so forth. If you analyze the most critical initiatives, you can decide which ones can be accelerated to move you faster toward your goals.

Acceleration is an initiative in itself. Take time to look at your business plan, and create a separate acceleration plan. Which goals can you accelerate? What actions can you take in the next 12 months to accelerate the attainment of your goals? List the resources you need to achieve this acceleration (capital, people, time, knowledge, etc.), as well as the factors that enable it and the factors that inhibit it. Acceleration requires setting priorities, focusing on key items, and having an action plan.

3

CHART YOUR TRANSACTION STRATEGY

In Chapter 2, we introduced the idea of the CEO (chief executive officer) as the accelerator of the company's success goals. Some of the most powerful tools for accelerating a business are strategic transactions, such as acquisitions, alliances, divestitures, private financings, and IPOs (initial public offerings).

The purpose of any transaction must be to develop the business, its goals, and its strategies for reaching those goals. An IPO is neither more important nor less important than any other transaction. It is merely one in a series of transactions that your company may undertake over time. Nor is an IPO an end in itself; it is a means to an end that should be clearly defined in advance.

As you build your business, there may be times when you need to consider acquiring a company. There will also be times when you need to finance or refinance your business. All transactions require a threefold perspective: You should aim to embark (1) on the right transaction, (2) at the right time, and (3) in the right way. Many companies have faltered by brilliantly executing the wrong transaction or by waiting too long or not long enough to act. Or it may have been that for a variety of reasons, the "postclosing" results did not materialize.

Depending on the goal, some transactions may be more "right" than others. One CEO, who needed to refinance the company's debt and raise more money for its operations, was considering borrowing $50 million. A loan from a bank would have required him to start repaying the debt immediately, but the company did not have the cash flow to do this comfortably. A better strategy for this CEO was a private placement with a cash-rich insurance company that did not require immediate payment.

As important as the rightness of the transaction is the timing of the transaction. This is especially obvious in the IPO market, which is notoriously volatile. The two extremes of the IPO market were particularly dramatic in 1998, the first half of which maintained the high levels of the previous two years, with 272 IPOs raising $24.8 billion. In the second half, however, following the stock market's decline, IPOs slowed considerably to just 124 issues and $18.9 billion.[1]

Even in a strong IPO market, a particular sector may be out of favor. An entrepreneurial insurance company was extremely successful, its stock trading at $80, until an analyst decided that the company's products were uniquely vulnerable to Year 2000 exposure. The stock plummeted.

In approaching an IPO, it is always wise to proceed with a backup plan in mind. Even if your company is well prepared and the market is favorable, the situation may shift by the date of your IPO. You should have the flexibility to take the company public with a two- or three-year window and a plan for a solid alternative.

Assuming you have chosen the right transaction and the right timing, you must still meet the challenge of managing that transaction in the right way. When the deal is closed, it is up to management to realize the benefits that they hoped for when they planned it. Research reveals that an overwhelming 77 percent of acquisitions fail to earn back the cost of capital.[2] Perceived synergies often disappear, as happened in the disastrous instance when Quaker Oats acquired Snapple for $2.43 billion in November 1994, only to be forced to sell it for $300 million in March 1997.

In advance of the IPO itself, CEOs of successful companies typically undertake additional transactions that help them achieve the maximum benefit from their IPO. If you intend to go public—or to undertake any other transaction—part of your strategy must be to enhance your credibility in the marketplace. Two examples of the many different transactions that can potentially add value to an IPO are: (1) an acquisition for the purpose of achieving critical mass, new product development, a distribution channel, or technological sophistication, and (2) a divestiture to align the company's competencies so that industry analysts can understand the business better.

---

[1]*Source:* Securities Data Corporation.
[2]*Fortune,* November 1996.

This chapter is divided into three sections: The first section, "Make Sure an IPO Is the Right Strategy for Your Company," considers the advantages and disadvantages of an IPO. The second, "Transactions That Can Enhance the Value of Your IPO," briefly describes a few types of transactions that can strengthen an IPO. The third, "Summary of Financing Alternatives," presents (in tabular form) the features, advantages, and disadvantages of various forms of financing.

MAKE SURE AN IPO IS THE RIGHT STRATEGY FOR YOUR COMPANY

Going public is not for everyone. The pitfalls are numerous and the stakes are high. Poor market timing or lack of adequate planning and preparation can jeopardize an IPO. The fairy-tale success stories we've all heard about are counterbalanced by many tales of plunging share prices accompanied by litigation conflicts, management shakeouts, and loss of control. Some of the unsuccessful public companies would have failed even as private companies, but others could have avoided disaster by canceling their IPO or just postponing it.

Many CEOs are daunted by the dimensions and rigors of managing a public company—even a successful public company. Is an IPO really the best strategy for you and for your company? To help you decide, in this section we review the benefits and drawbacks (Exhibit 3.1) of going public.[3]

Benefits and Opportunities

The benefits of going public are many and diverse. To determine whether they outweigh the drawbacks, you must evaluate them in the context of personal, shareholder, and corporate objectives. Some of the most attractive benefits include the following:

• *Improved financial condition.* Selling shares to the public brings money that does not have to be repaid, immediately improving the company's financial condition.

---

[3]The considerations discussed here relate mainly to going public with a share offering, but many are equally applicable to IPOs of debt securities.

EXHIBIT 3.1.   Weigh the benefits and drawbacks.

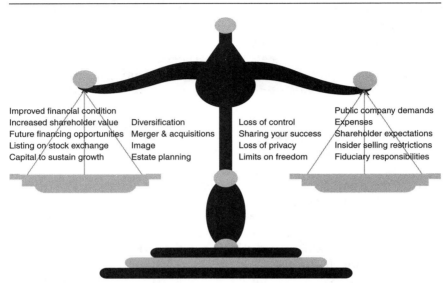

Improved financial condition
Increased shareholder value   Diversification   Loss of control   Public company demands
Future financing opportunities   Merger & acquisitions Sharing your success Expenses
Listing on stock exchange   Image   Loss of privacy   Shareholder expectations
Capital to sustain growth   Estate planning   Limits on freedom   Insider selling restrictions
                                                                              Fiduciary responsibilities

Benefits   IPO?   Drawbacks

• *Increased shareholder value.*   The value of the stock may increase remarkably, starting with the initial offering. Shares that are publicly traded generally command higher prices than those that are not. There are at least three reasons why investors are usually willing to pay more for public companies: (1) the marketability of the shares, (2) the maturity/sophistication attributed to public companies, and (3) the availability of more information.

• *Diversification of shareholder portfolios.*   Going public makes it possible for shareholders to diversify their investment portfolios. IPOs often include a secondary offering (shares owned by existing shareholders) in addition to a primary offering (previously unissued shares). You must ensure that potential investors and shareholders do not perceive the secondary offering as a bailout for existing shareholders. Underwriters frequently restrict the number of shares that can be sold by existing shareholders in a secondary offering.

Before you opt for diversification, you need to decide whether it is an appropriate goal. Spreading investment risk in this way may be as relevant an objective for the shareholders of a private company as it is for an institutional investor. However, many private companies earn returns well in excess of normal investment returns. You need to consider your company's prospects, the degree of inherent risk in your industry, and the return your company's shareholders earn now compared with what they could earn in alternative investments. Diversification may be a good idea, but this is not always the case.

• *Estate planning advantages.*   Going public also helps with estate planning because the liquidity of a shareholder's estate is increased by the sale of shares. Having an existing public market for shares retained also makes it easier for the company to hold future secondary offerings of shares. Should that future secondary offering be precipitated by the death of a major shareholder who is a key member of the management team, however, the offering may not be well received by investors.

The taxable value of a deceased investor's estate can be determined more easily if the shares owned are publicly traded. The value of those shares, moreover, will often be increased by a public market. Executors may be forced to sell a private company to pay estate taxes, whereas they can sell only a portion of the shares in a public company to pay them. Many of the estate tax benefits available to a privately held company also will apply once your company is public.

• *More capital to sustain growth.*   The net proceeds from the sale of shares in a public offering provide working capital for the company— an obvious benefit. The company can use this capital for general corporate purposes or specific projects. For example, it can use the capital to acquire other businesses, to repay debt, to finance research and development projects, and to acquire or modernize production facilities. Another plus is that raising equity capital through a public offering often results in a higher valuation for your company, through a higher multiple of earnings (or price-earnings ratio), as compared with many types of private financing. Thus, it often results in less dilution of ownership than with some other financing alternatives, such as venture capital. Raising capital in this way also avoids the interest costs and cash drain of debt financing.

• *Improved opportunities for future financing.*   By going public, a company usually improves its net worth and builds a larger and broader equity base. The improved debt-to-equity ratio will help you borrow additional funds as needed or reduce your current cost of borrowing. If your stock performs well in the continuing aftermarket, you will be able to raise additional equity capital on favorable terms. With an established market for your stock, you will have the flexibility to offer future investors a whole new range of securities with liquidity and an ascertainable market value.

• *A path to mergers and acquisitions.* Private companies often lack the financial connections and resources to assume an aggressive role in mergers and acquisitions. Well-conceived acquisitions can play a big part in corporate survival and success. A merger can be the route to instant product diversification and quick completion of product lines. It also can provide technical know-how, greater executive depth, economies of scale, improved access to financing, entry into otherwise closed markets, vertical integration of manufacturing operations, and new marketing strength. Going public enhances a company's financing alternatives for acquisitions by adding two vital components to its financial resources: (1) cash derived from the IPO and (2) unissued equity shares that have a ready market.

Public companies often issue stock (instead of paying cash) to acquire other businesses. The owners of an acquisition target may be more willing to accept your company's stock if it is publicly traded. The liquidity provided by the public market affords them greater flexibility—they can more easily sell their shares when it suits their needs or use the shares as collateral for loans.

The public market also assists in valuing the company's shares. If your shares are privately held, you have to estimate their value and hope the owners of the other company will agree; if they don't, you will have to negotiate a fair price. On the other hand, if the shares are publicly traded, the price per share generally is set every day in the stock market where the shares are traded.

• *Enhanced corporate image and increased employee participation.* Your company can improve its corporate image and indirectly strengthen its competitive position by having a public market for its securities. The attention of the financial community and press is focused on your company as it goes public, so you receive free publicity and word-of-mouth advertising from investors, boosting your corporate image. In addition, some of your customers and suppliers may purchase shares in your IPO, which may lead to new loyalties. But more importantly, they may want to do more business with your company!

Once you have established a public market for your shares, you may be better able to attract and retain key employees by offering them stock options, stock purchase plans, and stock appreciation rights. These popular compensation arrangements not only conserve cash and offer tax advantages, but also increase employee motivation and loyalty.

• *Listing on a stock exchange.* A goal of many companies that go public is to be listed on a stock exchange. A listing facilitates trading in your company's stock and fosters public recognition because listed companies are generally more closely watched by the financial press. (An expanded discussion of choosing among the various stock markets is included in Appendix B.)

Drawbacks and Continuing Obligations

The benefits must be weighed against the drawbacks of going public. Here again, you must view the possible drawbacks in the context of your personal, company, and shareholder objectives. In many cases, you can minimize the impact of these drawbacks through thoughtful planning backed by the help of outside advisors.

• *Loss of control.* Depending on the proportion of shares sold to the public, you may be at risk of losing control of your company now or in the future. Retaining at least 51 percent of the shares will ensure control for now, but subsequent offerings and acquisitions may dilute your control. A wide distribution of your shares will ensure that there is no concentration of voting power in a few hands, reducing the immediate threat to your control. Nevertheless, you may still be susceptible to an unfriendly takeover.

However, if the stock is widely distributed, management usually can retain control even if it holds less than 50 percent of the shares. You can also retain voting control by having a new class of common stock with limited voting rights. However, such stock may have limited appeal to investors and may therefore sell for less than ordinary common stock.

• *Sharing your success.*   By contributing their capital, investors share the risk of your business—and they also will share your success. But is their share of your success disproportionate? If you realistically anticipate unusually high earnings in the next two or three years, and you can obtain bank or other financing, you may wish to temporarily defer a public offering. Then, when you do go public, your shares will command a higher price.

• *Loss of privacy.*   Of all the changes that result when a company goes public, perhaps none is more troublesome than the loss of privacy. When your company becomes publicly held, the Securities and Exchange Commission (SEC) requires you to disclose much information about your company—information that private companies don't ordinarily disclose. And some of those disclosures are highly sensitive information: compensation paid to key executives and directors; special incentives for management; and many of the plans and strategies that underlie the company's operations. Although these disclosures need not include every detail of the company's operations, information that could significantly affect investors' decisions must be disclosed. These disclosures rarely harm your business. For the most part, employee compensation and the prices you pay for materials and receive for your products are governed by market forces—not by your disclosed financial results.

As a result of this loss of privacy, some companies feel that they should discontinue special arrangements with key personnel or other related parties that are normal for a private company but that might be misconstrued by outsiders. An example of such an arrangement would be the lease of assets from an entity that is wholly owned by the CEO of the public company.

• *Limits on management's freedom to act.*   By going public, management surrenders some degree of freedom. Whereas the management of a privately held company generally is free to act by itself, the management of a public company must obtain the approval of the board of directors on certain major matters; and on special matters, it must even seek the consent of the shareholders. (Obtaining directors' approval or consent need not be a significant problem. The board of directors, if kept informed on a timely basis, can usually be counted on to understand management's needs, to offer support, and to grant much of the desired flexibility.)

- *The demands of periodic reporting.*   As a public company, you will be subject to the periodic reporting requirements of the SEC. These requirements include quarterly financial reporting (Form 10-Q), annual financial reporting (Form 10-K), prompt reporting of current material events (Form 8-K), and various other reporting requirements, such as those for sales of control shares (shares held by controlling shareholders) and tender offers. The various reporting requirements, which include audited financial statements, usually result in the need for more extensive and more timely financial and other information. This may require improved accounting systems, more accounting staff, and increased use of lawyers, auditors, and other outside advisors. Securities analysts and the financial press also will make demands on your time and that of your executives. In short, some costs of doing business will increase.

- *Initial and ongoing expenses.*   Going public can be costly and will result in a tremendous commitment of management's time and energy. The largest single cost in an IPO is ordinarily the underwriter's discount or commission, which generally ranges from 6 percent to 10 percent of the offering price. In addition, legal and accounting fees, printing costs, the underwriter's out-of-pocket expenses (generally not included in the commission), filing fees, and registrar and transfer agent fees can typically add another $300,000 to $500,000. Costs depend on such factors as the complexity of the registration statement, the extent to which legal counsel must be involved, management's familiarity with the reporting requirements for a public company, and the availability of audited financial statements for recent years. These expenses generally are not deductible for income tax purposes. On the other hand, they also do not affect your reported net income because under generally accepted accounting principles (GAAP), they are treated as part of a capital transaction and thus deducted from the proceeds of the offering.

Beyond the initial offering, there are the continuing costs of the periodic reports and proxy statements filed with regulatory agencies and distributed to shareholders and the increased professional fees paid to attorneys, accountants, registrars, and transfer agents for additional services. The time that management will spend preparing the ongoing reports and statements also must be considered because this responsibility will divert management's attention from managing operations.

The company also may need to upgrade its management and accounting information systems to enable it to maintain adequate financial records and systems of internal accounting controls to meet the accounting provisions of the Foreign Corrupt Practices Act, which are included in the Securities Exchange Act of 1934. Upgraded systems also may be necessary to report timely financial information.

• *Dealing with shareholders' expectations.* Investors generally will expect you to maintain and continually improve your company's performance with respect to measures such as revenue, earnings, growth, and market share. Should the investors become disillusioned with your performance, your share price will suffer. Thus, you may be tempted to try to compromise long-term profitability in the interest of maintaining annual and quarterly reported results. Some shareholders will expect dividends when you believe that the company would be best served by reinvesting earnings. These shareholder pressures are real and must be weighed carefully. But a sound business strategy, adequately disclosed and explained to shareholders, may mitigate any adverse market reaction.

• *Restrictions on selling existing shareholders' shares.* Controlling or major shareholders of a public company are not free to sell their shares at will. The SEC has restrictions on when and how many shares insiders may sell. You must be aware of these restrictions when you plan an IPO and of the number of existing shareholders' shares (secondary offering) to be sold at that time. Additionally, under penalty of civil and criminal law, no one with inside information about your company may trade in its stock before that information becomes public. Other restrictions include the short-swing profit provisions, which require that certain insiders who realize a gain on your stock within six months of its purchase return that gain to the company, whether or not the trading was based on inside information.

• *New fiduciary responsibilities.* As the owner of a private business, the money you invested and risked was your own. As the manager of a public company, the money you invest and risk belongs to the shareholders. You are accountable to them, so you must approach potential conflicts of interest with the utmost caution. It also will be necessary to work with your board of directors to help them discharge their fiduciary responsibilities when acting on corporate matters.

TRANSACTIONS THAT CAN ENHANCE THE VALUE OF YOUR IPO

If you do decide to take your company public, it should be from a position of maximum strength. As we have mentioned, our research shows that the companies that had the most successful IPOs already had attained a superior competitive position at the time of the IPO. Among the elements you should consider in preparing your company for a successful IPO is the potential value you could add by planning one or more strategic transactions.

Your overall transaction strategy is comprised of much more than the IPO itself. Other transactions are useful for a variety of reasons. Not only will a well-planned and executed transaction add value to your IPO, it also will increase your credibility with market analysts and investors. Virtually any successful transaction demonstrates to analysts and institutional investors your ability to plan and execute a complex strategy, thus enhancing your management's credibility. It is well known that the quality of management is a major factor in the investment decisions of institutional investors. Our research shows that nonfinancial criteria—such as quality of management—constitute 35 percent of the investors' decision.

Many of today's transactions can also raise your own level of comfort with the IPO. When you already have interacted with institutional investors in such transactions as a private placement or an acquisition, you will have a more sophisticated understanding of their concerns.

There may be a period of time in which either your company or the IPO market is not quite ready for a public offering. You probably will need capital to sustain your growth in the meantime. *Bridge capital*—financing provided to a company that is expecting to go public within six months to two years—may be the answer. This type of financing is often structured to be repaid from the proceeds of the anticipated public offering. Almost any financing alternative (e.g., private placements) can be used as bridge financing, including venture capital and mezzanine financing in particular.

Whether you use them as bridge financing or as ways of strengthening your competitiveness, there are many creative transactions that can help you enter the IPO market in a stronger position. Among them are acquisitions, venture capital, private placements, mezzanine financing, joint ventures, and recapitalizations.

Acquisitions

There are many reasons for undertaking an acquisition. Your company might want to buy additional product lines, technologies, geographical focus, distribution channels, or manufacturing capacity. A good acquisition can be quicker and more cost effective than building, and it can also add people with expertise that the company needs. In addition to the obvious advantage of efficiencies of scale, there is also an opportunity to diversify the company's risks.

As we have already noted, a successful acquisition can add value to an IPO by increasing the momentum of the company's earnings and revenue, as well as by adding critical mass. It can demonstrate management's aggressiveness and skill, providing the market with evidence of management's credibility.

There are four stages to an acquisition: (1) the planning stage, in which the strategy is developed and targets are identified; (2) the valuation stage; (3) the negotiation stage; and (4) the post-acquisition integration. Although every stage is important, it is the last stage that is most critical and that should be carefully planned during the planning stage.

The most elusive element in an acquisition is making sure that the synergies that were planned come to fruition after the transaction. Many a company has entered into an acquisition with the best of intentions, only to be gravely disappointed in the months and years that follow. The difference between success and failure hinges on a variety of factors, but the critical ones are good professional advice and sound management of the integration of the two companies.

Venture Capital

Because they focus on future potential, venture capital firms often invest in companies that do not qualify for other forms of financing. As a result, venture capital is most appropriate for a fast-growth business with the potential to generate the exceptional returns that venture capitalists expect. However, bear in mind the basic nature of a venture capital relationship: at some point in the future, the venture capitalist supplying the funds will want to harvest, or cash in on, its investment.

Venture capital can take the form of common stock, preferred stock convertible into common stock, or debentures convertible into common stock. Whatever the form of the financial package, it is structured to allow the venture capitalists to liquidate their investment and realize their profits when the investment matures—which they usually expect within five to seven years. Some agreements call for a public offering after a specified number of years or at the venture capitalist's option. Others provide for a management buyout option, and still others result in the company being merged into or purchased by another company.

How active or passive a role the venture capitalists play will vary. Because their investment in the company is predicated on confidence in existing management and on the company's potential, they typically do not take over the company's management. Yet when serving as the lead investor, they closely monitor the company's performance and frequently require board representation, which is often a blessing because venture capitalists generally have the business experience to make a meaningful contribution to the company. Should management fail to perform up to the promised and expected standards, however, venture capitalists generally do not hesitate to move in to protect their investment.

Approaching venture capitalists may require some additional preparation beyond that required for other sources of financing. Recognizing their focus on your particular product or service and their prospective equity stake in its success, you will want to provide detailed plans and projections. Your plan should explicitly specify the amounts and timing of financing requirements, the applications of all such funds, year-by-year (and month-by-month for the first one or two years) sales and profit projections, the projected time frame for completion or maturity of the venture, and the way in which the venture capitalist will liquidate the investment and realize a profit. In preparing for the negotiations, you should also carefully consider how much of the company's equity you and the current shareholders are willing to give up, both now and in the future.

Many venture capital firms concentrate on specific industries or stages of investment, such as bridge financing. The valuable contacts, market expertise, and business strategy they can offer as a result of this specialization can be as important to you as the money they provide, so it is important to find potential investors whose skills, experience, goals, and reputations complement yours.

One of the most critical elements for a successful venture capital relationship is the close alignment of your objectives with those of the venture capitalists. At the very beginning, you must reach agreement on several key aspects: What are the investment objectives? What are the liquidity needs of the business? How much control are you willing to give up? Making sure that your needs are compatible with the venture capitalist's needs is probably the most critical step toward a successful outcome.

Private Placements

Going public may be feasible eventually, but how can your company obtain needed financing now? A *private placement*—selling stock directly to a few private investors instead of the public at large—can be faster and less expensive than a public stock offering. A private placement is *exempt* from the detailed and time-consuming SEC registration requirements. This is a significant advantage because it reduces paperwork, saves time, and costs far less than an IPO. (Appendix C provides an overview of more commonly used registration exemptions.)

Saving time and money for small companies in need of growth capital was exactly what Congress had in mind when it provided for registration exemptions in 1933. The aim was to simplify compliance with securities laws and to make it easier for companies to raise capital. The Small Business Investment Incentive Act of 1980 expanded exempt-offering opportunities, and the resulting changes in SEC regulations have made private placements an increasingly popular method of raising capital.

Although *exemption* is the key word, you have far from a completely free hand. For one thing, while your private placement may be exempt from federal registration, it may not be exempt from registration under state laws. Some states require registration, some do not. Also, private placements are not exempt from the antifraud provisions of the securities laws. This means that you must give potential investors the information that they need to make a well-informed decision about your company. You must exercise meticulous care neither to omit or misstate the facts nor to paint them them in a rosier hue than they deserve.

There are many factors to consider in a private placement, as your attorney or independent accountant will tell you. Broadly defined, the private placement market includes a wide variety of larger corporate finance transactions, including senior and subordinated debt, asset-backed securities, and equity issues. This sophisticated, highly developed market is dominated by institutional investors (including insurance companies, pension funds, and money management funds), larger corporate issuers, and investment bankers or other corporate finance intermediaries. If your company is contemplating a debt financing of $10 million to $15 million or an equity financing of $5 million to $10 million, your financial advisor can help you determine whether the institutional market is a viable alternative.

As privately negotiated transactions, private placements can be designed to meet the specific needs of your company. Debt securities can have amortization schedules tailored to match anticipated cash flow. By attaching warrants or other equity "kickers," you can improve returns on debt securities for investors while not causing any immediate dilution or control implications for current ownership. Equity financing has the advantage of requiring no current servicing, thus conserving the company's cash flow for investment in the business. Creative securities can be structured to minimize the transfer of control to outside investors.

Mezzanine Financing

If your company is beyond the early growth stage but lacks the resources from earnings to fund sales growth or capital projects, *mezzanine financing* may solve your dilemma. Although the term can be used to refer to any private placement of medium-risk capital, mezzanine financing often describes a subordinated debt instrument used by companies with sales of $5 million to $100 million. In addition to a fixed interest rate, the debt comes with warrants to purchase equity in your company—typically between 5 and 15 percent. Therefore, a lender may be willing to provide this type of financing to a company considered too high a risk for conventional debt.

Although the fixed interest rate may be relatively low, the interest combined with the equity provision is designed to give investors a total return that is 25 percent and higher than they would pay for collateralized or other senior debt, but lower than the rate-of-return requirements of a typical venture capital investor.

Also, the mezzanine investor, like the venture capital investor, will want to cash in the investment at some point. Usually, this will be accomplished through a buy-back provision. You must determine whether you will be able to go public or whether you will be otherwise able to fund the buy-back.

Several mezzanine capital funds, structured similarly to venture capital funds, specialize in this stage of capital. A variety of other financial institutions also provide mezzanine financing, including insurance companies, finance companies, and banks.

Joint Ventures and Other Strategic Alliances

Regardless of the label—strategic partnership, strategic alliance, or corporate venture—a collaboration with a larger, financially stronger company can provide you with the resources to meet your goals. A strategic partnership can contribute more than money to your company's success. Depending on your circumstances, your partner also might provide, for example, manufacturing or technological capabilities or marketing agreements giving you access to new or expanded distribution channels, particularly in international markets.

Although almost any structure is possible, a typical strategic partnership involves the sale of a minority interest in your business to a larger company. In addition to equity, your partner may also expect to benefit from your entrepreneurial talent and ability to innovate. The partner might gain access to your technology, add your product to its product line, or profit from a business opportunity you have identified. Because of these benefits, a strategic partner may require a smaller share of your equity than an investor seeking only a financial return on investment.

A minority investment by a larger company is only one way to structure a strategic alliance. Other forms of such alliances include setting up a separate legal entity (joint venture); establishing cooperative arrangements (e.g., to fund research and development or to exploit an idea or strategy); and a variety of cross-licensing or cross-distribution agreements.

Several issues are critical to the success of your strategic partnership. Surveys of corporate partners indicate that the three most common causes of failed alliances are (1) incompatible partners, (2) unrealistic expectations, and (3) ill-defined objectives. In evaluating compatibility, partners should consider management and corporate styles and individual personalities. For example, how can an entrepreneurial partner who is accustomed to quick actions best work with a large firm with a slower, multilayered decision-making process? Where will control be focused, and how will conflicts be resolved?

Both parties should assess their objectives and expectations and communicate them in a formal, written agreement. Issues such as timing, measurement criteria for determining the success of the project or relationship, and alternatives for ending the relationship should be defined up front and quantified to the extent that is possible.

Disappointment sometimes occurs when one partner learns that the other partner might not be the source of the unlimited funding that was initially expected. Here again, quantifiable milestones will help provide more realistic expectations. The ultimate success of a partnership requires compatible economic and strategic goals.

Recapitalizations

Today's private market offers owners great opportunities for recapitalizations. A leveraged recapitalization involves the sale of a substantial part of the company to an outside investor, followed by a borrowing and repurchase of shares from current owners. The owner receives cash and retains a substantial equity stake—(usually from 20 percent to 51 percent, but at least 5 percent). This restructuring of the balance sheet and equity ownership effectively transfers ownership from the current owners to a third party (the "equity sponsor") using funds borrowed from a bank or a private lender. And if properly structured under the accounting rules, a leveraged recapitalization avoids recognition of goodwill and its resulting drag on future earnings.

A recapitalization brings many advantages to the company. It allows management to focus on the operation of the business, and it enhances the company's credibility in the marketplace. It is particularly useful in positioning the company for an IPO by bringing in operational and financial sophistication.

For example, a company might need $30 million from the public market to provide investors with liquidity. Yet taking $30 million in cash from a public offering would not look good to the market. By entering into a leveraged recapitalization in advance of the IPO, the company could borrow the $30 million, use it to pay the existing owners, then make the public offering and use the $30 million raised in the market to repay the debt. This is a typical transaction and one that the market understands and accepts.

FINANCING ALTERNATIVES

Going public is not always the right answer. A wide variety of alternative sources of financing may be available for your company. Which source is best for you will depend on many different factors, including the amount required, when it is required, how long you expect to need it, and when you can repay it, whether you can afford to service it, the stage in your company's development, and your goals and objectives. Exhibit 3.2 is an outline of some financing alternatives for consideration.

EXHIBIT 3.2. Summary of financing alternatives.

Alternative	Terms and Uses	Security	Requirements	Advantages	Disadvantages	Sources
Bank lines of credit or revolving credit	1–3 years; borrowings often float as a percentage of receivables and/or inventory. Seasonal working capital use option.	Unsecured or secured by receivables, inventories, property, plant equipment, fixtures, etc.	Have collateral. Have established sales/earnings record. Have predictable cash flow.	No equity dilution. Support services. Interest deductions. Predictable interest. Flexibility to borrow and repay funds as need dictates.	May need collateral. Leverage can be expensive. Can impede additional financing. Restrictive debt covenants.	Commercial banks. Hybrid lenders. Commercial finance companies.
Revolver/term loan	1–2-year revolver converting to a 2–7-year term loan. Working capital use. Equipment needs. Acquisitions. Expansion.	Unsecured or secured.	Have collateral. Have established sales/earnings record. Have predictable cash flow.	No equity dilution. Support services. Interest deductions. Flexibility to borrow and repay funds. Principal payments at maturity.	May need collateral. Hard to obtain in difficult times. Leverage can be expensive. Can impede additional financing. Restrictive debt covenants.	Commercial banks. Hybrid lenders. Institutional lenders.

EXHIBIT 3.2. *continued.*

Alternative	Terms and Uses	Security	Requirements	Advantages	Disadvantages	Sources
				Provides long-term commitment. Able to package assets purchased over time into a single loan. May be able to renew revolving portion indefinitely, subject to performance.	Prediction of interest may be difficult with floating loan rates.	
Term loan	1–7 years. Equipment needs. Acquisitions. Expansions	Unsecured or secured.	Have collateral. Have established sales/earnings record. Have predictable cash flow.	No equity dilution. Support services. Interest deductions. Interest predictable with interest-rate protection.	May need collateral. Hard to obtain in difficult times. Leverage can be expensive. Can impede additional financing.	Commerical banks. Hybrid lenders. Commercial finance companies. Institutional lenders. Government sources.

| Mortgage note | 7–30-year amortization. 5–7-year maturity. Equipment needs. Real estate purchase. Expansion. | Real estate/equipment. | Have collateral. Have established sales/earnings record. Have predictable cash flow. | No equity dilution. Support services. Interest deductions. Interest predictable with interest-rate protection. Likely fixed rate of interest. Lower repayment terms over longer periods. | May be fixed-rate interest. Repayment over time. | Restrictive debt covenants. Interest rate may be higher. Need collateral. Prepayment penalty on fixed-rate loans possible. | Need collateral. Prepayment penalty on fixed-rate loans possible. | Commercial banks. Commercial finance companies. Institutional lenders. Government sources. |

EXHIBIT 3.2. *continued.*

Alternative	Terms and Uses	Security	Requirements	Advantages	Disadvantages	Sources
Subordinated debt	5–10 years. Working capital use. Equipment needs. Acquisitions. Expansion.	Unsecured.	Subordinated to other senior lenders. Have established sales/earnings record. Have predictable cash flow.	Interest deductions. Interest predictable with interest-rate protection. May be perceived as additional equity by senior lender. May be fixed-rate interest. Lower repayment terms over longer periods.	Possible equity dilution. Hard to obtain in difficult times. Leverage can be expensive. Restrictive debt covenants. Interest rate may be higher.	Commercial banks. Hybrid lenders. Institutional lenders. Public/144A market. Venture capital investment firm.
Asset-based lending	1–3-year contract. Working capital use. Semipermanent working capital. Equipment needs.	Secured. Advance rates vary with industry: • 65–90% of receivables. • 10–60% of inventory.	Have collateral. Have established sales/earnings record. Have predictable cash flow.	No equity dilutions. Support services. Interest deductions. Interest predictable.	Need collateral. Leverage can be expensive. Can impede additional financing. Restrictive debt covenants.	Commercial banks. Commercial finance companies.

48

		50–75% of orderly liquidation value of fixed assets. 50–75% of fair market value of real estate.	Flexibility to borrow and repay funds.	Interest rate may be higher. Lender controls cash.
Leases	Limited to life of asset leased. Equipment needs. Real estate.	Asset leased. Have collateral. Have predictable cash flow.	No equity dilutions. Support services. Interest deductions. Interest predictable. May be fixed-rate interest. Lower repayment terms over life of asset. May not be capitalized.	Need collateral. Interest rate may be higher. Payment may be required at end of lease. Commercial banks. Leasing companies.

49

EXHIBIT 3.2. *continued.*

Alternative	Terms and Uses	Security	Requirements	Advantages	Disadvantages	Sources
Corporate bonds/ debentures	5–30+ years. Permanent working capital use. Equipment needs. Acquisitions. Expansion.	Unsecured.	Established sales/earnings record. Have predictable cash flow. Bond rating may be required.	Support services. Interest deductions. Interest predictable. Lower repayement terms. May be perceived as additional equity. May be fixed-rate interest.	Possible equity dilution. Hard to obtain in difficult times. Leverage can be expensive. Can impede additional financing. Restrictive debt covenants. Interest rate may be higher. Generally not available to smaller companies.	Institutional lenders. Private and public/144A markets.
Franchising	Long term. Working capital use. Equipment needs.	N/A	Developed sound product. Recognizable individuality. Rapid growth of concept. Control over growth.	Immediate cash flow. No need to repay. No equity dilution. Low risk. Limited capital	Costs to franchise. Share profits with franchisee. Requires extensive testing of concept.	Franchisees.

				Advantages	Disadvantages	Sources
			Ability to develop good relationship with franchisees.	requirements. Ability to expand rapidly. Distributes start-up costs to others. Provides long-terms royalty stream.	Legal complexities.	
Venture capital (VC)	5–7 years. Exploiting new products, services, or market niches. Seeking equity capital in leveraged buyout (LBO). Equipment needs. Acquisitions. Expansion.	Equity in company.	Need start-up seed capital with potential for rapid growth. Need early-stage second- or third-round capital, with potential for rapid growth. Established and growing rapidly.	Management and financial expertise from equity investor. Strength of equity (i.e., greater leverage and cash flow). Enables company to mature enough to make public financing feasible. No cash drain for debt repayments or interest and liquidity needs.	Difficult to obtain. Heavy equity dilution. Process is time-consuming and difficult. No assurance of success. VCs have high expectations. VCs require various reports. Management often gives up economic control to VCs.	Individuals ("Angels"). Private venture capital funds. Investment bankers. Government venture funds. Public venture funds. Institutional venture capital pools. SBICs and SSBICs.

4

CHART YOUR PERSONAL STRATEGY

Your company is on a success track, and you and the other founders are the catalysts. In your enthusiasm to take your company public, you need to set aside time to focus on how the IPO will affect your personal financial situation. The IPO presents you with a unique opportunity to preserve and to create wealth because your company's value will increase dramatically. This is the time to minimize your income tax liability and to protect the assets in your estate with careful planning. In a recent survey, an astonishing 75 percent of senior executives surveyed did not have a personal wealth management strategy.

Planning early for the potential IPO should be at the heart of your strategy. You should consider gifting company stock to your heirs and setting up certain types of trusts well in advance of your company going public. By gifting and setting up trusts before going public, you may save considerably on estate and gift taxes. Every dollar of appreciation that you remove from your taxable estate could save you 55 cents in estate taxes.

This chapter examines your options. It briefly discusses how gifting to your heirs and creating partnerships and/or trusts will reduce tax liability and leave you and your family with more capital to spend and invest. The chapter explains how these techniques work and what they can do for you. It also highlights various income tax planning strategies you can put in place to protect your new wealth.

Although this chapter provides useful planning information and makes practical suggestions, we strongly urge you to discuss the important estate and income tax planning issues outlined here with your personal financial advisor, a Certified Public Accountant (CPA), or an estate planning attorney.

EFFECTIVE ESTATE TAX PLANNING BEFORE YOUR COMPANY GOES PUBLIC

The key to successful estate planning involves transferring assets to your beneficiaries so that you realize the least amount of estate or gift tax (often called "transfer tax liability"). One of the most effective ways to accomplish this end is to give away assets that have a low value but that you expect will increase dramatically in value in the future. Stock in a closely held company that may be the subject of a public offering is just that sort of asset.

You are probably aware that a federal estate tax is imposed on your estate when you die. A gift tax is also imposed if you transfer assets of more than $10,000 per person annually while you are alive. Both of these taxes are imposed at the same rate and are cumulative. This means that when you die, all of your previous taxable gifts are added to your estate and the tax is calculated on that amount. These "unified transfer tax" rates range from 18 percent up to 55 percent (see Exhibit 4.1).

To avoid or to limit the amount of tax you and your heirs must pay, you generally want to depress the value of the assets you transfer while you are alive or upon your death. The idea is to freeze the value when you calculate taxes but retain the true economic value.

Transferring your wealth to your beneficiaries or to a favorite charity may involve assets that are difficult to value; therefore, an expert appraisal is a critical element of a successful valuation freeze for transfer tax purposes. An effective appraisal takes advantage of all available discounts and yet will be likely to withstand a challenge by by the Internal Revenue Service (IRS).

Property that trades on an established market can be easily valued. For example, publicly traded stocks and bonds are valued based on the average of the high and the low selling prices on the date of a gift or on your death (or, if your executor chooses, the date six months after your death). However, interests in closely held businesses or partnerships, like your company before it goes public, must generally be appraised by taking into account the business's assets, earning capacity, and other factors.

You are probably familiar with the process of getting a home appraised for purposes of obtaining a mortgage or a home equity loan. It is especially important to have a certified appraiser with expertise in the type of property to be appraised. A CPA, an attorney, or a personal financial

EXHIBIT 4.1. Unified estate and gift tax rates (as of 1999).

1. Taxable transfers over	2. But not over	3. Tentative tax on amount in column 1	4. Rate of tax on excess over amount in column 1
$ 0	$ 10,000	$ 0	18%
10,000	20,000	1,800	20%
20,000	40,000	3,800	22%
40,000	60,000	8,200	24%
60,000	80,000	13,000	26%
80,000	100,000	18,200	28%
100,000	150,000	23,800	30%
150,000	250,000	38,800	32%
250,000	500,000	70,800	34%
500,000	750,000	155,800	37%
750,000	1,000,000	248,300	39%
1,000,000	1,250,000	345,800	41%
1,250,000	1,500,000	448,300	43%
1,500,000	2,000,000	555,800	45%
2,000,000	2,500,000	780,800	49%
2,500,000	3,000,000	1,025,800	53%
3,000,000	———	1,290,800*	55%

*Plus 5 percent of the cumulative transfers in excess of $10,000,000 but not exceeding $21,040,000.

planner can assist in identifying an appropriate person to appraise your company's worth for estate or gift tax valuation purposes.

Estate and Gift Tax Basics

Gifting keeps the value of your estate down and helps to accomplish your goal of keeping the valuation of your estate as low as possible—particularly if your estate is larger than $3 million, and thus subject to a 55 percent tax rate. (There is an additional 5 percent tax on taxable estates larger than $10 million.)

Annual Gift Tax Exclusion. The law allows an annual gift tax exclusion of $10,000 per donee. If you are married, you can elect to use up to a

$20,000 exclusion per donee. So you could give $20,000 worth of stock to each of 10 people every year with no gift tax consequences.

The annual exclusion can be especially useful if the value of the property gifted can be reduced for gift tax purposes. You could give 100 shares of stock worth $100 each, but you could give 200 shares if the value were reduced to $50.

Medical and Educational Expense Exclusions. An unlimited gift tax exclusion applies to the payment of medical and educational expenses for any recipient. This exclusion applies only if the payments are made directly to the medical care provider or to the educational institution. (The exclusion is especially helpful if you would like to help your grandchildren with their private school or college tuition payments. Parents' payments would not be considered "gifts.")

The Marital Deduction. The marital deduction is a feature of both the estate tax and the gift tax. If you are married, you are allowed an unlimited deduction for the value of property transferred to your spouse during your lifetime or at the time of your death. Simply put: You can give or bequeath as much as you want to your spouse, and neither you nor your estate will pay gift or estate tax. The estate tax marital deduction essentially permits you and your spouse to postpone paying estate tax until the second spouse dies.

Because of the unlimited marital deduction, many taxpayers commit the common error of leaving everything to their spouses when they die. This will result in a higher tax when the second spouse dies. It is important, therefore, that each spouse have an amount of *individually owned assets* at least equal to the unified credit equivalent that he or she can leave to someone other than his or her spouse (either directly or through a trust).

Credits. When determining the net amount of federal estate tax due, your estate's personal representative can claim certain credits against your or your estate's tentative tax. The best known credit is the unified estate and gift tax credit. (The credit is called a "unified credit" because it applies against both gift and estate taxes.) In 1999, each person is entitled to a unified credit of $211,300—the amount of tax generated by a transfer of $650,000. The amount of the unified credit equivalent is scheduled to rise in future years as follows:

Year(s)	Unified Credit Equivalent
2000–2001	$ 675,000
2002–2003	700,000
2004	850,000
2005	950,000
2006 or thereafter	1,000,000

Other death tax credits include a state death tax credit, a foreign death tax credit, and a credit for tax on prior transfers. The credit for tax on prior transfers applies to the federal estate tax for part or all of the estate tax paid on property transferred to you before your death or to your estate afterward.[1]

Minimizing Transfer Taxes

The time to save on estate taxes is before the IPO. You can do this in a variety of ways, four of which are:

1. Making outright gifts of stock to your chosen beneficiaries.
2. Setting up a trust or trusts to hold your beneficiaries' stock. (If you do this, your beneficiaries get the management of a trustee and the economic benefits of ownership, without having actual control.)
3. Setting up a Grantor Retained Annuity Trust (GRAT) and transferring stock in exchange for an annuity with the remainder going to your beneficiaries.
4. Establishing a Family Limited Partnership (FLP) with company stock and gifting partnership interests to your beneficiaries.

The first three methods allow the transfer of future appreciation (the premium on the IPO) to your beneficiaries at a relatively low transfer tax cost; the fourth method does the same but also allows the transfer of part of the current value at a low cost.

Deciding on a Method.   Which of the four methods you use is largely subjective. Do you want your beneficiaries to have an interest in the company, or have you and the other shareholders agreed not to share

---

[1]The prior transfer credit applies to transfers from someone who died between 10 years before your death and 2 years after your death.

interest in the company? Do you want to keep your beneficiaries' creditors safely away from the money by putting it in a trust? Or do you prefer a simple gifting arrangement because it's easier for you and because you believe your beneficiaries are fully competent to make their own financial decisions? These are questions that only you can answer.

Trusts. If you decide to take the trust route, your attorney will draft the trust agreement for you. You will then choose a trustee to manage the trust. If you decide to gift company stock directly or through a trust, remember that valuation is crucial. Because you are gifting stock in a closely held company and, because it is generally a minority interest, substantial discounts should be available from the normal appraised value of the stock. These discounts should apply even though the family as a whole may have a controlling interest in the company.

GRATS and FLPs are two of the useful techniques that can be used to minimize transfer taxes. Your professional advisor may be able to suggest others that are effective and use the same general principles.

A *GRAT* is a trust that allows you to transfer a large amount of your company's stock—or an interest in a partnership—to your children at a reduced gift tax cost. The GRAT is very effective for property that is expected to appreciate significantly, which no doubt applies to your IPO stock (see Exhibit 4.2).

To establish a GRAT, you transfer property to a trust for a fixed term of years. During the trust term, you receive a fixed stream of annuity

EXHIBIT 4.2. Grantor retained annuity trust (GRAT).

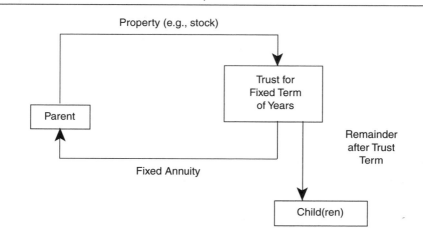

payments. When the term of the GRAT expires, any property remaining in the GRAT passes to your beneficiaries.

A *FLP* is designed specifically as a valuation vehicle. It allows you to transfer ownership of significant assets to family members—typically, children and grandchildren—during your lifetime without having to relinquish control of those assets. A FLP is also an ideal vehicle for dividing assets into portions to facilitate using the $10,000 annual gift tax exclusion and other large gifts. However, to be respected for tax purposes, the FLP must have a bona fide business purpose (e.g., your desire for centralized management of family assets).

Once the funds are transferred by means of a gift of a partnership interest, you have removed a portion of valuable assets from your estate, thus freezing your gift tax and estate tax burden. This protects the assets of the FLP from a "spendthrift" beneficiary and also provides a degree of protection from potential creditors who reach the partnership's underlying assets or who cause a dissolution of the partnership.

INCOME TAX STRATEGIES BEFORE AND DURING THE IPO EVENT

Income taxes will play a major role in the decisions you make when your company goes public. You can minimize those taxes by using legal techniques that allow you to avoid or to defer them. In this section, we will discuss in detail some income tax planning issues, including methods for avoiding the capital gains tax on your sale of stock to the public.

Minimizing Capital Gains Tax by Using a Charitable Remainder Trust

When you sell your company's stock to the public, you are subject to a 20 percent federal capital gains tax on the profit from the sale, in addition to any state and local income taxes. One of the most useful vehicles for avoiding at least part of these capital gains taxes is a Charitable Remainder Trust (CRT).

CRTs allow you to maximize tax savings after selling your company's stock, while contributing a portion of the value of your appreciated stock to your favorite charity and a portion (in the form of an annuity) to yourself or to your noncharitable beneficiaries, like children and grandchildren.

Instead of selling your stock directly, you transfer your stock into a CRT. The trustee then sells the stock, but because the trust is tax exempt, no tax is due at the time of the sale. The pretax proceeds are then reinvested by the trustee. The trust provides that at least annual payments be made to you or to any other designated beneficiary that is not a charity, either over a term not exceeding 20 years or over the lifetime of the beneficiary or beneficiaries. When the term or lifetime interest ends, the charity will have full use of the entire property. You can name a specific charity as the remainder beneficiary when you set up the CRT, or decide later on. You can also name your own private foundation as the beneficiary.

Although actual receipt of the charity's interest is deferred, you receive an immediate income tax deduction for the present value of the interest that passes to charity. Later the trust assets will be included in your taxable estate, but you will receive an estate tax charitable deduction for the value that goes to charity.[2]

Pooled Income Funds

Another form of charitable giving that shares many of the tax effects of a CRT is the Pooled Income Fund, in which donors pool their gifts into a fund that is in turn managed by a charity. The donors receive a pro-rata share of the Pooled Income Fund's earnings for life. After your death, your portion of the fund goes to the charity.

Pooling of funds allows for more diversification of investments than do trusts, making it possible to afford more expert management at a reduced cost. As with a CRT, when the Fund sells the stock, there is no tax liability. The distinction is that the managers of the Fund, rather than the trustee of a trust, retain investment discretion.

Minimizing Income Taxes in the IPO Year

The Charitable Lead Trust. A Charitable Lead Trust (CLT) is to some extent the mirror image of a CRT. It can be used for either estate or income tax planning purposes, and it may generate a large up-front income tax

---

[2]The tax law requires that CRTs be in the form of either a Charitable Remainder Annuity Trust (CRAT) or a Charitable Remainder Unitrust (CRUT). Differences between these two structures are beyond the scope of this chapter.

deduction or a low-taxed transfer to your beneficiaries. If you set up a CLT, the charity gets the income or lead interest, and the remainder interest (i.e., whatever is left in the trust when it terminates) returns to you or passes to beneficiaries of your choice.

If the remainder interest reverts to you, you may claim a current charitable income tax deduction equal to the present value of the income stream. However, the trust income will be included in your income as the charity receives it, and the remainder will be included in your estate. This results in a large income tax deduction in the year you establish the CLT. If the remainder interest passes to beneficiaries other than a charity, there may be no up-front charitable deduction. However, usually the income will not be included in your taxable income, the remainder will not be included in your estate, and the value of the beneficiaries' remainder interest will be low.

Other Tax Deductions.   In your IPO year, you will probably be in the highest tax bracket of your lifetime. Clearly, this is the time to consider taking advantage of as many tax deductions as you can. You may want to accelerate deductions into that year because the value of a deduction is higher the higher your tax bracket. Consider making outright charitable gifts of company stock after the IPO—you get a full-market-value deduction without having to recognize any gain.

Many entrepreneurs will establish a private family foundation or directed gift fund with a company stock contribution. This will allow the benefits of charitable giving to extend to future generations. Also, consider accelerating the payment of other deductible expenses such as investment interest, mortgage interest, real estate and state and local income taxes, and investment expenses.

Other Tax Saving Strategies.   There are numerous other tax saving strategies that you might want to consider and discuss with your advisors, including:

- Investing in tax-exempt securities.
- Generating capital losses to offset the gain realized on the IPO.
- Maximizing the use of tax-deferral vehicles, such as qualified retirement plans, nonqualified deferred compensation, life insurance, and annuities.
- Taking advantage of your children's lower tax brackets.

As with estate planning, the critical consideration is that your planning begin well in advance of the actual IPO. This allows you to structure your tax affairs in a rational and unhurried manner and to avoid or mitigate IRS challenges to the substance of any transactions.

OPTIMIZING YOUR INVESTMENTS

Now that you have converted what was an illiquid asset into cash by selling stock in the public market, a major concern is what to do in terms of reinvesting that cash. Because all investments are subject to some degree of risk and many vary in returns from year to year, how can you be sure to get the return you need with a level of risk you can afford? The answer is to diversify your investments so that you don't put "all your eggs in one basket." If you have gone through an IPO, you probably still have a large position in your company stock. Therefore, you will want to make sure that the cash you have received is diversified out of the company, and perhaps out of that industry or market segment.

You and your financial advisor can see to it that your investments achieve the level of diversity you desire. Choose your money manager carefully. Find out what his or her investment track record is. What type of return does this person typically achieve on the investments he or she makes for other clients? Don't hesitate to ask for references and to check them. Choosing the right money manager for your personal assets is just as important as choosing the right underwriter for your IPO.

CONCLUSION

Perhaps the most important bit of advice to take from this chapter is that your pre-IPO tax and personal financial planning process should begin well before you start your company's IPO planning. If you wait until shortly before going public to set up a GRAT or a FLP or to make outright gifts to beneficiaries, your company will receive a much higher valuation than it would have one year earlier. Generally speaking, a private company's valuation will increase as the date of the IPO approaches because the private company is worth much less than the public company.

Needless to say, higher valuations result in higher gift and transfer taxes for you and your beneficiaries. Even if you take action close to the time of the IPO, early planning will ensure that your results will be more effective.

It is critical for you to place as much importance on your personal financial situation as you do on your company's financial situation and to understand that the decisions you make should reflect your personal values, not someone else's idea of what is appropriate. For example, if you are dedicated to helping the homeless, you may decide to include a homeless shelter as the remainder beneficiary of a charitable trust. Or, if you strongly believe that your children need the advice of a money manager, place your gift to them in a trust so that its management will be overseen by a trustee. No matter what course of action you choose to follow, be sure that you follow the sound, objective advice of your investment and tax consultants.

5

CREATE THE
WINNING TEAM

As you continue your journey of transformation into a public company, your success depends to a great extent on a coordinated team effort. Your winning team includes three major segments: (1) a talented internal group of employees and executives, (2) a strong board of directors, and (3) a quality team of external advisors. A high-impact team will help you design and execute your business strategies and will provide invaluable expertise and support during the IPO process.

The time for creating a winning team is not during the three or four months preceding the public offering; the team needs to be in place and functioning well as far in advance of the IPO as possible. The leadership challenge of lining up a winning team involves reassessing your current team and possibly making additions and changes both in the composition of the team and in the way you manage and reward the team. For example, you will probably want to upgrade your executive compensation program, augment your board of directors and learn to get the most from them, and establish positive, ongoing relationships with underwriters and other investor groups.

In this chapter, we will consider the three major constituents of a winning team. The first section, "Your Internal Team," examines your company's executives and their role in the IPO process. It includes a special subsection on the critical issue of establishing an effective executive compensation program. The second section, "Your Board of Directors," includes the selection and compensation of board members, the structure of the board, and getting the most out of the board. The third section, "Your External Advisory Team," focuses on choosing and managing underwriters, auditors, attorneys, investor relations firm, and even your financial printer.

YOUR INTERNAL TEAM

Your company's executives are your inner circle and one of your most valuable assets. You will depend on their assistance every step of the way in the IPO process as well as during the strategic initiatives that precede going public.

Management represents your company to the financial community. As we have noted, our research shows that nonfinancial criteria—including, specifically, quality of management and the ability to attract and retain talented people—constitute 35 percent of an institutional investor's decision. Thus, you can expect that underwriters and investors alike will be closely assessing the strength of your management team.

The Role of Executive Management

Great demands will be made on management's time before, during, and after the public offering. Management must be prepared for these responsibilities and must be capable of assuming them. Before you embark on this critical part of the Value Journey, you will want to reassess your current executive team. Do they have the breadth and the depth that you need to achieve both short-term and long-term success as a public company? Consider the critical skills, character requirements, and experience of your team and look for gaps you need to fill. For instance, as CEOs contemplate a public offering, they frequently hire a CFO who has experience with a public company.

The difference between the top performer and the average company depends increasingly on the blend of skills at the highest levels. The typical 1970s executive headed a conglomerate; the 1980s leader was a takeover expert, and the 1990s company has been guided not by a single individual but by a balanced management team. At the top level of a successful company heading into the next millennium, there are likely to be two people: a CEO and either a CFO or a COO (chief operating officer) with traits that are different from but complementary to those of the CEO and very different roles.

The CEO would focus on relationships with the whole gamut of external stakeholders. He or she would be a confident, outgoing leader and an enthusiastic spokesperson for the company who is able to bond with the various new stakeholders. On the other hand, the CFO or COO would focus on running the business and on achieving the best possible performance. This individual would have to be comfortable and experienced with both numbers and systems.

These two leaders will spend a great deal of time on the road, particularly during major transactions like an IPO. It is likely that the company would also need another level of management—capable people who could independently manage such operations as production, sales and marketing, finance (controller), and management information systems (MIS). Some of these positions may have to be filled by outsiders and integrated into the company.

We have noted that the 1990s have been the decade of the management team. It is not clear how this trend will be viewed in future years. However, it appears that management teams have been able to bring together fragmented industries; and by making the industries more efficient and productive, these teams are serving shareholders well.

Executive Compensation Strategies for the Winning Team

To attract and to retain a strong management team, you must offer them a competitive and coherent compensation plan. Having the right compensation program is particularly important in today's environment because the market for talented executives is extremely competitive. Private companies face special challenges in developing competitive compensation programs because they cannot offer publicly traded stock, the form of compensation that has received considerable emphasis in the past 10 years.

As a public company, you will have two powerful new elements to add to your company's compensation plans: (1) outright stock grants and (2) stock options. A pre-IPO company has a unique opportunity. The perceived value of your stock may never be greater because of the jump in value that can be expected at the time of the IPO. Therefore, if you use it correctly, your stock may become your most powerful compensation tool for attracting and retaining key employees, thus enhancing company and shareholder value.

Before the IPO, 65 percent of the companies in our research survey made improvements in their executive compensation programs. This is a high-payoff endeavor. Analysts and investors pay considerable attention to the strategic aspects of compensation because it can improve the company's ability to attract and retain talented people while ensuring that compensation is aligned with shareholder interests. Even if your company already has an effective compensation program, you should reexamine it as you prepare for your IPO. You will be well advised to adapt your program to suit your new status as a public company and to use stock-based compensation to your advantage.

Your company's compensation program should be approached like any other major business investment with the goal of maximizing the company's return on investment. The compensation planning process involves careful and informed consideration of shareholder value, accounting rules, tax laws, leading-edge compensation practices, and much more. Many errors and costs can be avoided by consulting high-quality compensation consultants.

As a public company, you will be making compensation decisions in a public arena. In this new environment, you will need to communicate your pay policies not only to employees, but also to regulators, stock exchange officials, investors, and the public at large. Your board of directors—especially your compensation committee—will assume greater responsibility in developing and monitoring your compensation practices. Careful consideration must be given to the advantages and the disadvantages of stock-based arrangements, including the potential dilution impact compared to the concept of owning a "smaller piece of a bigger pie."

Ideally, a company that plans to go public should authorize and reserve a pool of stock in advance, a pool that contains enough to cover all pre-IPO option grants as well as expected grants for two or three years after the IPO. Authorizing the grants in advance sends a clear message internally and externally, helping you manage employee expectations while giving investors the information they need to make decisions regarding the potential dilution impact of the shares that are used for compensation. Planning in advance also eliminates the need to get shareholder approval shortly after the IPO to reserve additional shares for compensation programs.

Leading-Edge Compensation Practices.   Underwriters and analysts prefer a strong element of risk in compensation plans, especially in stock compensation plans. Our research reveals that this preference is borne out by the facts. We compared the compensation programs of the 50 Fortune 500 companies with the highest total return to shareholders to the compensation programs of the 50 Fortune 500 companies with the lowest total return. The result showed a clear correlation between greater emphasis on risk-based pay and increased return to shareholders.

Based on our experience and research, we have identified four "best practices" in compensation programs at top-performing companies:

1. *Companies are moving from* **fixed** *to* **variable** *pay.* The most fundamental change is the shift from *fixed* compensation components (i.e., base salaries, guaranteed deferred compensation, automatic base-pay increases, etc.) toward *variable* compensation or risk-based pay. Some common techniques to begin this shift toward variable pay are:
   - Freezing base salaries or reducing salary increases.
   - Introducing annual incentive plans or enriching existing annual incentive plans.
   - Extending existing annual incentive plans to more employees.

2. *Companies are replacing* **cash** *compensation with* **equity** *compensation.* The use of equity as a compensation tool has significantly increased in all industries. For many companies, the increase in equity-based compensation is accompanied by a decrease in cash-based compensation. Examples of this practice are:
   - Paying bonuses in restricted stock or stock options.
   - Receiving a premium award if stock is voluntarily accepted in lieu of cash.
   - Shifting more of the total pay mix toward equity devices.

3. *Companies are shifting* **short-term** *compensation to* **long-term** *compensation.* In addition to just shifting from fixed pay to variable pay, the variable pay portion is structured to reward sustained performance over a period in excess of one year. This trend is seen in programs like the following:
   - Annual cash compensation held back pending future company performance.
   - Increased use of equity devices with multiyear vesting provisions.
   - Performance-based reward systems that are linked to the achievement of specific milestones, regardless of when they are achieved. (These milestones are not directly measured on an annual basis.)

4. *Companies are implementing an* **ownership culture** *for top executives and more and more for middle management levels.* An ownership culture encourages employees to think and act like owners

and to operate the business as if they were self-employed. An ownership culture is fostered by vehicles such as the following:

- Communication and employee empowerment programs.
- Target stock ownership plans (requiring executives to own a specified amount of stock).
- Equity-based compensation programs (i.e., restricted stock, stock options, and employee stock purchase programs).
- 401(k) matches in company stock.

Strategic and Philosophical Considerations.   Your compensation strategy should be aligned with your business strategy, with the company's culture, and with your compensation philosophy. Compensation strategy is very complex. Considerations range from philosophical issues, such as the extent to which you want to adopt an ownership culture, to market issues, like benchmarking for competitiveness, and practical business issues, such as legal, tax, and accounting implications.

Benchmarking is indispensable in assessing the competitiveness of your plan. First you'll want to identify the peer group of competitors with which you wish to compare yourself. This peer group can consist of companies in the same industry or the same geographic area as well as companies from whom employees might be recruited. Size is often a criterion; however, it is best not to look at size in terms of where you are but in terms of where you want to be. A $20 million company that is on the road to becoming a $100 million company needs to have strategies in place that resemble those of a $100 million company.

The next step is to decide at what level of the competitive market consensus to benchmark each component. Depending on the situation and the specific position, you might want to be at the median, the 75th percentile, or the 110th percentile. The level of benchmarking depends on many factors, including supply and demand in the marketplace, the quality of the employee, total responsibilities and scope of the position, length of service in the industry, individual performance, and more.

In setting your compensation philosophy, consider the extent to which you want management and employees to be owners rather than traders. Owners buy and hold stock; traders use stock as a device to increase take-home pay. Owners think long term; traders think short term. Maximum alignment with shareholder interests occurs with employee owners. If you design your equity compensation programs to promote the sale of your stock, don't be surprised if your employee shareholders liquidate at the first sign of a market dip.

In many companies, management is expected to own a designated amount of stock. Such "target ownership plans" often identify the stock ownership requirements for key executives as a multiple of salary. Although financial planners may see this as putting too many eggs in one basket, shareholders' interests are better served by providing a bigger basket. You must decide whether you want to use equity as a compensation device or whether you really want your executives and employees to "own" the company. Although stock options are often used as a device to build equity, the difference between a shareholder and an option holder is significant. Option holders participate in future appreciation whereas shareholders have capital at risk.

It is important to realize that stock options have a cost. They reduce, or dilute, shareholder earnings by spreading the corporation's earnings over more shares. Many shareholders will welcome some dilution in the interest of aligning employee interests with those of the company. On the other hand, too much dilution may have a negative impact on the value of a company. Stock option dilution levels vary by industry and by the company's stage of development. At this stage, the challenge is to determine the optimal level of dilution for your company.

Last but not least, the success or failure of your compensation program depends on many technical and legal issues such as:

- The compensation issues that commonly concern the SEC, underwriters, shareholders, and institutional investors.
- The financial, tax, and accounting impact of alternative compensation programs.

Basic Compensation Components. The appropriate competitive level of total cash compensation is a combination of what is competitive for the position in the market and what is appropriate for the individual employee. Typically, senior-level executive compensation consists of the following components:

Component	Purpose
Base Salary	Should reflect market—competitive practices for similar positions in similar organizations.
	Often critical to attracting key individuals to the organization.
Annual Incentives	Should reflect market practices, but should be designed in a way to provide superior pay for superior performance.

Component	Purpose
	Also plays a role in attracting individuals to the organization, but should be primarily used for motivating individuals to achieve short-term results that are essential to organizational success.
Long-Term Incentives	Should reflect market-competitive practices, but should be uniquely designed to support long-term organizational strategies and objectives.
	Usually plays a role in motivating individuals to achieve long-term results that are essential to organizational success, but focuses on retaining key individuals and sharing in the ownership of the company.

The sum of the base salary and the annual incentive is referred to as *total cash compensation* (TCC) because these components are generally paid in cash. The sum of total cash compensation plus the annualized value of the long-term incentive is referred to as *total direct compensation* (TDC).

Conclusion. Your compensation plan is ongoing. It requires periodic updating as your company grows and as regulations and best practices evolve. Using your compensation philosophy as a foundation, you should continue to ask whether your current compensation packages are truly competitive enough to attract and to retain the level of executive you want.

YOUR BOARD OF DIRECTORS

Well before the IPO, your board of directors should play a key role in policy decisions. The composition of the board of directors is an important factor to investors who are evaluating a company. Outside directors (i.e., other than management and major shareholders) bring specialized expertise and an independent perspective to the boards of both private and public companies. Your company should consider inviting individuals with proven, relevant expertise to serve as directors. For example, CEOs or other executives of other companies may bring operations expertise; bankers may be able to provide financial advice; attorneys, accountants, and other professionals could bring legal and financial expertise; and academics might be invited for their recommendations on technical or operational matters.

Outside board members not only will help strengthen the management of your company by serving on the board and its committees, but will also enhance your credibility with the investment community. Strong outsiders can be especially valuable intermediaries and advocates if the company encounters a rough period after the IPO.

If your aim is to have your stock listed on a national exchange (e.g., New York Stock Exchange, American Stock Exchange) or on the National Association of Securities Dealers and Automated Quotations (Nasdaq) Stock Market, you will have to comply with the corporate governance requirements of the exchange—which include, among other things, requirements to have varying numbers of independent directors.

Companies going public often try to identify as candidates for directors those individuals with strong reputations in their industry, in other areas of the business community, or in public service. However, companies considering such individuals sometimes find them reluctant to assume the director role due to the liability they must legally assume when they only have limited familiarity with the company.

Under the Securities Act of 1933 (the 1933 Act), a director can be held liable if a registration statement contains any untrue statement of a material fact or fails to state a material fact that was required. As today's boards face the growing risk of litigation, companies are finding new ways to give their directors legal protection. In addition to paying increasing premiums for directors' and officers' (D&O) liability insurance coverage, many companies are changing their corporate charters to permit indemnification of directors. Although the Securities and Exchange Commission (SEC) historically has not favored indemnification for securities law violations, the majority of public companies obtain D&O insurance for directors and have amended their corporate charters to permit indemnification of directors.

Size

As with any group, a larger board provides greater expertise and breadth of experience. This, however, must be weighed against the disadvantage that a larger group may be unwieldy and therefore not be able to function as effectively. The average size of the board of directors varies according to industry group, asset size, and sales volume.

According to the American Bar Association's *Corporate Director's Guidebook*, complex corporations tend to have larger boards, averaging about 15 members, while smaller industrial concerns average 8 or 9 members. This is consistent with the notion that relatively smaller boards provide an opportunity for board members to become more involved in discussions and deliberations. Corporations that have larger boards tend to operate in committees, which permit a more manageable operating size.

In determining the appropriate number of board members, many companies look to the complexity of the company's operations, the number of issues that either require board involvement or would benefit from the board's involvement, the size of their competitors' boards, and the cost of obtaining and retaining highly qualified board members.

Term

There are no specific laws or regulations that dictate the length of service of board members or the frequency of reelection or replacement of board members. Some companies elect their entire board on an annual basis, expecting, however, that there will be minimal turnover from such annual proceedings. Other companies, concerned both with continuity and protection against unsolicited offers, will establish longer terms for board members (e.g., three to five years) and stagger the elections so that only a percentage of the board will stand for election in a given year. Some companies have established their own rules regarding the maximum number of terms a member may serve, and some have established a mandatory retirement age for board members.

Basic Responsibilities

The basic duty of a corporate director is to advance the interests of the corporation. A director is often said to be performing this duty by demonstrating behavior that can be described as diligent and loyal. Although these concepts may appear obvious, it is important that directors understand them. Failure to understand the responsibilities of directorship can lead to liability for both the director and the corporation.

Diligent behavior refers to acting in good faith, with the care that an ordinarily prudent person in a like position would exercise, and in a manner believed to be in the best interests of the corporation. Diligence includes such important attributes as consistently attending board meetings and taking the time before a meeting to ensure that one is fully informed by obtaining and reviewing all the pertinent information that is needed to make an informed decision. In doing so, directors may rely on the reports of experts such as independent accountants or the corporation's legal counsel.

Loyal behavior is such that directors act in the interest of the corporation's shareholders and not in the director's own interest or in the interest of another person or organization. Directors should remain alert for any issue that may be construed as conflicting with the best interests of the corporation and generally should recuse themselves from voting on matters that could involve a conflict of interest.

Directors should be responsive to shareholders in that their primary role is overseeing the activities of management. After the IPO, the company will have a significant responsibility to its new shareholders.

Independent Directors

The board of directors of a public company (or one that is about to go public) should be organized to function as an independent observer and evaluator of the company's affairs and performance.

The composition of the board will be a major factor in determining the group's effectiveness in promoting the objectives of the corporation. Boards are usually comprised of both management and independent directors. A *management director* is one whose primary duty is as an employee (typically a senior executive) of the corporation. Although these members are important because of their expertise in running the company and their day-to-day familiarity with its operations, boards are increasingly comprised primarily of independent directors.

As we have noted, independent directors are a requirement for publicly traded companies. The independent director is valued because of his or her ability to be objective about the company's affairs. Boards comprised of members who simply rubber stamp the recommendations of management are prime targets for shareholder lawsuits. A strong board will be perceived positively by the investment community and will serve to strengthen the company as it begins the process of going public.

Committees of the Board

Many public companies have found the committee structure to be the most efficient and effective way for their boards to function successfully. The committee approach is especially useful for outside directors who have extensive commitments elsewhere. In addition, the committee structure allows independent directors to specialize and to cultivate greater depth of knowledge about specific areas, ranging from financial reporting and internal financial controls to management selection and compensation.

On most committees, the majority of members are independent directors. The number and size of the various board committees vary among industry groups and companies within those groups. As with the issue of the size of the board itself, the primary advantage of large committees is the broader experience base represented by the members. The disadvantage is that larger committees may become unmanageable and make it difficult for the chairperson to keep the committee meetings focused. Each company must determine the appropriate size for its unique circumstance. A discussion of the activities and composition of the more common committees follows.

Audit Committee. First recommended by the New York Stock Exchange (NYSE) in 1939, the audit committee has emerged as the most prevalent board committee. Today the NYSE, the American Stock Exchange (AMEX), and the Nasdaq Stock Market all require audit committees for their listed companies. The NYSE requires the committee to be comprised entirely of independent directors, whereas the AMEX and Nasdaq require that a majority of the members be independent.

The overall duties of an audit committee may be relatively similar from company to company, but its style and methods of operation need not be. Rather, the style and operational methods should be closely tailored to the objectives, needs, and circumstances of the organization the committee is designed to serve. The background and experience of directors, the depth of their knowledge of the company's financial position, and the specialized industry regulatory requirements are key factors that should determine the nature and scope of an audit committee's activities.

Typically, the audit committee is established through a formal board resolution. The audit committee must distinguish its oversight responsibility from its involvement in the day-to-day management of the company and the conduct of the audit. The committee must not be considered an adversary of management; rather, it is part of the corporation's governance and oversight process.

The audit committee is responsible for overseeing the financial reporting process, the work of internal audit, and the work of the independent auditors. To perform its function effectively, the audit committee needs to understand the company's business, the industry and its attendant risks, and the financial reporting process itself. The audit committee will be aided in its oversight duties by maintaining open communication with both internal auditors and the company's independent auditing firm.

The most important key to success for an audit committee is effective communication among the committee and management, the full board, the internal auditors, and the independent auditors.

Although the size of audit committees varies—the Treadway Commission suggests at least three members—each member should be an active participant in committee activities. Several research studies show that between three and five members is fairly standard.

Typically, audit committee charters require that only outside directors be members, and this practice has been encouraged by most research studies and regulatory agencies. Most important, members must be committed to the task and have adequate time to devote to the committee's work. Exhibit 5.1 illustrates a model audit committee charter.

The role of audit committees has been the subject of heightened interests in the financial community for the past several years. For example, the NYSE and the National Association of Securities Dealers (NASD) sponsored the Blue Ribbon Committee on Improving the Effectiveness of Corporate Audit Committees (the Blue Ribbon Committee), which was charged with developing a series of recommendations intended to empower audit committees to function as the ultimate "guardian of investor interests and corporate accountability." The Blue Ribbon Committee's February 1999 report[1] contained a series of recommendations for the securities exchanges, the SEC, and the American Institute of Certified Public Accountants (AICPA) aimed at improving the effectiveness of audit committees. However, before any of the Blue Ribbon Committee's recommendations became rules or regulations, they must be acted on by the SEC, the securities exchanges, and the AICPA's Auditing Standards Board. You can get updated information on the status of the rule-making

---

[1]The report is available electronically on Ernst & Young's web site (www.ey.com) and on the web sites of the NYSE (www.nyse.com) and the NASD (www.nasd.com).

EXHIBIT 5.1.   Sample audit committee charter.

Organization

The audit committee of the board of directors shall be comprised of [at least three] directors who are independent of management and the Company. Members of the audit committee shall be considered independent if they have no relationship to the Company that may interfere with the exercise of their independence from management and the Company. All audit committee members will be financially literate, and at least one member will have accounting or related financial management expertise.

Statement of Policy

The audit committee shall provide assistance to the directors in fulfilling their responsibility to the shareholders, potential shareholders, and investment community relating to corporate accounting, reporting practices of the company, and the quality and integrity of financial reports of the company. In so doing, it is the responsibility of the audit committee to maintain free and open communication between the directors, the independent auditors, the internal auditors, and the financial management of the company.

Responsibilities

In carrying out its responsibilities, the audit committee believes its policies and procedures should remain flexible so as to best react to changing conditions and assure the directors and shareholders that the corporate accounting and reporting practices of the company are in accordance with all requirements and are of the highest quality.

In carrying out these responsibilities, the audit committee will:

- Obtain the full board of directors' approval of this Charter and review and reassess this Charter as conditions dictate (at least annually).
- Review and recommend to the directors the independent auditors to be selected to audit the financial statements of the company and its divisions and subsidiaries.
- Have a clear understanding with the independent auditors that they are ultimately accountable to the board of directors and to the audit committee as the shareholders' representatives, who have the ultimate authority in deciding to engage, evaluate, and, if appropriate, terminate their services.
- Review and concur with management's appointment, termination, or replacement of the director of internal audit.

(continued)

EXHIBIT 5.1. *continued.*

- Meet with the independent auditors and financial management of the company to review the scope of the proposed audit and timely quarterly reviews for the current year, the procedures to be utilized, and the adequacy of the independent auditor's compensation and, at the conclusion thereof, to review such audit or review, including any comments or recommendations of the independent auditors.
- Review with the independent auditors, the company's internal auditor, and financial and accounting personnel the adequacy and effectiveness of the accounting and financial controls of the company, and will elicit any recommendations for the improvement of such internal controls or particular areas where new or more detailed controls or procedures are desirable. Particular emphasis should be given to the adequacy of internal controls to expose any payments, transactions, or procedures that might be deemed illegal or otherwise improper. Further, the committee periodically should review company policy statements to determine their adherence to the code of conduct.
- Review reports received from regulators and other legal and regulatory matters that may have a material effect on the financial statements or related company compliance policies.
- Review the internal audit function of the company, including the independence and authority of its reporting obligations, the proposed audit plans for the coming year, and the coordination of such plans with the independent auditors.
- Inquire of management, the internal auditor, and the independent auditors about significant risks or exposures and will assess the steps management has taken to minimize such risks to the company.
- Receive, prior to each meeting, a summary of findings from completed internal audits and a progress report on the proposed internal audit plan, with explanations for any deviations from the original plan.
- Review the quarterly financial statements with financial management and the independent auditors prior to the filing of the Form 10-Q (or prior to the press release of results, if possible) to determine that the independent auditors do not take exception to the disclosure and content of the financial statements, and will discuss any other matters required to be communicated to the committee by the auditors. The chair of the committee may represent the entire committee for purposes of this review.
- Review the financial statements contained in the annual report to shareholders with management and the independent auditors to determine that the inde-

(continued)

EXHIBIT 5.1. *continued.*

pendent auditors are satisfied with the disclosure and content of the financial statements to be presented to the shareholders. Review with financial management and the independent auditors the results of their timely analysis of significant financial reporting issues and practices, including changes in or adoptions of accounting principles and disclosure practices, and will discuss any other matters required to be communicated to the committee by the auditors. Also review with financial management and the independent auditors their judgments about the quality, not just acceptability, of accounting principles and the clarity of the financial disclosure practices used or proposed to be used and, particularly, the degree of aggressiveness or conservatism of the organization's accounting principles and underlying estimates, and other significant decisions made in preparing the financial statements.

- Provide sufficient opportunity for both the internal and the independent auditors to meet with the members of the audit committee without members of management present. Among the items to be discussed in these meetings are the independent auditors' evaluation of the company's financial, accounting, and auditing personnel and the cooperation that the independent auditors received during the course of audit.
- Review accounting and financial human resources and succession planning within the company.
- Report the results of the annual audit to the board of directors, and, if requested by the board, will invite the independent auditors to attend the full board of directors meeting to assist in reporting the results of the annual audit or to answer other directors' questions (alternatively, the other directors, particularly the other independent directors, may be invited to attend the audit committee meeting during which the results of the annual audit are reviewed).
- Review the nature and scope of other professional services provided to the company by the independent auditors and consider the relationship to the auditors' independence.
- On an annual basis, obtain from the independent auditors a written communication delineating all their relationships and professional services as required by Independence Standards Board Standard No. 1, *Independence Discussions with Audit Committees.* In addition, review with the independent auditors the nature and scope of any disclosed relationships or professional services and take, or recommend that the board of directors take, appropriate action to ensure the continuing independence of the auditors.
- Submit the minutes of all meetings of the audit committee to, or discuss the matters discussed at each committee meeting with, the board of directors.
- Investigate any matter brought to its attention within the scope of its duties, with the power to retain outside counsel for this purpose if, in its judgment, that is appropriate.

and other information about audit committees on Ernst & Young's web site (www.ey.com).

Compensation Committee.   Executive compensation recently has become one of the most hotly debated issues of corporate governance. The debate centers around the question of whether the often-lucrative salary and benefits packages of the CEO and other senior executives are justified by the performance of the executives and the corporation.

Whereas a privately held company need not disclose the compensation of its key executives, a public company must disclose the compensation of its CEO and its other four most highly compensated executive officers. A responsible compensation committee of the board of directors can aid the board in assessing the performance and resulting compensation of key executives.

Strategically, the compensation committee should consider how the achievement of the overall goals and objectives of the corporation can be aided through adoption of an appropriate compensation philosophy and an effective compensation program. This is an important issue for a company about to go public because, as we have noted, compensation plays an important role in attracting and retaining management talent.

Administratively, the compensation committee reviews salary progression, bonus allocations, stock awards, and the awards of supplemental benefits and perquisites for key executives and compares them to the compensation objectives and overall performance of the company. Generally, the compensation committee is concerned only with the compensation levels of senior executives. In order to be an effective tool for corporate governance on behalf of the shareholders, the committee should be composed of independent directors.

A compensation report is not required in a registration statement; however, the SEC requires that a report to shareholders by the members of the compensation committee (or another group functioning in that capacity) be included in a proxy or other information statement relating to an annual meeting. The report should discuss the company's compensation policies for executive officers and the committee's basis for determining the compensation of the CEO and certain other highly compensated employees for the prior year.

Just as the audit committee has access to outside advisors to determine the integrity of the firm's financial controls, the compensation committee may seek assistance from compensation consultants. Specialists can advise them as to the competitiveness of the company's compensation structure within the same industry, as well as with companies of similar size in different industries. Many compensation committees have responded to the requirement of providing a detailed compensation committee report by retaining consultants to assist in the determination of compensation, as well as in the drafting of the report.

Executive Committee.   Historically, the executive committee has served as a key link between the board and management, especially during periods between board meetings. The committee usually is granted broad powers to ensure that important matters that cannot wait until the next scheduled meeting receive timely attention. Executive committees also can help the full board function more efficiently, particularly when the board is large. It may serve as a sounding board for general management problems involving matters that affect the corporation as a whole.

Companies often assign retired CEOs or other senior members of management to serve on this committee because their experience in managing the company is often valuable. The chairs of other key board committees often serve as members of the executive committee as well. Given its orientation toward management issues, it is not surprising to find the greatest percentage of management directors sitting on the executive committee.

Finance Committee.   In this era of acquisitions, mergers, and general financial uncertainty, the finance committee's role is growing more critical, particularly in larger companies. This committee is most likely to be present in larger corporations with complex financial structures.

The finance committee is primarily involved with financial decisions and planning. Its responsibilities include:

- Staying informed on a timely basis about the company's financial status.
- Evaluating the financial information it receives and developing conclusions as to any plan of action needed.
- Advising corporate management and the full board on financial matters. Although usually not empowered to act on its own, the finance committee is sometimes authorized to make decisions on behalf of the full board during the periods between board meetings.

Nominating Committee.   As it becomes increasingly difficult for corporate America to find qualified candidates willing to serve on boards of directors, the job of the nominating committee becomes ever more critical. For a company deciding to go public, such a committee would be given the responsibility of thoroughly searching for and screening candidates for initial board positions or board vacancies. To achieve this, the nominating committee must consider the broader issues of the composition and the organization of the board, including committee assignments and individual board membership. In addition, the nominating committee evaluates the board itself and its members and reviews the company's management succession planning.

Candidates recommended to the nominating committee for board membership often have had prior contact with CEO and other board members. Increasingly, though, nominating committees are relying on outside consultants. These advisors generally help screen candidates to provide greater assurance that the candidates selected are independent in fact and in appearance.

In general, all nominees recommended by the committee stand for election by the corporation's shareholders. In some instances, though, boards have the authority to elect a director to fill a vacancy for the remainder of a term.

How to Work Effectively with the Board

A strong relationship between the CEO and the board of directors is more important today than ever before. Two separate trends drive home this point:

1. The current business environment increases the need for a cooperative relationship, especially as conditions continue to be unstable. Typical pressures range from consolidations and downsizings to international competition, economic turmoil, and constantly accelerating change. If the CEO and the board work as a team, they can more easily meet challenges as they arise; they can create and sustain a strong business strategy; and they can adapt quickly when changes need to be made.

2. The tendency is for today's board of directors to be much more active than in years past. An active board can be an asset to the company. Experience shows that companies with active boards generally perform better. *Business Week*'s "best 25 boards" far outpaced the Standard &

Poor's (S&P) 500 in 1997, producing annual shareholder returns of 27.6 percent, compared with an S&P average of 19.8 percent.[2] Conversely, boards that have had low levels of power and involvement have been associated with poor financial performance.[3]

A CEO can do much to skillfully manage the board's expectations, even in the worst-case scenario of an unsympathetic board. He or she can encourage the board to participate in strategic planning, can explicitly define roles and responsibilities, can keep the board thoroughly informed, and can communicate frequently and honestly.

• *Encourage board participation.*   The board's buy-in to the CEO's strategic plan is a corporate-governance must. A recent survey showed that boards spend an average of one-fourth of their time on corporate strategy.[4] While it is ultimately the CEO's job to create and implement a winning strategy, that strategy should either be created in tandem with the board or it should be approved by the board.

If the CEO is new and the board is inherited, the new CEO should make a special effort to understand the board and its goals for the organization. The better the CEO understands the board's agenda, the easier it will be to develop and implement a strategic plan that is endorsed by the board.

• *Explicitly define roles and responsibilities.*   The division of responsibility between the board and management should be clearly defined. Especially with an inherited or an unsympathetic board, explicit job descriptions of the board and the CEO are advisable.

Clear criteria for the CEO's effectiveness will eliminate sources of conflict before they arise. Ideally, the CEO should set performance goals in conjunction with the board. At the very least, the board's annual performance goals for the CEO should be agreed on by both parties. Just as the CEO should be willing to accept the board's performance goals, the board should be willing to establish similar criteria to evaluate itself and the performance of its members. According to *Business Week*, the best boards conduct both self-evaluations and peer reviews.[5]

[2]"The Best and Worst Boards," *Business Week*, December 8, 1997, pp. 91–98.
[3]"The Effects of CEO-Board Relations on Hospital Performance," *Health Care Management Review*, June 22, 1997.
[4]"Opening the Door to the New Age of Corporate Governance," *Corporate Board*, March 1997.
[5]"The Best and Worst Boards," *Business Week*, December 8, 1997, pp. 91–98.

• *Keep the board thoroughly informed.* A critical part of the CEO's job is to keep the board informed about market trends and the company's progress. It is particularly important that the CEO not withhold any negative information from the board. Unpleasant surprises tend to undermine trust.

It is best if information flows both ways. Just as the CEO can provide information to the board, a strong board can often contribute knowledge to the company, along with access to the board members' network of business and personal relationships.

• *Communicate frequently and honestly.* The purpose of effective communication with the board is to gain credibility and support in creating and implementing the company's strategy. If there is good communication, the company's strategic initiatives can become cooperative ventures involving the CEO and the board, enabling the board to take an advisory role in the company's major decisions. Such a cooperative relationship allows the CEO and the board to maintain a shared focus.

Good communication eliminates misunderstandings and uncertainties in advance. To facilitate good communication, the CEO needs to be available on a regular basis to respond to the board's concerns. A lack of responsiveness is likely to generate distrust and concern. Regular meetings allow the CEO to keep the board informed and the board to give the CEO feedback on how he or she is doing. Any potential issues or conflicts can be addressed before they become problems.

To summarize, the best relationship between the CEO and the board is one of mutual respect, cooperation, and shared responsibility. The CEO should communicate regularly and honestly with board members, should remain accessible, and should encourage open discussion of all relevant company matters.

YOUR EXTERNAL ADVISORY TEAM

If you choose your outside directors well, they will add to the sophistication and quality of your winning team. Equally important is your selection of professional advisors. For example, your underwriters will be absolutely critical to the success of your IPO because they will help you present your company to investors and they will actually sell your securities. You will need a law firm that has considerable SEC experience and an accounting firm that fully understands all of the nuances involved in taking your company public.

The quality of your external advisory team can make an enormous difference in the success of your IPO. The more successful companies have close relationships with these professionals and maintain open and honest communication with them in good times and bad.

Your Underwriters

Few companies attempt to sell their own shares through a public offering without the help of underwriters—and with good reason. The underwriting syndicate has the distribution channels, the contacts, and the experience to reach a much broader group of investors than the company could on its own. It will lend more credibility to your offering; and will target specific investors for whom your shares are likely to hold the most investment appeal. The syndicate also has the resources to invest in this time-consuming effort, as well as the expertise to avoid the potential liabilities and other consequences that can result from an improperly handled selling effort.

In addition to their primary role in the initial sales effort, underwriters typically play a significant role in maintaining a strong and stable aftermarket for your securities. They serve as market makers for your shares, buying and selling shares on the interdealer market and generally helping maintain interest in your shares among analysts and investors.

Navigating the Underwriting Firm.   Like any brokerage operation, an investment bank has two sides: (1) the issuers of securities, who are called "clients," and (2) the investors, who are called "customers." The investors, who buy and sell securities daily and are the firm's bread and butter, are known as "the franchise."

Your investment banker works on your behalf, advising you and representing your interests in a very complicated firm. At the pricing meeting, however, the investment banker moves to the other side of the firm. Ultimately, he or she has to protect the firm's financial interests and answer to its sales force and their customers.

The CEO of a company making an IPO will work very closely with the research analyst, who straddles both sides of the firm. A research analyst is the ultimate broker, selling your company to investors while representing investors in your company. The analyst has to have credibility with both investors and clients like you. Finally, you should get to know the capital markets experts who actually price the deal, manage the "book," and make the deal happen.

The Preliminary Selection Process. Your underwriters will play the central role in selling your securities. Your direct contact is your lead, or managing, underwriter. The managing underwriter will have the primary responsibility for determining the initial price of the shares to be sold. Your shares are distributed through an underwriting syndicate—assembled by your managing underwriters—consisting of a number of other underwriters who also sell the shares to individual and institutional investors.

Selecting the right managing underwriter is crucial to the success of your IPO. For some small companies, the reputation of the underwriters can be one of the more important factors that investors consider in evaluating your offering. A variety of firms actively underwrite IPOs, from major national investment bankers to smaller regional brokerage firms with investment banking divisions. Many of the smaller firms specialize in specific industries.

Selecting the managing underwriters best suited to your situation should begin with a self-evaluation of your company and its future plans. Consider the current and potential market for your product. If your geographic coverage is national or international, it may be best to retain a national firm to capitalize on and to enhance your corporate image in the United States and in select areas abroad. If your sales market is regional, a regional firm may be able to serve you equally well.

If your industry is specialized, you may want to seek underwriters who specialize in your industry. If you plan to diversify, through acquisition or internally, consider using an investment banking firm that also has experience in that new industry. You can avoid having to repeat the selection process by choosing underwriters that can fill both your current and anticipated needs; then you can focus on building a long-term professional relationship.

The selection process is mutual. Some underwriters will not be interested in your offering. Some do not handle IPOs, and some are interested only in offerings above certain minimum amounts. Others may decline on the basis of their assessment of your company's or your industry's future prospects. The underwriters' reputation hangs largely on the success of the offerings they underwrite. Because underwriters are compensated only if the offering is completed (except for any expenses you agree to reimburse), they will not want to commit time and resources unless they are reasonably confident that the offering will be completed.

Underwriters examine a company and its prospects in much the same way that an investor would, but much more intensively. Their examination begins with your business plan. Your business plan will either spark their interest or lead to rejection, so it should be well prepared and it should present your company in its best possible light. But here and in all future dealings with your underwriters, you must scrupulously avoid any misrepresentation. If the underwriters find they have been misled, they will abort the offering—leaving you with delays, lost time, and a tarnished reputation.

If the underwriters decide to investigate further, they will delve into almost every aspect of your business. They will interview key executives, scrutinize your financial statements, challenge your accounting policies, and examine your financial projections. Often they also will meet with your auditors to obtain their views. They will evaluate your products in relation to your industry; talk to your suppliers and customers; and assess your market share, technological sophistication, and market growth potential. The intended use of the proceeds of the offering also will be taken into consideration. In short, they will perform a thorough evaluation of your company to decide whether to handle your offering and, if they are selected, how to price and promote your offering.

The next step is to develop a list of underwriters who appear to meet your selection criteria (e.g., national or regional, industry specialization). Your auditors, attorneys, and bankers can help you identify those firms and perform a preliminary evaluation of their qualifications. Although you must consider other factors, the most important selection criteria are the *reputation of the firm* and the *quality of the research analyst*. Here is some detail about those criteria, as well as others you will consider:

Reputation.   Prospective investors consider the reputation of your managing underwriters. Sometimes their reputation can overshadow the merits of your offering. A well-respected underwriting firm will be better able to form a strong underwriting syndicate to sell your securities. Underwriters earn their reputations by providing top-quality, reliable service to their clients—and they will strive to safeguard their reputations by providing good service.

Research Capability.   A very important component of developing and maintaining market interest is the underwriters' analysis and distribution of information about your company and your industry. Your underwriters' research department should have the resources necessary to produce that information, and it should have a reputation that commands the respect of investors—particularly institutional investors—and the respect of the financial community in general.

One very effective way to investigate the quality of a firm's research staff is to call other underwriting firms and ask them which sell-side analyst they really like in your sector. In looking for analysts, it is helpful to ask prospective analysts for copies of all the reports they wrote for companies that went public, both during and after the IPO. Consider how complete they made the reports, whether they followed up on their initial enthusiasm, and how they handled difficult periods (whether they remained loyal to clients they took public).

Experience. Your underwriters should have extensive experience in underwriting IPOs and the particular type of security you intend to offer (e.g., equity, debt, or a combination). It is beneficial if your underwriters also have experience in your industry as a basis for pricing your stock, for selecting an appropriate underwriting syndicate, and for providing credibility to investors and industry analysts.

Syndication and Distribution Capability. Depending on the size of your offering, the number of geographic markets in which you wish to offer your securities, and the mix of investors you hope to reach (retail or institutional), your managing underwriters may need to establish a syndicate that could range from as few as 3 to up to 50 underwriters. A broad distribution not only will provide a larger market for your shares but also will help avoid concentration of major blocks of shares in the hands of a few persons.

Your underwriters' ability to attract institutional interest in your offering may be a big factor in your success. Most successful IPOs require substantial participation from institutional investors. Accordingly, your underwriters should have appropriate syndication experience, a broad client base, and a retail and institutional investor orientation that is consistent with your needs.

Aftermarket Support. Providing aftermarket support for your shares is an important part of the underwriters' service. This is accomplished by having the managing underwriters and some or all of the syndicated underwriters act as market makers in your shares. Market makers offer to buy shares from or to sell shares to the public (or in the interdealer market) at a firm price, and generally they sustain the financial community's interest in your shares by disseminating information about your company's progress. You can evaluate the underwriters' aftermarket performance by tracking recent post-IPO share-price movements for a sample of IPOs underwritten by the firm.

References.   Reputable underwriters will often encourage you to contact the management of several of the companies they have recently underwritten for a recommendation. It would be helpful to include your comparable companies in this exercise, perhaps focusing on how the research analysts handled a volatile market situation.

Some questions you may wish to ask are:

- Did the underwriters provide all the services they promised to your satisfaction?
- Did the underwriters display an interest in and knowledge of your industry and company and maintain interest after the IPO?
- Did the underwriters significantly reduce the stock split ratio or estimated selling price during the registration process?
- Did the underwriters present any last-minute surprises or demands?
- Are you satisfied with the breadth of the underwriting syndicate and the placement of your shares?
- What happened to your share price in the aftermarket? To what extent do you believe price movements were related to the appropriateness of the initial offering price, the level of aftermarket support from the underwriters, or other factors?
- Do the managing underwriters continue to promote your company through regular research reports and to provide you with other financial advice?
- Would you use the same group to underwrite another offering and recommend them to other companies?
- Is there anything else I should know about this underwriting firm?

Continuing Financial Advisory Services.   The managing underwriters should have the resources to continue to provide your company with investment banking services. This would include providing assistance in obtaining additional capital as the need arises (whether from private or from public sources), advising on proposed mergers or acquisitions, and, in general, offering a full range of investment banking services.

Narrowing the Field.   Once you have formally or informally evaluated a number of underwriters, you can develop a short list of underwriters to approach directly. There are varying opinions as to the number of underwriters with whom you should negotiate at the same time. One school of thought warns against shopping for underwriters and recommends approaching only one firm at a time. Another viewpoint holds that some shopping—and the resulting competition—would be to your advantage.

The number of underwriters you approach will depend partly on the attractiveness of your offering. If the offering is small and highly speculative, the aim may be to find one investment banker willing to underwrite the offering. In a relatively small offering, the underwriter's commission also will be modest. Under these circumstances, underwriters will be less willing to spend a significant amount of time investigating your company and negotiating with you unless they are sure of getting your business.

On the other hand, if your offering is large and likely to be attractive to underwriters, you may be well advised to approach three or four underwriters on a preliminary basis. However, be sure to let them know that you are approaching other underwriters, and be candid about every other aspect of your company and the offering as well. If the offering is attractive, underwriters will happily spend the necessary time with you.

Approaching those underwriters on your short list may be handled directly by you or indirectly through your auditors, attorneys, bankers, or business acquaintances. You also should consider whether you wish to retain more than one managing underwriter. The use of comanaging underwriters, particularly for larger offerings, can be advantageous with respect to initial market coverage, research capabilities, and aftermarket support.

While holding discussions with these underwriters, and in selecting your managing underwriters, bear in mind that you will have a relationship with the individuals assigned to your account. Therefore, you should feel comfortable with them on a personal level.

Letter of Intent.   The final underwriting agreement is usually not signed until just before the registration statement is declared "effective." (See "Declaring the Registration Statement Effective" in Chapter 8.) Ordinarily, there is no legal obligation for either your company or the underwriters to proceed with the offering until that time. Generally, neither the underwriters nor the company will abort a public offering after the registration process has begun, except under the most unusual circumstances, and then it is typically by mutual consent (for example, if the window has closed for IPOs in a particular industry).

In the early stages of an offering, underwriters prepare a letter of intent that describes the preliminary understanding of the arrangement (e.g. underwriters' commission, estimated offering price, and other negotiated terms) but that does not create a legal obligation for either your company or the underwriters to proceed with the offering. However, the letter may create a binding obligation for you to pay certain expenses incurred by the underwriters if the offering is not completed.

Underwriting Agreement. There are two common types of underwriting agreements: (1) firm-commitment and (2) best-efforts. In a *firm-commitment* underwriting agreement, the underwriters agree to purchase all the shares in the offering and then to resell them to the public. Any shares not sold to the public are paid for and held by the underwriters for their own account. This type of agreement provides you with the most assurance of raising the required funds, and it is used by most of the larger underwriters.

Often the underwriters ask for an "over-allotment option," which allows them to purchase up to a specified number of additional shares from the company in the event they sell more shares than the underwriting agreement stipulates. Over-allotment options take various forms: in some situations, the company will issue additional shares if the option is exercised; in other situations, the additional shares will be provided from the holdings of existing shareholders. The existence of an over-allotment option (or "green shoe" option, named after the Green Shoe Manufacturing Company, which introduced this technique) must be disclosed in the prospectus.

In a *best-efforts* underwriting agreement, the underwriters simply agree to use their best efforts to sell the shares on behalf of your company. Some best-efforts are all-or-nothing arrangements—the offering is withdrawn if the shares cannot all be sold. Others set a lower minimum number of shares that must be sold before the offering can be completed.

The obvious drawback of a best-efforts underwriting arrangement is that you are not assured of obtaining the required amount of capital. You could receive less capital than you need but still be saddled with the responsibilities and costs of being a public company.

Offering Price.   Underwriters generally will not (and cannot) guarantee an offering price (or, in the case of debt securities, an interest rate) and total proceeds in advance. The offering price is not finalized until just before the registration statement becomes effective because it must be responsive to current market conditions. Underwriters are usually unwilling to predict a precise offering price, but they generally will estimate a range for the offering price based on existing market conditions at the time of their estimate. Although their estimates are not binding and will most likely change in response to changing market conditions up to the effective date of the offering, they will reduce the chance of misunderstandings and last-minute surprises.

Underwriting Costs.   Although the costs of underwriting are substantial and cannot be ignored, they should not be a top criterion in selecting your underwriters. In the early stages of evaluating prospective underwriters, you may not be able to directly compare costs because commissions and other forms of underwriters' compensation are a matter of negotiation. However, you can get a good idea of the potential range of underwriting costs by doing your homework. Get a list of recent IPOs of similar size (and in your industry, if possible), and review the IPO prospectuses. The underwriting fees will be prominently listed. The underwriting agreement will be filed as an exhibit to the registration statement. Carefully reviewing the underwriting agreements for recent transactions will give you time to consider all the nuances that you will negotiate with your underwriter during the offering process.

Underwriting costs are generally the single largest expense in a public offering. These costs primarily consist of the underwriting commission, but they also may include other forms of compensation. All parties should clearly agree on the compensation arrangements before starting the registration. Underwriting costs may consist of the following:

Underwriting Commissions.   For recent IPOs, underwriting commissions have generally ranged from 6 to 10 percent (somewhat less for debt offerings). In determining the rate of commission to charge, underwriters consider a number of factors that affect how much effort they will have to expend in selling your shares. These factors include the size of the offering, competitive rates for offerings of similar size, the type of underwriting (i.e., firm-commitment or best-efforts), and the marketability of the shares. There also may be a trade-off between the rate of commission and other forms of compensation, particularly for smaller offerings.

Underwriter Warrants.   Some underwriters will negotiate for stock warrants in addition to their commission. Such warrants are more common when dealing with smaller underwriters and smaller offerings. If the granting of stock warrants can be traded for lower commissions, the obvious advantage is increased net proceeds from the offering, although some dilution of shareholders' equity will result. Be sure to reach agreement on the number and the terms of the warrants in advance to avoid last-minute misunderstandings.

Reimbursement of Underwriters' Expenses.   It is common, particularly in smaller offerings, for the managing underwriters to request reimbursement of some of their expenses incurred for your offering. For example, legal fees incurred by the underwriters' counsel to review compliance with state securities laws (commonly referred to as "Blue Sky" laws) are ordinarily reimbursed by the issuer. By complying with these Blue Sky laws, you will be able to offer your securities in more states, thus broadening the market for your offering. You may therefore wish to discuss the area of geographic syndication in the negotiation stage, before the underwriting syndicate is established by your managing underwriters. You may also be able to negotiate a limit to the amount of underwriters' expenses you will be required to reimburse.

Rights of First Refusal.   Some underwriters will request a right of first refusal on any future underwritings by your company. Such a request may seem innocuous, but it can adversely affect future offerings. Other underwriters will be reluctant to invest the time and resources necessary to evaluate a proposed offering if they know they may be preempted by another underwriter's right of first refusal. If a right of first refusal cannot be avoided, you should consider negotiating either a time limit after which the right expires or a provision that the right expires any time it is available but not exercised.

Optimizing the Relationship with Your Underwriters.   Contrary to the opinion of some, share price is not the most important concern. At best, your relationship with your underwriters is a long-term one, and most veteran CEOs would agree that the second offering will be more important than the first. At the second offering, the company not only gets more liquidity but actually returns to the market to see how well its first offering was received.

You will work closely with your managing underwriters in the preparatory stages of your public offering, through the completion of your offering, and often long into the future on subsequent public offerings, mergers, or acquisitions. Good chemistry is therefore important. Optimizing that relationship also requires conscious attention to maintaining frequent and meaningful communications.

Your Auditors

Your independent auditors play a significant and varied role in the complex process of going public. You will want to select an experienced professional services firm that has enough depth and breadth to serve as your trusted business advisors throughout the IPO Value Journey and beyond. It is wise to choose a firm with a strong national reputation as well as experience in securities offerings and in dealing with the SEC. A full-service accounting firm has the resources to provide a full range of accounting, auditing, tax advisory, and management consulting services.

Advisory Role. Your auditors should become involved in the early stages of a public offering. They will help you assess the relative advantages and disadvantages of going public. They will advise you on alternative sources of financing and help you investigate those alternatives. They also will advise you on corporate and personal tax implications, as well as on estate planning considerations. They can help you assess and approach underwriters and advise you on negotiating with them.

Technical Assistance in Meeting SEC Requirements. Having highly capable auditors on your team of professional advisors not only will help you avoid costly delays and errors in the registration process, but will provide you with continuing counsel and assistance in dealing with SEC reporting and with many other obligations of a public company.

Your auditors also will help you prepare one of the most important aspects of the prospectus—the financial disclosure package. For an established private company, the historical audited financial statements and financial highlights are the evidence of your size and earnings record. You also may need to supplement or update your business plan (see

Chapter 2 and Appendix A) to include current cash flow analyses, sensitivity studies, industry and competition studies, and marketing analyses. Your auditors can help you prepare and present the financial disclosure package clearly, concisely, and in accordance with SEC rules and regulations. They also can anticipate SEC concerns so that you can address them before the initial filing.

One of the SEC's financial disclosure requirements is a summary of selected financial data for a period of five years (not required for small business issuers). Although the SEC will require audited financial statements for only three years (two for small business issuers), some underwriters prefer that all years listed in the table of selected financial data be audited. In addition, many SEC disclosures and interpretations of GAAP differ from those applicable to private companies and therefore require careful consideration in preparing a public offering. These SEC interpretations can necessitate significant changes in the financial information you present. This underscores the importance of establishing a relationship with a professional services firm and having annual audits performed well in advance of a public offering.

Your auditors typically will provide *comfort letters* at the request of your underwriters. The underwriters will rely on the letters as part of their due diligence with respect to certain financial information in the prospectus and the registration statement.

A good working relationship developed early with your professional services firm not only will facilitate the registration process but will prove valuable as you become a mature public company.

Your Attorneys

Your attorneys will play an instrumental role in helping you prepare and execute your public offering. Their primary responsibility is to assist you in complying with all applicable federal and state securities laws and regulations and to advise you on the selection of any exemptions for which you may be eligible.

Because of the highly complex nature of securities law, it is important to select a firm with broad experience in securities law and in handling IPOs. If your general counsel does not have the necessary SEC expertise, they may be able to recommend a firm that does. Your auditors can also advise you on the selection of experienced SEC counsel. Many companies retain a firm that specializes in securities law specifically to make sure they meet all of the applicable SEC requirements, while at the same time retaining their general counsel to handle the company's routine corporate matters.

Your attorneys will assist you throughout the planning and execution phases of the Value Journey. They will review your existing contractual obligations and will suggest any necessary changes and revisions. Your attorneys will help you amend your articles of incorporation and bylaws as necessary. They also will recommend and help implement any changes to your capital structure that may be required to facilitate the public offering and to minimize the effect of SEC restrictions on the sale of "restricted" shares after you go public.

Attorneys often assume a coordinating role in the preparation of your prospectus and your registration statement, working closely with your management team and other professional advisors. Your attorneys will coordinate all correspondence with the SEC staff. They will review the entire prospectus and the registration statement and will advise you on the type of information that is legally relevant. For certain parts of that information, they will advise you on the form of presentation and the procedures necessary to verify its accuracy.

Throughout the registration process, and particularly while preparing the registration statement, you will be working closely with and relying heavily on your attorneys. Careful selection of attorneys will enhance the smooth completion of your registration.

Your Investor Relations Firm

Selling your shares and maintaining investor interest in the aftermarket is not dissimilar from selling your products or services to customers. Both are aided by name recognition, advertising and publicity, a product support system, and good distribution channels. Your underwriter and the underwriting syndicate will provide the distribution channels. However, you need to create your corporate image and to build the foundation for a strong investor relations program.

Many companies find that a good investor relations firm is of great value as a member of their external team. These firms know the institutional market and can help you design your institutional road show and plan your disclosure strategy. Creating your corporate image takes time, so you should start working with an investor relations firm well in advance of the IPO. Bear in mind, too, that the SEC imposes restrictions on any new forms of advertising or publicity in which you may engage once you have started the registration process by retaining an underwriter. (These so-called "quiet period" restrictions are discussed in Chapter 8.)

The first step in creating a public image is to perform a thorough self-evaluation of your company and its future. Consider your potential geographic appeal. Depending on the nature of your product and your geographic product market area, your shares may be limited to a regional market, or they might attract national or even international interest.

In what industry will your company be categorized? That could bear on your company's appeal to investors. Certain industries are more attractive to investors than others and thus command a higher price-earnings ratio. If your business could be classified in more than one way, aim for the industry classification that would result in the highest price-earnings ratio. Some companies with diverse product lines may be identified only with one of their better-known products. A good publicity campaign can create a broader based image for your company.

Your Financial Printer

The selection of a financial printer for your prospectus and registration statement is a seemingly mundane issue. However, an experienced financial printer contributes to the timeliness and efficiency of the registration process. Significant time demands are placed on the printer in the final stages of the registration process. Revised drafts are often required on a same-day basis, and the prospectus is often printed the night before the red herring is circulated and again the night before the registration statement becomes effective.

Your financial printer should have up-to-date knowledge of SEC rules and requirements with respect to paper size, format, type size, and related technical matters, and they should have the specialized facilities to deal with the accuracy, timing, and security needs of a public offering. Your financial printer also will help you file your registration statement electronically on EDGAR, the SEC's automated system for *Electronic Data Gathering and Retrieval.*

6

COMPLETE YOUR
IPO PLATFORM

At this point, you already have carefully laid the foundation for a successful IPO. You have defined success, chartered your business strategy, prepared your business plan, and, perhaps, undertaken one or more strategic transactions. Your winning team is in place. Will the interests of your company and your shareholders best be served by a public offering?

A common mistake some CEOs (chief executive officers) make is to start executing their IPO before they are ready to meet the demands of being a public company. You have now progressed from the planning phase to the execution phase, and you are moving toward the starting line of the IPO event. Before the actual event takes place, your challenge is to pull all the pieces together and complete the many different items on your pre-IPO "to do" list.

This is the time to set your priorities for the critical months just before your IPO. You are actually starting the process of becoming a public company. This phase of the Value Journey will help you ensure that when you do become publicly financed, you will meet your own definition of success and that, at the same time, you will meet and exceed the expectations of the market.

During the months preceding the IPO event, successful CEOs consider the following questions:

- What operating, personal, and transactional milestones have yet to be completed before we are ready to move into the IPO?
- Do we have a clear plan for using the proceeds of the IPO, and has that plan been communicated to investors and analysts?

- Have we completed our "corporate housekeeping"?
- Is the market ready for our IPO at this time?

Your responses to these questions can be the key both to the success of your IPO and to the ongoing performance of your shares in the aftermarket.

COMPLETE YOUR IMPROVEMENT AGENDA

This is the time to revalidate your decision to go public after having implemented all the changes you planned during the earliest stages of the IPO Value Journey. Is your company where it needs to be in order to go forward into an IPO? You will want to review the goals, strategies, and initiatives you set forth in the early phases of the journey (see Chapters 2 through 5) and to make sure all your building blocks are in place.

Consider whether the elements of your operating and transactional strategies have come to fruition. Perhaps you planned to make three acquisitions to move the company from $25 million to $100 million. Similarly, you may have reengineered your inventory control systems to gain efficiency and credibility. Just going through the externals of a transaction or an improvement program does not guarantee that you will reap the benefits. Your company has changed significantly in the wake of these acquisitions or improvements, and you have added considerable uncertainty.

You have to be sure you were able to integrate the new businesses and their people into the daily operations of the company. You must ensure that the new inventory system actually operates as planned and achieves your objectives. If you try to go public without integrating the new companies and/or systems, you will be unlikely to be able to meet your earnings estimates.

This step in the Value Journey is an important opportunity to review your preparation efforts and to fill in any remaining gaps. Its purpose is to be sure you have fully integrated all the initiatives that propel you to the threshold of your IPO. You'll want to ensure that all those initiatives are adding value and that you are secure enough in your future direction to meet your earnings forecasts quarter after quarter.

IS YOUR COMPANY READY?

There is no formula or universal rule to determine whether a company is sufficiently large, mature, or profitable to go public. A review of recent successful offerings, however, can provide some useful generalizations about what investors look for in a newly public company.

Size

Underwriters have had their own rules of thumb—based primarily on revenue and net earnings—for what constitutes an adequate size to support a public offering. Today, however, size is often measured in terms of market capitalization or float.

The phenomenal multiples of Internet companies have highlighted the importance of nonfinancial factors. A considerable number of IPOs have been Internet companies and other companies with minimal revenue, many of which have never shown a profit. These start-up companies normally have other attractions—such as an innovative new product with a potentially significant market and a proven management team—that compensate for the lack of a financial track record. Our research shows that more and more investors and bankers are looking at such criteria.

Nevertheless, if your company appears to lack the size or the earnings to support a successful public offering, you have other avenues to explore. You might consider merging with another company in your industry that also is too small for an IPO. Such a merger could result in an amalgamated company whose combined assets, earnings, and management will make a public offering feasible.

Growth

Underwriters and investors look for a record of consistently high growth, as well as a demonstrated potential for continuing that growth in the future (e.g., 15 to 25 percent per year for the next several years). If the momentum is not there when the company goes public, investors will turn to more promising opportunities, and the offering may fizzle. Having an innovative product, a significant market share, or proven potential in a new market and being part of an emerging industry all contribute to your real and perceived prospects for growth.

Profitability

Many successful IPO companies have a demonstrated track record of stable revenue and earnings. In exceptional cases where companies have excellent earnings trend lines, investors may trade off prospects for exceptional growth and price appreciation for lower risk and a reliable dividend stream.

But there are no hard-and-fast rules. Each company must evaluate its present circumstances and its prospects, bearing in mind that few elements in the overall picture will impress the investor as much as momentum. Nevertheless, every year, start-up companies in "glamor" or "hot" industries go public. Many of these companies have never posted a profit; some have never even reported revenues.

Although a perfect trend line is optimal, it certainly isn't always necessary. Even mature companies with aberrations in their earnings trend lines have successfully executed their IPO strategies—particularly if the aberration was caused by some unusual, one-time, or non-recurring charge that is unlikely to have an impact on future operating results. In the final analysis, the critical success factor is not short-term earnings, but rather the ability to sustain your financial performance over the long term.

Management Capabilities

Underwriters and investors will carefully consider size, growth, and profitability in evaluating your company. But weaknesses in any of these areas will not necessarily preclude a public offering. The single issue on which underwriters and investors rarely will compromise is management strength. Strong management translates into the most important intangible element—investor confidence.

Now is the time for your senior executives to analyze whether they can comfortably adjust to the public's scrutiny of the company's actions. Are they ready to cope with the requisite loss of freedom and privacy? Are they ready to admit outsiders to the decision-making process? Do they have the leadership capability to grow as the company grows?

CREATE AND COMMUNICATE A PLAN FOR USING THE IPO PROCEEDS

As you move closer to the IPO, you need to have a clear strategy for communicating with underwriters, investors, and employees. The success of your road show will depend on the coherence and the credibility of the story you tell. Investors are looking for a *compelling* reason why you are raising funds in the public market. General working capital is not a strong enough reason. Highly successful companies have a clearly articulated and persuasive plan for the proceeds of the IPO.

If you are not absolutely sure of your plan for using the proceeds, your first step is to review the initiatives in your business plan. Can you use the proceeds to reposition your company strategy, to reengineer processes, to reconfigure your infrastructure, to revitalize your culture? The market looks favorably on a plan to pay off debt from a recapitalization. You need to evaluate the uses of the proceeds from a perspective of whether each proposed initiative creates high shareholder value or low shareholder value, as well as whether the value created will be long-term or short-term.

As you begin to form a communication strategy for both external and internal audiences, notice that your story has changed because you have made many changes and you are contemplating a public offering. What, exactly, is the new story? Investors and employees alike need to understand the company's direction and the way in which its improvement agenda is affecting the creation of value.

COMPLETE YOUR CORPORATE HOUSEKEEPING

Before you proceed into an IPO event, you may need to do some corporate housekeeping. This involves considering whether the existing corporate, capital, and management structures are appropriate for a public company and whether your transactions with owners and management have been properly documented and recorded.

Corporate housekeeping generally begins during the planning stage and may not be completed until the registration statement is filed with the Securities and Exchange Commission (SEC). The following are typical questions to be considered during this phase:

- *Should the company's capital structure be changed?*   Restructuring may have tax implications, but you can mitigate any tax disadvantages with appropriate planning. You may want to simplify a restructuring by issuing common shares in exchange for preferred stock or special classes of common stock.

- *Should additional shares of stock be authorized?*   Additional shares might be needed for the public offering or for future acquisitions or sales.

- *Should the stock be split before you go public?*   To improve the common stock's marketability, companies frequently split their stock— after consulting with underwriters—so that the offering price of the stock will be between $10 and $20 per share.

- *Should affiliated companies be combined?*   A public company generally is organized as a single corporation, perhaps with subsidiaries. Affiliated companies might provide services to each other, might compete with each other, or might sell related products and services. The combined entity may well be more attractive to investors and thus command a higher price in the market.

- *Should the company's article of incorporation or bylaws be amended?*   A private company may have special voting provisions that are inappropriate for a public company, or the board of directors may need to establish certain committees, such as audit and compensation committees.

- *Are the company's stock records accurate and current?*   Accurate shareholder information is a must for a public company. (While reviewing the stock records, be alert for problems with previous issuances of unregistered securities.)

- *Are the company's transactions or arrangements with the owners and members of management appropriate for a public company, and are they adequately documented?*   The SEC requires public companies to fully disclose all significant related-party transactions. Such transactions should be identified and discussed with the company's legal counsel early in the process.

- *Are the company's contractual obligations appropriate for a public company?*   Your legal counsel can assist you in challenging the appropriateness of your contractual obligations by performing a "legal audit" of significant contracts (including employment contracts, stock option or purchase plans, debt and lease agreements, shareholder or management loans, rights of first refusal, corporate charter and bylaws, and major supply contracts).

• *Have important contracts and employment agreements been put in writing?* Do they need to be amended?

• *Should a stock option plan be implemented?* Should additional options be granted under existing plans?

EVALUATE YOUR INFORMATION SYSTEMS

A public company is required to provide timely and reliable financial information to investors. If the company's management and accounting information systems are inadequate, now is the time to put them in first-class working order. There are legal liabilities for reporting false or misleading information, not to mention the loss of investors' confidence if the information is not timely and accurate.

EVALUATE YOUR SYSTEM OF INTERNAL CONTROL

Many companies have long recognized the importance of strong internal controls. An effective internal control structure can help you achieve established financial goals, can prevent loss of resources, and can prepare reliable financial statements.

Companies considering an IPO need to take a close look at their systems of internal control and evaluate their effectiveness. The importance of internal controls became clear with the enactment of the Foreign Corrupt Practices Act of 1977 (FCPA). The FCPA was a direct result of investigation and a public scandal that revealed that more than 400 U.S. companies had secretly made kickbacks, bribes, or other questionable payments to foreign officials to obtain or to maintain business connections.

There are two major provisions to the FCPA. The first provision, the conduct provision that affects all U.S. companies, makes it illegal for any U.S. business to pay or to authorize payment of anything of value to foreign officials to obtain or to maintain business relationships. As a result of the provisions of this part of the FCPA, many companies have established written codes of conduct that address these issues.

The second major provision, which relates to accounting issues, applies only to companies that file reports with the SEC under the Securities Exchange Act of 1934 (1934 Act). Two major requirements are mandated by the accounting provisions of the FCPA: (1) Registrants must establish and maintain books, records, and accounts that accurately reflect the transactions of the registrant; (2) registrants must establish a system of internal controls adequate to meet the following four requirements:

1. Transactions are executed in accordance with management's general or specific authorization.
2. Transactions are recorded in such a way as to permit preparation of financial statements in conformity with GAAP (generally accepted accounting principles, or any other applicable criteria) and to maintain accountability for assets.
3. Access to assets is permitted only in accordance with management's authorization.
4. The recorded accountability for assets is compared with the existing assets at reasonable intervals, and appropriate action is taken with respect to any differences.

The accounting provisions of the FCPA, which are the responsibility of management, amend the 1934 Act and are subject to SEC enforcement.

ENHANCE YOUR CORPORATE IMAGE

Creating your corporate image takes time, so you should start well in advance of the public offering. Bear in mind, too, that the SEC imposes restrictions on any new forms of advertising or publicity in which you may engage once you have started the registration process by retaining an underwriter.

The first step in creating a public image is to perform a thorough self-evaluation of your company and its future. Consider your potential geographic appeal. Depending on the nature of your product and your geographic product market area, your shares may be limited to a regional market, or they might attract national or even international interest.

In what industry will your company be categorized? That could bear on your company's appeal to investors. Certain industries are more attractive to investors than others and thus command a higher price-earnings ratio. If your business could be classified in more than one way, aim for the industry classification that would result in the highest price-earnings ratio. Some companies with diverse product lines may be identified only with one of their better-known products. A good publicity campaign can create a broader based image for your company.

IDENTIFY POTENTIAL INVESTORS

Consider what types of investors you can attract or wish to attract. There are obvious advantages to luring institutional investors—they control a hefty portion of America's investment capital. But they also often have various technical investment restrictions relating to, for example, the number and the price of your shares on the market, earnings history, dividend policy, and stock exchange listing. These restrictions initially may limit your company's institutional appeal, or they may spur you to take steps to improve it.

Once you have determined your target market of investors and the corporate image you plan to project, you must find ways to reach that market. You may wish to hire an investor relations firm and prepare a corporate brochure describing your company and its products, markets, and operations. If you already engage in product advertising, your advertising campaigns might include a corporate focus to help build investor interest in your company. Many companies use the power of the Internet to promote their businesses with creative web sites.

Try to identify the securities analysts and members of the business media who follow your industry, and make a special effort to reach them, either through a personal meeting or by including them on your mailing list. Building a good relationship with the press—including both trade publications and the national or local business and financial press—will help keep publicity flowing during and after your public offering.

EVALUATE THE RISKS AND
THE TIMING OF THE IPO

Risks

Many risks are involved in an IPO. The most obvious risk, perhaps, is that the offering will not be completed and the costs that have been incurred will have been wasted. This may occur because changes in the market or disappointing financial results cause the underwriter to back out. Another risk is that the stock may have to be offered at a lower price per share to attract investors. This will either result in lower proceeds from the offering or greater dilution to current shareholders.

If your public offering is made prematurely, there is the risk of serious long-term consequences. If your company falters shortly after going public—whether because of unstable management, technological difficulties, market forces, or other reasons—its credibility will be undermined. You may even find your company and its executives subject to litigation by disgruntled shareholders. It will be difficult to regain investor confidence.

Timing

Suppose you have weighed all the pros and cons and have decided that the best thing for the company is to go public. But is now the best time to go public? If the capital you need is available from nonpublic sources at reasonable cost, you may want to delay going public. If funds raised from other sources can be used to increase the company's growth potential, the value of the company's stock may increase. At a later date, the increased stock value may result in raising more capital or selling fewer shares.

Timing is crucial. The market for initial offerings has been known to fluctuate dramatically, often within a single year. In deciding whether the time is right to go public, you should consider several questions: Is the mood of the market right? Is the market strong, or is it slumping? Are prices rising or falling? Is trading volume up or down?

Investor acceptance of new issues is cyclical but often not predictable. Infatuation with a particular industry can significantly increase the share price for IPOs in that industry. But the window for new issues, and for your industry in particular, can unexpectedly close just as quickly as it opened.

A complex, ever-changing capital market virtually necessitates the advice of an underwriter or investment banker in determining the optimal time to go public. When the market is favorable, many companies go to the market to obtain funds that they will not need until some time in the future, thereby eliminating the need to speculate on future market conditions.

SUMMARY: PREPARATION IS THE KEY TO SUCCESS

We hope that the message of these first six chapters is loud and clear: Take the time you need to enter the IPO arena thoroughly prepared. As we have noted, our research showed that the highly successful IPOs were those companies that had systematically positioned themselves to act like successful public companies months or years in advance.

The well-prepared company that has addressed all the issues will be able to move swiftly when the market is right. In the next chapter, we will guide you through an exercise we call "Be the Public Company"— areas in which you can actually practice the many policies and procedures that are required of a public company.

7

BE THE PUBLIC COMPANY

Major differences in mindset and a variety of management challenges—not to mention legal requirements—distinguish a public company from a private company. There are many new procedures and behaviors to learn. Too often companies rush into an IPO and are forced to climb the learning curve afterward—with unhappy results. Our research shows that the most successful IPO companies started acting like public companies well before the offering.

We suggest that you practice being a public company for six months or a year before the event actually takes place. Think of it as a series of dress rehearsals in preparation for the IPO. You should simulate complying with as many Securities and Exchange Commission (SEC) requirements as possible. For example, you can set a timetable for closing your books, convene the board and report your quarterly earnings, and draft a press release that you send to your attorneys and to the board for review.

You can prepare financial statements that are in accordance with SEC requirements. You can even rehearse the lengthy process of writing your Management's Discussion and Analysis (MD&A). You can ask your accountants to perform quarterly reviews and to consider interim cut-off issues and interim tax issues. Most important, perhaps, you can and should practice comparing forecasted earnings to your actual performance for a few quarters. Accuracy in forecasting earnings is critical to an IPO's success.

If you do all these things for two or three quarters, you will see an enormous difference in your comfort level, and you will greatly increase the likelihood that your IPO will be a success in the critical first few quarters as you attempt to gain and to keep investor confidence.

Your practice exercise should not be limited to the CEO (chief executive officer) and top management. It should include any and all employees who will be involved in the relevant operations, from your controller to the clerk who closes the books. You will want to be sure that your people are fully informed about the SEC's confidentiality issues and that they will be careful what information they reveal to their families and associates.

In this chapter, we will review the following relevant areas: budgeting and forecasting systems, benchmarks and comparables, external financial reporting, financial statements, federal securities law, and IPO accounting and reporting issues.

IMPROVE YOUR BUDGETING AND FORECASTING CAPABILITIES

Your systems and processes for internal budgeting and forecasting are likely to need attention far in advance of the IPO. Public companies are expected to be able to budget and forecast their operations quarterly for one to two years in advance—and then hit their targets. This ability to meet your projections is so critical that it should be very near the top of your "to do" list. Your underwriters will be keenly interested in how well you have been able to predict your performance, whether you have had frequent "surprises, " and if so, whether you have been able to rectify any problems in the critical months before going public.

At least a year before the IPO, you should have your internal forecasting and budgeting systems in place. This will give you time to fine-tune them from quarter to quarter as you approach the IPO date. The rule of thumb is to "underpromise and overdeliver." Your management challenge is to learn to position the company's performance expectations so that you will achieve your forecasts. Because you want to exceed those expectations, it is advisable to set them low, holding the tide against bankers and others who may pressure you to raise them. Overpromising carries dire consequences in the public markets.

UNDERSTAND YOUR BENCHMARKS AND COMPARABLES

Another major element in the IPO is the performance expectations held by the analysts for your industry or sector. With which companies will the analysts be comparing your performance? What metrics are standard in your industry? This is the time to align your company's performance measurement practices with the demands of the market. For example, if you are in a retail industry, the key metrics may be same-store sales or sales per square foot. Technology companies are benchmarked by revenue per employee or book-to-bill ratio, whereas Internet companies measure the number of subscribers and revenue per subscriber as key performance indicators. If you are in steel, it may be costs per ton; if you are in textiles, it may be sales per yard. Being the public company means becoming familiar with your competitors and with the accepted terms of comparison. Performance criteria and performance measures must be clearly defined. Once you know your comparables and the relevant measurement criteria, you can work closely with your research analyst, your management team, and your outside advisors to position your company against those benchmarks and comparables.

Become familiar with your company's competitive position. Remember that our research shows that the highly successful IPO companies entered the IPO in a leadership position from the perspective of *all* of the following 8 financial criteria and 15 nonfinancial criteria (see "Anatomy of a Winner" in Chapter 1):

Financial Performance	Nonfinancial Performance
Sales	Quality of Management
Profitability	Quality of Products and Services
Return on Assets	Level of Customer Satisfaction
Cash Flow	Strength of Corporate Culture
Sales Growth	Quality of Investor Communications
Income Growth	Effectiveness of Executive Compensation
Market Share	New Product Development Capability
Cost Control	Innovativeness/Research Capability
	Research Productivity
	Strategic Planning
	Strategy Execution
	Management Credibility
	Ability to Attract and Retain Employees
	Quality of Major Processes
	Market Position/ Leadership

ENHANCE YOUR EXTERNAL FINANCIAL REPORTING

Most private companies will need to improve their external financial reporting capabilities substantially to get them up to speed. It is not at all unusual for a private company to prepare monthly financial statements a month or two in arrears and to take up to six months after year-end to close the books and get them ready for an annual audit. When you are a public company, you will have to report information with regimental frequency.

The following is a checklist of questions that can start your thinking process about the reporting issues you may need to address before the IPO:

- Is someone in your finance or accounting group ready to take on the responsibility of preparing your financial reports?
- Are your systems capable of producing reliable monthly and quarterly financial data?
- In order for your current systems to be reliable, do they require you to take a full physical inventory each time you prepare financial statements for external use?
- Do your monthly financial statements and management reports include all the necessary adjustments that are necessary for a fair presentation of interim results (for example, sales and receiving cut-off, routine accruals, depreciation expense)?
- Does your finance and accounting group have to make material adjustments at year-end to cleanup the balance sheet?
- Are you often surprised by year-end cleanup or audit adjustments?

Annual Financial Statements

Many private companies routinely prepare annual financial statements and have them audited by an independent auditor; however, their reporting capabilities are often limited. The main focus of their annual audit is typically to provide financial information only to creditors (as required by debt agreements) and to a limited number of owners.[1]

---

[1]In November 1998, the SEC proposed to accelerate the due dates for reporting annual (60 days) and quarterly earnings (30 days) in Form 8-K. Refer to SEC Release No. 33-7606A for additional information on the proposed changes.

All too often, owners/managers and shareholders of privately held companies are not concerned about the timeliness of their annual financial statements—as long as they are available in time to satisfy provisions of debt agreements. If a private company goes public, all that will change. As a public company, your annual report to the SEC will be due by the 90th day following the end of your fiscal year.[2] But in order to meet expectations for earnings releases, annual shareholder reports, and proxy solicitations, many companies find that their real deadline is much earlier than that.

Interim Financial Statements

Another extremely important but sometimes overlooked aspect of being a public company is the need to have reliable interim (quarterly) financial data. As a public company, you will have to report earnings quarterly in condensed financial statements within 45 days of the end of the first three quarters of each fiscal year. Many private companies are able to generate reliable annual financial data but do not prepare monthly and quarterly financial statements with the same degree of care.

Depending on the timing of your IPO, you may well need interim (stub period) financial statements in your IPO registration statement. This may be the first time you have had to present interim financial statements to anyone other than management or the board of directors. If your systems are not ready, you should start now to fill any gaps so that you will be ready to report interim financial information reliably when the time comes.

Close Schedules

If you have already bolstered your internal control and accounting systems and are capable of producing accurate financial data for interim and annual periods, consider establishing more aggressive monthly financial-close schedules. Challenge your finance and accounting group to close the books by the fifth working day after the end of each month.

If this is a problem, find out why. Delays in the monthly financial-close process can often be rectified quickly by a simple analytic procedure.

---

[2]Ibid.

Map out your process on a chalkboard. Identify the inputs, processes, and outputs of each subprocess that is needed to get the books closed on time. Measure how long each subprocess takes and whether the outputs of each subprocess are really necessary.

You may find that some processes and outputs do not add value. Eliminate those, and focus on improving the processes that are really critical to the monthly close. Identify the root cause of any problems, brainstorm solutions, and implement them. Implement the quick fixes first. If quick fixes alone do not solve the root causes of the problems, you may need a more comprehensive (and probably more expensive) solution—perhaps replacing your data processing systems.

Infrastructure

Is your system capable of producing all the financial and nonfinancial information you will need to generate after you become a public company? The only way you will really know for sure is if you start now. Instruct your finance and accounting group and your corporate information officer to begin preparing and producing press releases and reports as if you were already a public company. This will help you evaluate whether your infrastructure (people, systems, policies, and procedures) is adequate to ensure that you will be able to comply with the SEC reporting requirements without missing a beat after the IPO. By addressing these issues now, you will be in an advantageous position when you begin the daunting task of gathering all the information that will be needed in your IPO registration statement (see Chapter 8). For example, you may want to:

* *Have the person you have selected to handle investor relations routinely prepare press releases about significant company events and developments.*

* *Prepare quarterly earnings releases, just as you will have to do after you go public.*   Set a target for their completion. Many public companies announce quarterly earnings just a few days after the end of the quarter. Although some take longer, most make their announcements by the end of the calendar month following the end of the quarter. Perform a survey of the earnings release dates of your competitors and other similar-sized companies in your industry. Analysts will generally expect you to conform to the norm of your peers.

• *Prepare Form 10-Qs or 10-QSBs (the quarterly reports filed with the SEC) each quarter.*   Have the mock reports reviewed by your independent accountants and attorneys, and make sure the reports and all necessary reviews are completed before the 45th day after the end of each quarter.

• *Prepare a Form 10-K or 10-KSB (the annual report public companies file with the SEC) for your latest fiscal year*—including MD&A and all the other required information. Virtually all the information in this mock annual report will be needed in your IPO registration statement anyway. Preparing the disclosures in advance will significantly expedite and streamline the offering process. Have your independent accountants and attorneys review your report to identify any material omissions or areas of concern.

• *Upgrade the current knowledge and skills of your financial reporting group.*   Are they ready to take on these new reporting obligations? If not, will your current staff be ready to take on the challenge with a little focused training? Do you need to hire new talent from outside? Ask your auditors to recommend appropriate SEC-specific accounting and reporting training courses, seminars, or self-study materials, and encourage your staff to complete any necessary training.

The SEC's quarterly and annual reporting requirements go well beyond simply preparing financial statements. Your financial statements will have to be supplemented with many new disclosures, such as earnings per share and specified financial data by operating segment. (See the section "Consider Potential IPO Accounting and Reporting Issues" later in this chapter.) In addition to financial statements, you must report a substantial amount of nonfinancial data (such as MD&A) in periodic reports filed with the SEC. To comply with these new requirements, you should make sure your financial reporting systems are capable of providing the necessary data. Your independent accountants and attorneys can help you identify the new disclosures that will be required.

GET YOUR FINANCIAL STATEMENTS IN ORDER

It is of paramount importance that you make sure that you have or can obtain all the necessary audited financial statements—not only for your company but also for any predecessor companies, recently acquired companies or probable acquisitions, and significant investee companies (among others). A company will not be allowed to go public if its financial statements have not been audited.

The prospectus[3] for your IPO generally must include audited financial statements for the past three years (two years if you are eligible to file as a small business issuer.[4]). Your prospectus also may be required to provide certain financial information for the past five years. These disclosure requirements generally apply only for the years in which your company has been in existence. However, they also may apply to a predecessor.[5]

Some companies have proceeded with great haste toward their IPO—and wasted a great deal of time and money in the process—only to find at the last minute that they are unable to comply with one or more financial statement requirements. For example, you could find out at the last minute that you need audited financial statements for a business you acquired two years ago. As is often the case, you may not have access to the books and the records or to the management of the seller. Your auditors may inform you that it is impossible to complete an audit in these circumstances. As a result, you will have to put your IPO on hold until the preacquisition financial statements of that business are no longer needed.

Or your company might have a material investment in a joint venture (i.e., greater than 20 percent of total assets) that is accounted for using the equity method. The joint venture agreement prohibits both you and your venture partners from publicly disclosing financial information about the venture. You assumed all along that your venture partners would waive the nondisclosure provision. At the last minute, you find out that they are not willing to waive the provision and that the only way for you to go public is either to buy out your venture partners or to sell your interest to them. There are many similar potential mishaps—all of which are completely avoidable if you pay attention to these issues and resolve them in a timely manner.

The SEC's financial statement requirements are quite complex. The first step is to determine which financial statements are required. You will

---

[3]The *prospectus* discloses information about the company and the offering and is distributed as a separate document or booklet to prospective investors.

[4]Generally a company is eligible to use the small business disclosure system if it is a domestic U.S. or Canadian company and has revenues and public float of less than $25 million.

[5]See Appendix D for information about SEC reporting requirements for predecessor companies.

also need to determine the companies for which you will need financial statements, the periods for which you need the statements, and how current those statements must be at the filing and effective dates of the registration statement. Even if you already have audited financial statements for all the requisite periods, GAAP (generally accepted accounting principles) and the SEC's rules may require that they be augmented to include additional disclosures (mostly in the footnotes). You also may need pro forma[6] financial information (see the subsection "Common Pro Forma Disclosure Requirements in IPO Registration Statements" later in this chapter) if the historical statements do not accurately portray the ongoing entity (for example, when there have been acquisitions, divestitures, debt restructurings, etc.).

The Importance of Early Planning

Well before the IPO, you must make plans to ensure that you will be able to comply with all the SEC's requirements for both audited and unaudited financial statements. Many private companies routinely have annual audits. These companies are in a much better position to go public on short notice than those that do not have annual audits. Private companies that have not had annual audits face a significant challenge. Some companies may ultimately be able to comply with the audit requirements (by engaging their auditors to perform a multiple-period audit), but others will not be able to comply for several years. It is imperative to know where you stand early in process.

Plan for Your Audit Requirements. At least a year before the IPO, you should meet with your independent auditors to thoroughly consider the sometimes complex SEC requirements for audited financial statements and to identify all the gaps that need to be addressed before the offering. The importance of involving your independent auditors as early as possible cannot be overstated. Not only will your independent auditors play a key role in helping make sure that your financial statements are in order; they also will help you determine whether you will need separate financial statements for any other companies, whether your financial statements comply with public company GAAP and the SEC's financial

---

[6]Pro forma financial information is historical information adjusted "as if" a given transaction had occurred at an earlier time.

statement disclosure rules, and when (or if) you will need to update the financial statements in your IPO prospectus.

If your company's financial statements have not been previously audited and if you're even only *thinking* about going public in the next several years, it is imperative that you address your audit requirements immediately. Your auditors *may* be able to perform a multiple-period (three years, two years for small business) audit in anticipation of a public offering. However, a multiple-period audit is a time-intensive process that is likely to delay your offering timetable, and you could miss a market window. A multiple-period audit could also cause credibility problems or even kill the deal if the auditors find material unexpected adjustments to current and prior years' earnings.

It is possible that your auditors will conclude that it is *not feasible* to do a multiple-period audit. For example, if you have significant inventories, your auditors must observe and test your annual physical inventory counts in order to issue an unqualified or "clean" opinion (required by the SEC's rules). They cannot perform these tests after the fact, and the SEC will not accept anything less than a clean opinion on your financial statements. If a multiple-period audit is impossible, you may have to delay your plans for going public until you can comply with the audit requirements. This could mean a three-year (two-year for small business) delay.

Consider the Requirements for Acquired Businesses. Make sure your auditors are thoroughly familiar with the history of your company, including the details about all the acquisitions, mergers, and investments you have made over the past three to five years.

Some companies run into problems when they make acquisitions during the three years (two years for small business) before they decide to go public, especially if the acquired business did not have annual audits performed. Even if the acquired business was previously nonpublic—or perhaps was just part of a business—the SEC's rules may require that your IPO registration statement include separate audited financial statements for one to three years prior to the acquisition. If audited financial statements are not available or if it is impossible to complete an audit, you could be precluded from going public or at best delayed for up to three years.

To avoid these potential pitfalls, always consider the audit requirements whenever you make, or even consider, an acquisition. If an audit has not already been completed, negotiate an audit report for one or more years as a condition for closing. If this is impossible, at least make sure you will have access to the books and records and to the seller's personnel so that you can have the audit performed after the acquisition.

Keep in mind that it may not be possible to perform the audit after the fact, and carefully consider the potential impact this will have on your plans for going public. You may decide that a particular acquisition is a tremendous opportunity—key to your strategic plan. In this case, it is probably of primary importance to complete the acquisition while you have the chance. On the other hand, you may decide that remaining IPO-eligible is more important and that you can seek similar acquisition opportunities that will not cause problems with your IPO. In that case, you might consider canceling the acquisition. In any event, you will want to keep the SEC's audit requirements in mind whenever you make decisions about business acquisitions.

Anticipate Your Underwriter's Needs. Even though the SEC's rules may require you to have audited financial statements for only three years (two years for small business), your underwriters may insist that your financial statements be audited for all five years that will appear in the table of selected financial data. If you expect this to be a problem, you will need to consult with your independent auditors to explore the alternatives and, based on the alternatives, reach a timely agreement with your underwriters.

Financial Statement Requirements
for a Registration Statement

What financial statements must the "registrant" (i.e., the company that is issuing registered securities) produce in an IPO registration statement? First, you must determine whether you are eligible to file using the small business disclosure system (under Regulation S-B). If you do not meet the criteria for Regulation S-B, you must comply with Regulation S-X (refer to Appendix E—Simplified Registration under the Small Business Disclosure System—for additional information on the eligibility criteria and benefits of this system). You will also need to determine whether your company has a "predecessor"[7] and, if so, whether you will need to include the predecessor company's financial statements.

---

[7]See Appendix D for information about SEC reporting requirements for predecessor companies.

Basic Financial Statements. IPO registration statements must include the following (audited and unaudited) financial statements:

- *Audited balance sheets* as of the end of each of the past two fiscal years (one year for small business issuers under Regulation S-B).
- *Audited statements of income, cash flows, and shareholders' equity* for each of the past three fiscal years (two years for small business issuers under Regulation S-B). In addition, you may need to include a separate statement of comprehensive income or to disclose information about other comprehensive items[8] in the income statement or in the statement of shareholders' equity.
- *Unaudited interim financial statements* for the three, six, or nine months after the end of the most recently completed fiscal year (together with comparative statements for the corresponding period of the preceding fiscal year). These interim statements may be required if the registration statement is declared "effective" more than 134 days after the end of a fiscal year (see Exhibit 7.1).

Additional Financial Statement Requirements. If your company has been in existence for less than three years (two years for small business), and it was originally formed solely for the purpose of acquiring an operating business, that business would be considered your predecessor under the SEC's rules. If the date you succeeded to the business of a predecessor falls within the two- or three-year period for which you must provide audited financial statements of your company, you will also need separate audited financial statements for the predecessor for one or more periods prior to the succession. You may also need older data (to the extent required in the five-year table of selected financial data) for the predecessor business. (See Appendix D for additional information about SEC reporting requirements for predecessor companies.)

In addition to providing audited financial statements of your company and its predecessor(s) in your IPO registration statement, you also may need to file separate financial statements (audited and unaudited)

---

[8]"Other comprehensive items" includes, for example, unrealized appreciation or depreciation on certain investments in marketable securities, certain changes in pension liabilities and the effects of certain types of foreign currency translation gains and losses. Accounting rules require that such items of "other comprehensive income" be charged directly to shareholders' equity, rather than including them in net income.

EXHIBIT 7.1. Age of Financial Statements in IPO Registration Statements

Type of Financial Statement[a]	Expected Effective Date of IPO Registration Statement		
	January 1, 2000, to February 14, 2001	February 15, 2001, to May 14, 2001	May 15, 2001, to December 31, 2001
The most recent *audited* financial statements must be:	As of a date no earlier than[b] December 31, 1998.[c]	As of a date no earlier than December 31, 1999.	As of a date no earlier than December 31, 1999.
The most recent condensed *unaudited* interim financial statements must be:	As of a date no earlier than[d] September 30, 1999.	None.	Most recent quarter (3/31, 6/30, or 9/30) ended more than 45 days before the effective date.[e]

[a]Examples assume company has a calendar (12/31) year-end.
[b]If the annual audited financial statements included in the registration statement are not recent (e.g., nine months old at the effective date), your underwriters may require you to have your interim financial statements audited—even though the SEC rules don't require audited interim financial statements.
[c]Unless more recent audited financial statements are available.
[d]In addition to the condensed unaudited interim financial statements, financial information describing the results of subsequent months may be necessary to prevent the registration statement from being misleading (e.g., if the company incurs operating losses or develops severe liquidity problems).
[e]Filings made 134 days or more after the company's fiscal year-end must include an unaudited balance sheet as of an interim date within 135 days of the date of filing.

for certain affiliates and other acquired businesses or properties under the following conditions (see Appendix D for more detail):

- *Equity method investees*—if your investment in an affiliated company that you account for using the "equity method" (i.e., you don't consolidate) meets certain size tests[9] relative to your company's consolidated financial statements.
- *Subsidiaries that have guaranteed publicly registered debt*—if you plan to issue public debt and one or more subsidiaries guarantee the

[9]S-X Rule 3-09.

debt,[10] or if you pledged the stock of one or more subsidiaries as collateral for the debt.

- *Recently completed or probable business acquisitions*—if they meet certain size tests in comparison to your consolidated financial statements.[11]
- *Recently acquired real estate operating properties*—if they meet certain size tests provided in the SEC's rules.[12]

PREPARE TO COMPLY WITH FEDERAL SECURITIES LAWS

When you become a public company, you and your officers, directors, and some shareholders will be subject to a myriad of complex federal securities laws. The primary purpose of the federal securities laws is to protect the interests of investors and the public. Protection of investors is accomplished principally through disclosure requirements and by prohibiting fraud and manipulative practices in securities transactions. Federal securities law is principally embodied in six acts of Congress that were passed between 1933 and 1940, in the wake of the 1929 stock market crash. The most important of these are the Securities Act of 1933 (the 1933 Act) and the Securities Exchange Act of 1934 (the 1934 Act). In addition to these laws, the SEC has adopted numerous rules and regulations, and there have been countless court rulings and interpretations.

The 1933 Act was designed to protect investors by setting truth in securities disclosure standards. It requires that companies provide investors with extensive information about the securities being offered and about the issuing company. Essentially, the 1933 Act ensures that potential investors receive adequate information in the registration statement and in the prospectus to make an informed investment decision. The 1933 Act also prevents issuers from misrepresenting material facts or from engaging in other fraudulent practices in the sale of securities to the public. It subjects the issuing company, its officers, directors, "control" persons, and others (accountants, underwriters, attorneys) to substantial

---

[10]S-X Rule 3-10. However, under certain circumstances, you may be able to omit separate financial statements of subsidiaries that issue guarantees of parent or holding company debt. Instead, you may only need to provide condensed summarized financial information about the guarantor subsidiaries.
[11]S-X Rule 3-05 and Staff Accounting Bulletin No. 80.
[12]S-X Rule 3-14.

penalties if they make false and misleading statements or if they fail to disclose material facts.

The 1934 Act seeks to ensure fair and orderly securities markets by, among other things, requiring public companies to make periodic reports and disclosures. Companies that have registered a class of securities under the 1933 Act or that have become subject to the 1934 Act because of meeting certain size and ownership tests must update information contained in their initial registration statement with annual and periodic reports to the SEC. These companies must send certain additional reports (e.g., annual reports, proxy statements) directly to their shareholders. The 1934 Act also contains provisions regarding proxy solicitations, tender offer solicitations, insider trading, margin trading, and exchange trading practices.

Both the 1933 Act and the 1934 Act impose significant responsibilities on public companies as well as on their officers, directors, and certain shareholders. Well before you begin your public offering, you should meet with your company counsel to discuss your obligations and your potential liabilities under the federal securities laws and to develop guidelines for complying with them. You might consider holding one or more seminars for your employees, or at least having your attorneys provide all affected individuals with a summary of what they can and cannot do after you become subject to the federal securities laws.

A few of the more significant aspects of the current legal requirements, liabilities, and restrictions of a public company are discussed below.

Timely Disclosure and Public Relations

As a public company, you must promptly disclose material information (both positive and negative) to investors, unless you have a sound business reason for keeping the information confidential. Examples of a sound business reason are such events as pending merger discussions, preliminary discussions concerning strategic alliances, and possible new product launches. Being a public company will require that you disclose information that you never thought about divulging when you were a private company.

Both before and after you become a public company, you will issue frequent press releases to disclose material information to the public. Many public companies designate one person in the company to be their information officer. This person responds to requests for information from securities analysts, the business press, shareholders, and other interested parties, and he or she reviews all proposed press releases as well as the texts of presentations and speeches by corporate executives.

You may want to limit the number of people who are authorized to speak to the press and have those people attend seminars and conferences on what to say and what not to say to the press. It is a good idea to get into the habit of writing press releases now—before you file the registration statement—to build interest in your company. Appoint someone in your company to monitor developments and to draft and distribute press releases.

This person should begin working with your public relations firm a year or more before the IPO to begin building your corporate image and your name or brand recognition. Make sure he or she routinely consults legal counsel concerning the releases and knows when the federal securities laws limit or restrict such activities. For example, during the IPO, the SEC rules severely restrict almost all forms of communication because they might be construed as premature selling efforts, or "gun jumping."

Dealing with Unregistered Stock and Selling Shareholders

When you file your IPO registration statement, only the shares actually sold by the company and any selling shareholders in the offering will become publicly tradable. Because of the practical limitations on the percentage of existing shareholders who will be allowed to "bail out" in the IPO, many of your shareholders will be left with unregistered shares after the IPO. Their shares may have been obtained in a private placement or in some other type of exempt transaction. If so, their unregistered stock may be subject to resale restrictions that are designed to limit trading.

If you have shareholders who wish to liquidate some or all of their holdings to take advantage of the increased share price that usually comes with going public, you should inform them that they will generally have to wait at least 90 days after the IPO before they can sell any restricted shares. (Your underwriters could insist on longer holding restrictions.) Even after the 90-day waiting period, those shareholders may be subject to further volume restrictions that limit the number of shares they may sell in any three-month period. (See "Sale of Restricted and Control Stock— Rule 144" in Chapter 8.)

Securities Law Liabilities Regarding Registration Statements

The 1933 Act imposes a high standard of conduct on directors and officers of public companies who are associated with a registered public offering of securities. The signers of the registration statement, as well as the directors, officers, and others, are liable for any untrue statement of a material fact contained in a registration statement or for any failure to state a material fact.[13] The law allows purchasers of a registered security to sue the issuer, its director or partners, underwriters, accountants who are named as having prepared or certified the registration statement, and company officers who sign the registration statement.

The statute was designed to promote compliance with the disclosure provisions of the 1933 Act by imposing strict liability standards on the parties who play a direct role in registered security offerings. To establish a claim, investors must show only that they purchased a security pursuant to a registration statement and that the registration statement included a material misstatement or omission.

The liability of the issuer of a registered security is virtually absolute. However, other parties who play a role in the offering (e.g., directors, officers, and underwriters) may avoid liability by establishing a "due diligence" defense—which entails making a "reasonable investigation" and having reasonable grounds to believe in the accuracy of the non-expertized, company-produced portions of the registration statement. (An *expertized* portion is one in which a third party recognized as an expert, for example, an auditor or an attorney, has rendered an opinion.) With respect to portions of the registration statement that are expertized, officers and directors may avoid liability by proving that they had no reason to believe (and did not believe) there was a material misstatement or omission in the registration statement.

Because of the statutory due diligence defense, which also applies to the underwriters in a registered securities offering, the parties to the registration statement will undertake a thorough due diligence investigation of your company during the IPO process. The scope of the due diligence investigation varies considerably, and the adequacy of a party's due diligence defense is a question of law—best left for the courts to decide. (See Chapter 8 for more detail about the due diligence process.)

[13]Section 11 of the 1933 Act.

Other Securities Law Liabilities

The 1934 Act contains broad antifraud provisions that apply not only to documents filed with the SEC, but also to misstatements and omissions made in negotiated transactions as well as in press releases or other communications. The SEC brings enforcement actions against violators of the antifraud provisions.

The general antifraud provisions of the 1934 Act prohibit manipulative or deceptive practices in connection with the purchase or the sale of a security via the mail, the Internet, any means of interstate commerce, or any national securities exchange.[14] The Act prohibits any device or scheme to defraud, making an untrue statement of a material fact, or omitting material facts that are necessary to make a statement not misleading. It also prohibits engaging in any act, practice, or course of business that is intended to defraud any person. The 1934 Act also creates a liability for false and misleading statements contained in any report or document filed with the SEC.[15]

In order to recover an investment loss under the antifraud provisions, a person must have relied on the false and misleading statement to his or her detriment. The person who made the statement or caused the statement to be made may avoid liability by showing that he or she acted in good faith and had no knowledge that the offending statement was false and misleading.

The 1934 Act also expressly prohibits the falsification of corporate books and records. Directors and officers are prohibited from making false, misleading, or incomplete statements to an accountant in connection with an audit of company's financial statements. In addition, the Foreign Corrupt Practices Act of 1977 requires public companies to keep books, records, and accounts that, in reasonable detail, accurately and fairly reflect the transactions and asset dispositions of the company. Public companies are also required to maintain an adequate system of internal control.[16]

Although senior management and the board are obviously not expected to be personally involved in recording transactions in the accounting records, they have important responsibilities to monitor and to evaluate the adequacy of the company's records and control systems. The audit committee of the board, too, should assist with the responsibility of

[14]See Section 10(b) of the 1934 Act and Rule 10b-5 thereunder.
[15]Section 18 of the 1934 Act.
[16]Rule 13b2-1 under the 1934 Act.

overseeing and monitoring the effectiveness of the company's financial accounting and reporting systems (see Chapter 5).

Controlling Insider Information

When you become a public company, you must be careful not to release any material information to someone who may rely on that information to buy or to sell your stock, unless you immediately release the same information to the investing public. For example, if you disclose information such as projected earnings to an analyst, you must disclose the same information to everyone. This is because the antifraud provisions of the 1934 Act prohibit anyone from trading on inside information.

Corporate insiders who are privy to nonpublic information and who take advantage of their position to make significant profits (or minimize losses) at the expense of less informed investors may be held liable for fraud violations. These provisions apply not only to insiders—your officers, directors, and employees—but also to anyone outside the company who improperly gains access to inside information. They also apply to a *tippee*— one who *receives* inside information (knowingly or unknowingly) from a source who has obtained access to the inside information.

A special treble damages penalty may be imposed for insider trading. You will need to implement policies and procedures not only to make sure that your insiders are aware of these provisions, but also to ensure that they comply with them. For example, most public companies establish "black out" periods just before and after earnings releases and at other times when material undisclosed developments are known to a few persons within the company but cannot be disclosed in a press release (for example, if confidential merger discussions have begun).

We want to add a word of advice about electronic mail (e-mail) systems. There have been instances in which confidential information was leaked outside a company through corporate e-mail networks or even through the Internet. If such a leak were to occur during the "quiet period" of your IPO, you could be forced to terminate or to substantially delay your offering.

Shareholder Reporting Obligations

After the public offering, your officers, directors, and other insiders will be subject to the beneficial ownership reporting obligations under the

1934 Act.[17] *Beneficial ownership* is defined as voting power or investment power with regard to the company's common stock, whether or not the person has a monetary interest in that stock. The reporting obligations apply to every person who is directly or indirectly the beneficial owner of more than 10 percent of any class of equity securities that is registered under Section 12 of the Exchange Act and to every director or officer of the issuing company.

Your corporate officers, directors, and principal shareholders will be required to file public reports to the SEC to disclose their ownership and changes in their ownership of your company's stock. If your stock is listed on a national securities exchange, they also will be required to file reports with the exchange.

The purpose of these periodic reporting requirements is to discourage the abuse of inside information. The requirements are based on a belief that prompt public disclosure of insider securities transactions gives investors information about purchases and sales by insiders that might indicate the insiders' personal opinions about the company's prospects. Those who are subject to this reporting requirement must report to the SEC all their non-exempt transactions in your company's securities.

The company bears the responsibility of monitoring and overseeing compliance with shareholder reporting and must disclose any failure to file the required reports on time. The SEC encourages public companies to help their officers and directors comply with the shareholder reporting obligations. Three basic forms are used for insider reporting:

- *Form 3 is the initial statement of beneficial ownership of securities.* It must be filed within 10 days of qualifying as a Section 16 reporting person (i.e., an officer, a director, or a 10 percent holder).
- *Form 4 is used to report any changes in beneficial ownership.* Form 4 must be filed on or before the 10th day after the end of the month in which a change in beneficial ownership occurs.
- *Form 5 is an annual report that must be filed within 45 days of the company's fiscal year-end* by every person who was an insider at any time during the fiscal year.

[17]Section 16.

Short-Swing Profit Liability and Short-Sale Prohibitions

The 1934 Act provides for an automatic recovery of any profits an insider makes on securities that were purchased and sold within a six-month period (short-swing profits).[18] An insider's short-swing profits can be recovered regardless of whether the insider was actually in possession of material nonpublic information.

The 1934 Act also prohibits the sale of any equity security of the company if the selling insider either does not own the security (i.e., a short sale) or does not deliver it within 20 days after sale or mail it within 5 days (i.e., a short sale against the box).[19] Obviously, you will need to educate every person who may be affected by these provisions to avoid problems after the IPO.

CONSIDER POTENTIAL IPO ACCOUNTING AND REPORTING ISSUES

The financial statements of a company entering the public markets for the first time must comply with numerous accounting and reporting requirements that do not apply to private companies. Many of these additional requirements are dictated by GAAP (e.g., earnings per share, operating segment disclosures), whereas others are required by the SEC's rules (e.g., detailed requirements for financial statement line items, mezzanine treatment of redeemable stock).

Fortunately, most of the differences between public company GAAP and private company GAAP do not affect the way transactions are recognized in the financial statements. That's because the SEC relies on the private sector to establish accounting standards, and the private sector accounting-standards-setting bodies (e.g., Financial Accounting Standards Board [FASB], American Institute of Certified Public Accountants [AICPA], Emerging Issues Task Force) decided a long time ago that there should not be any differences in the recognition and measurement provisions of GAAP based on the size of the company.[20] But public companies generally must disclose substantially more information in their financial statements than is required by GAAP in financial statements of private companies.

[18]Section 16(b).
[19]Section 16(c).
[20]However, some SEC rules and interpretations specify recognition and measurement principles for public companies that differ from those applicable to private

The purpose of this section is to highlight some of the more common accounting and reporting issues that companies going public face and to provide guidance for dealing with those issues. If any of these accounting issues appear to apply to your company, consult your independent auditors early in the IPO planning phase. Most of these issues can be resolved expediently during the early planning phase, but your options may be much more limited down the road than they are now.

Earnings per Share

Public companies must present earnings per share in their annual and interim financial statements. Current accounting rules do not require private companies to disclose earnings per share,[21] and many companies do not even make the computations until just before they file their IPO registration statements. Because of the nuances of these often complex calculations, earnings per share can be a tricky proposition for some companies, particularly those with complex capital structures that have issued numerous types of equity instruments in the recent past.

The rules require that two measures of per share data be shown in the financial statements for both annual and interim periods: (1) *Basic earnings per share* is a very straightforward calculation—simply divide the income available to common stockholders by the weighted-average number of common shares outstanding for each period. (2) *Diluted earnings per share* is a bit more complicated. It reflects the assumed conversion of all *dilutive securities* such as options, warrants, convertible debt, or preferred stock for each period since they were issued (assuming they are dilutive, i.e., decrease earnings per share). The mechanics of computing diluted earnings per share when you have dilutive securities can be quite difficult for private companies, particularly if the company has no objective evidence for the market value of its common stock for each period within the three to five years before the IPO.

To avoid delays in the registration process, make sure you have appropriate documentation for the market value of your common stock for all necessary pre-IPO periods. Typically, such documentation would

companies for certain types of transactions or presentations (e.g., allocation of overhead costs and parent-company interest expense in financial statements of subsidiaries, divisions, or lesser components; gain recognition on the sale of a business or operating assets to a highly leveraged entity; gain recognition on sales of stock by subsidiaries or equity investees).

[21]FASB Statement No. 128, *Earnings per Share*.

be either a comparable cash sale of your common stock to an unrelated third party or a third-party valuation by an investment banker or another independent specialist. Your independent accountants can help you determine the information that will be needed, and your investment banking firm can assist you in determining the appropriate values.

Segment Disclosures

One of the new disclosure requirements you may face when you go public relates directly to how your internal reporting systems roll up information and report it to top management. Most private companies do not present segment information in their financial statements. Thus, the new requirement to present disaggregated information can be a tremendously time-consuming matter if you wait until the last minute to address it. The amount of information you must separately disclose (e.g., number of segments you must separately report) will be driven by your management reporting systems and by how you manage and allocate resources to each business unit or line of business.

Under FASB Statement No. 131, *Disclosures about Segments of an Enterprise and Related Information,* you may be required to make disaggregated disclosures about individual (or groups of) business units or lines of business in both your annual and interim financial statements. Determining whether you have separately reportable segments of your business—and which ones they are—requires careful consideration of the facts and circumstances.

In addition to the complexities of deciding what information will have to be reported, you will also want to consider the competitive aspects. For example, as a public company, you may have to disclose information about a segment of your business that has only one or two nonpublic competitors. Obviously, this could be to your disadvantage. Your competitors may have much more financial information about your business unit than you will have about theirs.

To avoid last-minute surprises, have your finance and accounting staff and your independent accountants analyze your company according to the requirements of FASB Statement No. 131, and prepare draft disclosures. When you see them, you may decide that this is not a problem. On the other hand, you might decide that the disclosures convey too much competitive information. If so, you may be able to implement changes in your corporate organizational chart, your internal management reporting systems, or both. At this point, you still have time to make the changes you think are necessary. Later in the offering process, you will not have the same degree of flexibility because of the time constraints of the process— nor will you have time to completely restructure your management team and reporting systems.

The segment disclosure rules require that you present disaggregated information about your company (in the notes to financial statements or in the Description of Business section of registration statements and periodic reports) using a "management approach." This means that you determine which parts of your company must be broken out in the segment disclosures on the basis of how you manage and evaluate the various parts (segments) of your business. Once you determine what parts of your business must be separately disclosed, you must disclose the following information about each reportable segment in your annual financial statements (less detailed disclosures are required in quarterly statements):

- Types of products and services.
- A measure of profit or loss.
- Total assets.
- Revenues (separately) from (1) external customers, (2) transactions with other operating segments, and (3) interest.
- Interest expense.
- Depreciation, depletion, and amortization.
- Unusual items.
- Equity in net income of investees accounted for by the equity method and the carrying amount of those investees in the balance sheet.
- Income tax expense or benefit.
- Extraordinary items.
- Significant noncash items other than depreciation, depletion, and amortization.
- Total expenditures for additions to long-lived assets.

The rules also require certain narrative disclosures; a reconciliation of total income and assets for all reportable operating segments (combined) to consolidated net income and assets; and certain other disclosures about products, markets, and foreign operations.

Pre-IPO Stock Issuances—Cheap Stock

Many companies that go public implement stock-based compensation strategies for their key executives and board members (see Chapter 5).

The most common forms of stock-based compensation are stock options and outright grants of restricted stock, which vest over several years after the IPO. Current accounting rules provide two options for accounting for stock options:

1. Accounting Principles Board Opinion No. 25 (APB 25). Does not require the company to recognize compensation expense for stock options in its financial statements if the grant meets certain conditions. Among other things, to avoid recognizing compensation expense, the exercise price of the options at the date of grant (or the consideration paid by the recipient for any restricted stock or award shares) must be at least equal to the fair value of the underlying common stock. If the exercise price of the option or the price paid by the recipient for any shares purchased is less than the fair value, compensation expense must be recognized for the "intrinsic value" (determined at the date of grant or award) over the vesting period.

2. FASB Statement No. 123 (FAS 123). Requires that compensation expense be recognized over the vesting period based on the fair value of the options as determined at the grant date.

For obvious reasons, very few companies choose to follow FAS 123. Instead, most follow APB 25 for purposes of determining compensation expense and disclose (on a pro forma basis) what net income and earnings per share would have been if they had followed FAS 123.

It is a good idea to get help from a knowledgeable accountant in structuring the terms of your stock option grant. The SEC staff carefully scrutinizes all pre-IPO issuances of options and stock to determine whether all compensation expense has been (or will be) recognized. When companies use APB 25, the SEC staff generally challenges whether the fair value determined by management is appropriate, and it looks for evidence that a higher value should have been used to determine compensation expense.

The SEC staff often assumes that the IPO price is the best evidence of fair value in the year of an IPO. This routinely leads to frequent staff questions about potential compensation accounting for pre-IPO stock, warrants, or options issued to employees at a price that is below that of the IPO. Such a rigorous SEC review can significantly disrupt the timing of the registration process.

In evaluating the reasonableness of fair values, the SEC staff has stated that it seeks "persuasive evidence" to support significant value increases between the date of grant and the IPO date. The SEC staff looks, in particular, for evidence that focuses on the registrant's own specific facts and circumstances. Although general market and industry conditions also might be helpful, they appear to be secondary in the staff's analysis. Also, the staff considers the proximity of the purchase or the grant date to the IPO date, and generally expects more recent grants to be very closely related to the IPO price.

Several elements of company-specific evidence may be helpful in convincing the SEC staff that the grant date fair value was appropriate even though it is lower than the IPO price. First, and most helpful, is a cash sale of similar stock to an independent party at the approximate time of the grant. Second, a concurrent appraisal from an independent recognized expert, such as an investment banker, should be helpful. (However, the SEC may challenge both the credentials of, and the assumptions used by, the appraiser.) Third, support for the increase in value can be provided by identifying specific company events that occurred between the grant and the IPO dates. Examples of such events might include the introduction of new products, opening of new markets, acquisitions, increases in sales or profits, or the favorable resolution of a contingency such as a lawsuit. Although valuing the stock of a private company is a subjective process, the more objective and specific the evidence supporting the valuation, the more convincing it will be. In the staff's view, the burden of proof is on the registrant.

Underwriters believe that the fair value of a company's common stock in the pre-IPO period may be less than the IPO price for a number of reasons. These include:

- The risks and greater uncertainties that investors often perceive with the illiquid securities of private companies.
- Uncertainty surrounding a private company actually going public— as demonstrated by the number of registrations that do not become effective.
- The fact that IPO proceeds often are used to pay off existing debt or preferred stock, subsequently enhancing the value of the publicly traded common stock.
- The rapid growth that companies about to go public often have immediately before the IPO.
- The frequent correction of existing company weaknesses and deficiencies by the IPO process itself.

Furthermore, most valuation experts acknowledge that a nontradeable share of stock is worth less than one that trades on a public market.

The SEC staff may object to an approach that applies a range of reasonable discounts to the IPO price based on the length of time between the purchase/grant date and the IPO. Instead, the staff expects a registrant to defend its positions based on the facts and the circumstances that existed at the date of grant or issuance.

Occasionally, the only significant sales of company securities that might provide a relevant common-stock-pricing reference are for convertible preferred shares. However, it is important to be aware of the differences between the common and the convertible stock. Careful consideration should be given to the respective terms of the two securities (with the help of an independent appraiser, if possible) before using the convertible preferred as a basis for estimating the value of the related common stock.

Among the factors that need to be compared and analyzed in using convertible preferred securities as a benchmark for determining the market value of common stock are the rights for conversion (often 1 : 1), dividends, and voting and liquidation preferences. To the degree that the rights of the common stock are substantively similar to those of the convertible preferred, their value also should be similar. Where significant differences in value between the preferred and the common stock are considered appropriate—preferred stock may have significant liquidation preferences—you will need evidence to support the lower value of the common stock. The opinion of an investment banker or another third-party specialist would be appropriate.

Pre-IPO issuances of stock, options, or warrants may require consideration not just from the perspective of compensation expense, but also from the perspective of special treatment in computations of diluted earnings per share. The SEC staff requires registrants to treat certain nominal issuances of shares of stock, options, or warrants during the five years preceding an IPO as if they were outstanding for all periods presented in computing diluted earnings per share.

Mandatorily Redeemable Equity Securities

Mandatorily redeemable preferred stocks are equity securities that either are subject to mandatory redemption requirements or are redemptive outside the control of the issuer. These shares are often referred to as "mezzanine" capital because they must be reported on the balance sheet between liabilities and stockholders' equity.

The SEC prohibits classification of manditorily redeemable preferred stocks under a general stockholders' equity heading.[22] This applies to any equity security with similar redemption characteristics, such as redeemable common stock. Redeemable preferred stock may not be presented in a total that includes nonredeemable preferred stock, common stock, and other stockholders' equity.

Because private companies can classify these securities as equity, this issue often comes as an unpleasant surprise during the IPO process. Some companies do not find out until late in the process that substantial quantities of their equity cannot be classified as equity because of this SEC rule.

Changes in Capitalization at the Time of the IPO

Many IPO strategies involve a recapitalization of the company at or near the IPO date. Examples are (1) debt or redeemable preferred stock that converts to common stock, and (2) changes in capital structure resulting from a change in legal form (partnership or limited liability company to corporation) or tax status (Subchapter S to Chapter C companies). When there is such a change in capitalization, questions routinely arise as to whether there should be retroactive restatement of the balance sheet for all periods presented.

In general, the SEC staff will object to a retroactive restatement of the financial statements to reflect these types of changes for any period before they occurred. If redeemable preferred stock converts to common stock on the effective date of the IPO, management often believes that the redeemable preferred stock should be shown in permanent equity for all prior periods because the stock will not be redeemable after the IPO. However, the SEC will not allow the prior-period financial statements to be restated either to present the redeemable preferred stock as common stock or to reclassify the redeemable preferred stock as permanent equity. The SEC requires the redeemable preferred stock to be shown in the mezzanine until the date of conversion.

Generally, the historical balance sheet or statement of operations should not be revised to reflect conversions or term modifications of outstanding redeemable preferred stock that become effective after the last balance-sheet date presented in the filing. Pro forma data presented with the

[22]Rule 5-02 of Regulation S-X.

historical statements would generally be required if the conversion or the modifications have a dilutive effect.

Material changes in the capitalization of a registrant that will be affected at the time of the closing of the IPO should be presented in a separate pro forma balance-sheet column beside the historical balance sheet in the primary financial statements. The pro forma column should reflect only the change in capitalization as if it occurred on the latest balance-sheet date included in the filing.

In addition to historical earnings per share, registrants should present pro forma earnings per share data on the face of the statement of operations, giving effect to the change in capitalization as of the beginning of the latest fiscal year carried forward through the most recent interim period presented in the filing. Pro forma data should be clearly labeled, and a note to the financial statements should explain the basis of the presentation.

Common Pro Forma Disclosure Requirements in IPO Registration Statements

Pro forma financial information is historical information adjusted "as if" a given transaction had occurred at an earlier time. It generally includes a condensed income statement for the latest year and any subsequent interim period and a condensed balance sheet as of the end of the latest period presented.[23]

Because pro forma information ordinarily is not prepared until the filing date of the registration statement, there really is not much advance planning that you can do to prepare for these requirements, other than making sure that you obtain any necessary historical financial statement information (e.g., for acquired businesses or predecessors).

As we have noted, pro forma information generally must be provided for significant business acquisitions and dispositions, reorganizations, unusual asset exchanges, and debt restructurings (among other situations). Pro forma financial information also is required when the historical financial statements are not indicative of the ongoing entity (for example, tax or other cost-sharing agreements will be terminated or revised).

When cash dividends are declared by a subsidiary after the date of the latest balance sheet included in a registration statement, the SEC staff

---

[23]The SEC's rules that govern the form, content, and preparation of pro forma financial statements are contained in Article 11 of Regulation S-X.

requires that such dividends be reflected in a pro forma balance sheet and presented alongside the latest historical balance sheet included in the filing. If a distribution will be paid to current shareholders out of the proceeds of an IPO or if dividends paid in the year before the IPO exceeded earnings during that period, the SEC staff requires pro forma earnings per share to be disclosed, giving effect to the number of shares whose proceeds would be required to pay the dividend.

In addition, any significant distribution or planned distribution to owners that is not reflected in the historical balance sheet requires the presentation of a pro forma balance sheet alongside the historical balance sheet. The pro forma balance sheet should reflect the distribution but should not reflect any proceeds from the offering.

Escrowed Shares

Sometimes there are questions about the value of a company as it prepares to go public. In order to facilitate the IPO, underwriters may request that some or all shareholders (some or all of whom may be employees) of the privately held company place a portion of their shares in an escrow account. The escrowed shares generally are legally outstanding and may continue to have voting and dividend rights. The shares are to be released from escrow if the company achieves such performance measures as specific earnings or market price levels. If the specified levels are not achieved, the escrowed shares are returned to the company and canceled.

These shares are reported as legally outstanding on the face of the balance sheet. However, the SEC staff considers the placement of such shares in escrow to be a recapitalization similar to a reverse stock split. When the shares are released, the SEC staff considers that there has been a grant of restricted stock awards under a performance-based plan. Under GAAP, this has to be recognized as compensation expense, potentially lowering earnings per share.

The SEC staff believes that the escrowed share arrangement should be accounted for as a variable stock award plan, with compensation expense determined based on the fair value of the shares at the date the performance measures are achieved. Any such expense would be recorded over the earning (vesting) period, starting when probable of being earned.

However, this applies only to "active" shareholders who are officers, directors, employees, consultants, or contractors. No compensation expense would generally need to be recognized for shares that are released to a person who has no relationship to the registrant other than as a shareholder (anyone who is not an officer, director, employee, consultant, or contractor).

SUMMARY: THE IMPORTANCE OF BEING THE PUBLIC COMPANY

Any theater professional will tell you that a dress rehearsal is indispensable in building confidence and in positioning a performance for success. If you have practiced "being the public company" as suggested in this chapter, you are probably ready to go forward with your IPO. You will have improved your budgeting and forecasting systems, familiarized yourself with your benchmarks and comparables, enhanced your external financial reporting, prepared financial statements that meet SEC requirements, and addressed other important accounting and reporting issues. When you have completed these exercises successfully, your company is already acting like a public company. You are now well positioned to enter the IPO arena.

8

THE IPO EVENT

As we have tried to show throughout this book, an IPO is a process, not an end in itself. The actual event occurs in the middle of this process, following many months or even years of careful preparation. During the IPO, the CEO will probably serve as the company's major spokesperson, delivering the company's story to the world.

All inside and outside parties—everyone from investors and analysts to your employees and relatives—will be looking to you for leadership. The challenge here is to be the director and the star of what is most certainly your show. This implies rehearsing well, performing at the top of your form, resolving any conflicts, and managing the entire process.

The CEO will be involved in setting the strategic direction for the SEC registration statement. As the statement is being drafted, the CEO can also spend some time providing high-level direction to the content of the presentation for the upcoming road show—a whirlwind tour of the company's prospective investors and analysts. Two useful exercises should help you focus your efforts: (1) List five selling points about the company that you would want analysts and the financial press to know. (2) List five possible objections that analysts might raise to your company's current situation, and carefully prepare responses to those objections.

The road show is your opportunity to tell your story to the people who will help you sell your securities (i.e., members of the underwriting syndicate), to people who will influence potential investors (analysts), and to key prospective investors. It also lets you meet many of the people who will follow your company after the public offering—analysts and market makers who will participate in your quarterly conference calls and will issue critical buy, hold, or sell recommendations. It is easy to understand that all these people will be keenly interested in you and in your executive management team's abilities.

This audience tends to be sophisticated and skeptical. They have heard many a presentation and may be seeing between 5 and 10 similar presentations that very day. Your challenge is to capture their imagination, while at the same time keeping up your own excitement and passion about the company, even though you may be making the same presentation 50 times or more.

The road show is so challenging that no one can ever be completely prepared. Your task as the company's spokesperson is not to sell the stock but to sell the *company*—what it has done and what it will do in the future. Basically, you will do best if you present a balanced view of your business and your competition, selling your advantages and not placing emphasis on the disadvantages of the competition.

In addition to providing input into the creative process for the registration statement and the road show, the CEO can answer the questions of investors and analysts, making sure they understand the company correctly. Of course, because of legal restrictions, at this time, you must be extremely careful not to cross the line and engage in an activity that could be construed as selling securities in advance of the offering.

If you have not already done so, you should be sure to review your own personal financial plans. Our survey showed that 73 percent of the respondents failed to take advantage of the unique pre-IPO opportunities to put their financial and estate plans in place (see Chapter 4). The window for making the most of this opportunity will close on the date of the IPO.

As the event progresses, you are likely to see some clashes among the agendas of various team members. You may be able to head these clashes off by reviewing the priorities of all the important stakeholders. Keep open the lines of communication with all your constituencies, and carefully manage any conflicts that may arise. This new role of managing expectations will not end with the IPO; it will intensify and become one of your principal responsibilities as CEO of a public company.

The IPO event generally lasts between 90 and 120 days, but some take up to six months. It includes preparing and filing your registration statement, the road show, and the closing. Thereafter, there will be a few followup events such as your first periodic reports, proxy solicitation, and dealing with any remaining restricted stock. In this chapter, we will outline in some detail the procedures and the requirements involved in the registration process, give some tips on how to conduct a successful road show, and describe some of the reporting requirements you will face immediately after the IPO.

EXHIBIT 8.1. Example of timetable for an initial public offering.

Day 1	First "All-Hands" Meeting
Day 45	First Draft of Registration Statement
Day 50	Second "All-Hands" Meeting—Revisions Agreed On
Day 55	Third "All-Hands" Meeting
Day 60	Filing of Registration Statement with the SEC
Day 70–100	Road Show
Day 90	Receipt of SEC Comment Letter
Day 90–110	Revisions and Pricing
Day 115	Effective Date
Day 120	Closing

THE REGISTRATION PROCESS

The registration process begins, for the SEC's purposes, when you have reached a preliminary understanding with an underwriter on your proposed public offering. From that point on, you become subject to SEC regulations on what you may and may not do to promote your company. The heart of the registration process is preparing the registration statement.

Overview of the Process

Although it is difficult to generalize, few IPOs are completed in less than three or four months, and almost all are more expensive than any other source of financing. Many factors can affect the timing and the costs of an IPO. A brief review of the offering timetable may give you an idea of what to expect.

Two to three months generally elapse from the date a company engages an underwriter for an IPO to the date the registration statement is initially filed with the SEC. The SEC staff then takes approximately 30 days to issue its first comment letter, but it may take longer to complete its initial review. (See Exhibit 8.1 for a sample timetable for going public.[1]) The

[1]Keep in mind that the exhibit is merely intended to illustrate the major phases of the IPO process. This is an example timetable for an IPO; it is not unusual for time periods to exceed 120 days.

effective date of the registration statement can be as soon as two days after the SEC staff's comments are resolved.

The process begins with the first "all-hands" meeting, attended by all members of the working group—company executives, attorneys, auditors, underwriters, and underwriters' attorneys. At this meeting, the terms of the offering are discussed, as is the registration form to be used and the financial statement requirements. The company's counsel will usually prepare a very detailed timetable and assign responsibilities for the preparation of various portions of the registration statement and completion of numerous tasks. This document also includes target completion dates for each task (see Exhibit 8.2).

EXHIBIT 8.2. Example of working group assignments and schedule for an IPO.

Diversified Industries, Inc.

IPO Registration

Working Group Assignments and Detailed Registration Timeline

July 10–November 21

Working Group Members:	Registrant (R)
	Registrant's Counsel (RC)
	Underwriters (U)
	Underwriters' Counsel (ULC)
	Independent Auditors (IA)

July 10	Execute nonbinding letter of intent with underwriters (R, U, RC, ULC).
July 11	Hold organizational meeting (all).
July 12	Begin drafting Registration Statement and Prospectus (R and RC).
July 17	Complete and distribute time schedule and allocation of duties (RC).
July 20	Complete and distribute first draft of underwriting section of prospectus and underwriting agreements (ULC).
July 25	Prepare form of questionnaire for officers and directors (RC).
July 31	Distribute preliminary draft of prospectus (R).
Aug. 7	Mail questionnaire to officers and directors (R).
Aug. 15	Submit financial statements for all periods prior to the latest fiscal year (R and IA).
Aug. 16	Receive and review questionnaires from officers and directors (RC and ULC).
Aug. 17	Review draft Registration Statement (all).
Aug. 21	Send first draft of Registration Statement to printers (RC).
Aug. 22	Submit audited financial statements for latest fiscal year and unaudited financial statements for any interim periods required (R and IA).
Aug. 24	Send completed financial statements to printer (RC).
Aug. 31	Hold all-hands meeting (all).
Sept. 21–22	Review draft Registration Statement at printer (RC).

EXHIBIT 8.2. *continued.*

Sept. 22	Submit revisions to printer (RC).
Sept. 24	Conduct subsequent events review (R and IA).
Sept. 25	Hold all-hands meeting (all).
Sept. 25	File Registration Statement (electronically) with the SEC (R and RC).
Sept. 26	Distribute preliminary ("red herring") prospectus (U).
	[Although the preliminary prospectus may be distributed on filing of the initial registration statement, many companies delay distribution at least until filing the first amendment. Distribution is delayed to avoid the possibility of having to redistribute the preliminary prospectus in the event that significant changes must be made to the prospectus in response to SEC staff comments or other events.]
Sept. 27	Begin road show (R and U).
Sept. 29	Make Blue Sky filings (ULC).
Oct. 2	File stock exchange listing applications (R, RC, ULC).
Oct. 10	Select registrar and transfer agent (R, RC).
Oct. 12	File NASD application (ULC).
Oct. 24	Receive comment letter from SEC staff (R and RC).
Oct. 25	Discuss SEC comment letter, make changes as necessary (all parties), and draft response letter (RC).
Oct. 26	Send draft of amendment to printer (RC).
Oct. 30	Review and revise proof of amendment (all parties); return corrected proof to printer (RC).
Nov. 1	Hold due diligence meeting (all).
Nov. 2	Conduct subsequent events review (R and IA).
Nov. 2	Preclear changes with SEC staff (RC). [Note: In the event that there are relatively few comments to address, the SEC staff may allow the registrant to preclear comments by reviewing draft responses or changed pages of the registration statement. Final clearance, however, will not be received until the SEC staff has reviewed the final amendment.]
Nov. 3	File amendment with SEC, and provide response letter to SEC staff (RC).
Nov. 10	Receive clearance from SEC staff, and request acceleration of effective date (R and RC). [This timetable assumes that only one letter of comment is received from the SEC staff. In many circumstances (e.g., complex transactions, contentious accounting, or disclosure issues), the SEC staff will issue additional comments on amendments, which could delay the completion of the registration process.]
Nov. 13	Meet to set price of securities (R and U).
Nov. 14	Deliver first comfort letter to company and underwriters (IA).
Nov. 14	File pricing amendment with SEC (RC).
Nov. 14	Underwriters sign agreement among underwriters.
Nov. 14	Underwriters and registrant sign underwriting agreement (R and U).
Nov. 14	Registration statement becomes effective.
Nov. 14	Securities offered to public.
Nov. 21	Deliver second comfort letter to company and underwriters (IA).
Nov. 21	Conduct closing meeting (R, RC, U, and ULC).

Shortly after the first all-hands meeting (if it hasn't already been done), a nonbinding letter of intent between the company and the lead underwriter should be formalized. The nonbinding letter of intent confirms the intended nature of the underwriting (e.g., best-efforts or firm-commitment), the underwriters' compensation, the number of shares or the principal amount of securities expected to be issued, and the anticipated price. A binding underwriting agreement is not signed until the registration statement is about to become effective.

Preparing the first draft of the registration statement can take 45 days or more. When initial drafts of all assigned portions of the registration statement have been provided to your attorneys, they will consolidate the various sections and circulate a rough draft to all members of the working group. At subsequent meetings, the members carefully review and discuss the draft and agree on revisions.

In our example, the third all-hands meeting, usually held at the financial printer's facility, is attended by all parties. At this meeting, the printer's proof of the registration statement is reviewed, and the signature pages are executed.

After the initial filing, the members of the working group stay busy completing their due diligence and preparing state and National Association of Securities Dealers (NASD) applications while awaiting SEC comments on the filing. As soon as the SEC comment letter is received, draft amendments are prepared to respond to SEC comments. If required, the prospectus information, including financial statements, is updated.

The road show may begin as soon as the registration statement is filed, but many companies choose to wait and begin the road show after the registration statement is cleared by the SEC. On the road show, company executives and managing underwriters meet with prospective members of the underwriting syndicate and with investors to discuss the company and the offering.

After the road show (assuming a favorable response from investors), members of the working group will reconvene to review and approve amendments to the registration statement and to finalize the pricing. The final registration statement is then filed with the SEC, and if all SEC comments have been addressed to the satisfaction of the SEC staff, they will, at your request, declare the registration statement effective. The culmination of the process is the closing, where the securities are issued to the underwriters and the company receives the proceeds of the offering.

Registration Expenses

The greatest expense is the underwriters' discount or commission and will be influenced by the type of security, as well as by the size and the structure of the offering. For example, underwriting costs are generally lower for debt offerings than for equity offerings. The underwriters' commission also will depend on market conditions, competition for underwriting business, and the relative stability of your company and industry. A highly speculative offering may require more effort to sell and thus command a higher rate of commission. Usually, the underwriters' commission for initial public equity offerings ranges between 6 percent and 10 percent of the total offering proceeds. Most underwriters also require you to pay some (or all) of their out-of-pocket expenses.

Legal fees generally represent the second largest expense. They include fees not only for preparation and review of the registration statement, but also for the various related tasks required in anticipation of a public offering, such as a review of contracts and other legal housecleaning chores.

Furthermore, you are often required to pay the legal fees incurred by your underwriters' attorneys for their review of compliance with state securities laws. Because of the complexities of these laws, the underwriters' attorneys often perform this work on your behalf. Fees can range from just a few thousand dollars to more than $100,000, depending on how many and in which states the offering will be made.

Printing costs usually exceed $50,000 and sometimes can reach over $150,000. Numerous revisions, a large press run, and the use of color photographs will contribute to higher printing costs. You may also use your financial printer to file the registration statement on the SEC's EDGAR (Electronic Data Gathering and Retrieval) system. Depending on the length and the complexity of your filing, the electronic filing can add substantially to your total bill from the financial printer. Large numbers of lengthy legal documents filed as exhibits to the registration statement will further increase your EDGAR filing costs.

Accounting fees can vary and depend significantly on whether audits have been performed in the past. The fees also will be affected by the relative strength of a company's system of internal controls, the ability of the internal reporting system to generate industry segment data and other required disclosure information for public companies, the timing of the offering and the resulting need to include interim financial statements, and the extent of the procedures required to complete the comfort letter.

Other expenses include the SEC filing fee (a percentage of the maximum aggregate offering price), the NASD filing fee (also a percentage of the maximum aggregate offering price up to a ceiling), indemnity insurance premium (if required by underwriters, and if obtainable), state Blue Sky filing fees (dependent on number of states and the size of the offering), and registrar and transfer agent fees.

The final element of cost (usually not quantifiable) is the heavy commitment of executive time required for an IPO. This time commitment begins with the selection of your underwriters and other professional advisors, continues throughout the registration statement preparation process, and may intensify during the road show that precedes the effective date of the offering. (The road show can be quite expensive, particularly if it involves several people or foreign travel expenses.)

Although you won't be able to completely control the costs of your IPO or the length of time your IPO event will last, there are some things you can do to limit the cost and to expedite the process. Here are a few tips on how to save time and money:

• *Underwriters' compensation.*   You should not select your managing underwriters solely based on their compensation. In negotiating with your underwriters, bear in mind the factors they consider in determining their fees. A well-prepared business plan will help sell your company to the underwriters and reduce the amount of effort needed to sell your shares. With smaller underwriters and for smaller offerings, you may be able to trade off up-front commissions for underwriter warrants. (Outstanding warrants increase the potential dilution of the shares being offered and thus may reduce the price you can obtain for your shares.) Also, the reimbursable amount of your underwriters' attorneys' fees for compliance with state securities laws depends largely on the number of states in which you register your offering.

• *Legal fees.*   You cannot avoid legal fees incurred directly for preparation of the registration statement, due diligence, and other related legal services. But fees for some legal services can be held to a minimum. For example, you can reduce the extent of required legal housecleaning by consulting regularly with counsel in the years preceding a public offering on such matters as employment contracts, employee stock option and award plans, and any other contracts that may present a problem when you decide to go public.

- *Accounting fees.* The fees directly related to the registration process are unavoidable. These include review of financial information, attendance at all-hands meetings, reading prefiling drafts, assistance with responding to SEC comments, and preparing comfort letters. But accounting fees are often driven up by weak systems of internal control, inadequate internal reporting systems, and the absence of audit opinions on prior years' financial statements. Annual audits and reliable internal controls reduce both the time and the expense of a public offering.

- *Printing costs.* Excessive revisions are the biggest culprit in printing cost overruns. Keeping drafts in word processing format as long as possible will help reduce the number of printer's proofs required. Inevitably, some revisions will be made after the initial printer's proofs are obtained as items are challenged in the context of other disclosures and in response to changing market conditions. But you can hold the number of revisions to a minimum by having all text, charts, diagrams, graphs, and even type style, format, and color approved in advance.

Printer's proofs are expensive, especially when you demand immediate turnaround and cause the printer to incur overtime charges. By appointing one individual to coordinate all comments and revisions, you can reduce the likelihood of overlooked comments and incomplete revisions and, thus, the number of printer's proofs. Your attorneys sometimes assign an associate or a paralegal to perform this task.

- *SEC review.* The time required for the initial SEC review of your registration statement is largely beyond your control. Although the SEC's goal is to issue its first comment letter within 30 days of the filing of the preliminary registration statement, this sometimes takes longer during periods of heavy market activity. Delays, both in issuing the first comment letter and in resolving SEC concerns, also may occur if you are unwilling to make changes recommended by the SEC staff or if your attorneys or auditors are inexperienced in dealing with the SEC.

Overall, an IPO will be both time-consuming and expensive. But advance planning and preparation, careful selection of your professional advisors, and the cooperation of all parties can keep costs and delays to a minimum. In addition, today's technologies, particularly the Internet, are enabling issuers and their professional service firms to gain efficiencies and cost savings throughout the IPO process. There are companies that have created systems that allow for secure, on-line communication and for collaboration in both document management and transaction management.[2] Such systems result in measurable cost savings in the document creation process, and these systems also help reduce the time to market, which is often a critical factor in the IPO process. Additional efficiencies are expected as the use of the Internet continues to expand.

Due Diligence Investigation

As we noted in Chapter 7, under the Securities Act of 1933 (the 1933 Act), a company is absolutely liable for any material misstatements or omissions in its registration statement. However, the directors, controlling shareholders, underwriters, experts, corporate officers, and others who sign the registration statement may claim a due diligence defense if such deficiencies come to light. As a result, during the IPO process, every party who is subject to potential liability under Section 11 of the 1933 Act will devote considerable time and attention to completing a due diligence investigation.

Certain common due diligence procedures have evolved over time and in response to various court cases. For example, the courts have held that you and the others involved in the registration statement cannot assign responsibility for a due diligence entirely to your attorneys or to some other person. This does not mean, however, that every individual must personally verify each statement or disclosure made in the prospectus; for example, you may rely on statements made by your independent auditors and other experts as long as you have no reason not to believe those statements.

At a minimum, each person involved in preparing the registration statement should read it in its entirety. You can also expect your attorneys and your underwriters' attorneys to probe deeply into your company and its affairs in carrying out their due diligence procedures. Your company's officers and directors should candidly answer any questions about the company, statements in the prospectus, and the offering. The questions will delve into management's experience, their compensation arrangements, and their contracts or transactions with the company.

In carrying out their due diligence procedures, your underwriters typically ask your auditors to supply a comfort letter detailing the specific procedures they have carried out with respect to the unaudited financial data contained in the registration statement. The letter may provide

[2]Ernst & Young's proprietary system Deal Space and Intralinks are examples.

"negative assurance"—a statement that nothing came to the auditors' attention that indicated that the unaudited financial statements and other financial data were not prepared in accordance with GAAP (generally accepted accounting principles) applied on a consistent basis. Generally, the letter is dated both as of the effective date and as of the closing date, or a separate letter is issued on each of those dates. A draft of the comfort letter typically is provided to the underwriters shortly after the initial filing of the registration statement to obtain preliminary agreement on the specific procedures to be performed.

Finally, a due diligence conference is generally held shortly before the effective date. This meeting brings together your managing underwriters and the underwriting syndicate; your company's CEO, financial executives, attorneys, and auditors; and the underwriters' attorneys. This meeting is held primarily to give members of the underwriting syndicate an opportunity to raise any last-minute questions about the offering and your company. Questions at this meeting will mainly focus on events or financial performance of the company that have occurred since the registration statement was initially drafted. If significant events have occurred that would be important to investors, the registration statement should be revised to discuss such developments.

Preparing the Registration Statement

The first step in preparing the registration statement is the initial all-hands meeting, which includes company executives, attorneys, auditors, underwriters, and underwriters' attorneys. At this meeting, responsibility is assigned for gathering information and for preparing various parts of the registration statement. Typically, the attorneys play a coordinating role in directing this team effort.

The entire working group ordinarily participates in the initial drafting of the registration statement. The company and its legal counsel generally prepare the nonfinancial sections. (If the company's legal counsel is inexperienced in preparing registration statements, the underwriters' counsel assists.) The managing underwriter and underwriters' counsel prepare the description of the offering. The company prepares the required financial statements and schedules, as well as other financial disclosures. The independent accountant usually advises the company about the financial statements and disclosures.

As the various sections of the registration statement are assimilated, disclosures are reviewed, considered, and often redrafted. Two purposes of the prospectus, often viewed as conflicting, will become evident at this stage:

- *The prospectus is a selling document.* It will be used by your managing underwriters in forming an underwriting syndicate and by the syndicate to sell your securities. Therefore, you will want to present your company and the offering in the best possible light.

- *The prospectus also is a disclosure document.* It serves as protection against any liability for misleading and omitted material information on the part of controlling shareholders, executives, directors, underwriters, and experts providing information for the registration statement. As a result, all concerned will want to stress that all negative factors or investor "risk factors" related to your offering and your company are given at least equal prominence with the positive factors.

The experienced advice of your attorneys, auditors, and underwriters can help you balance these conflicting purposes. Even if the final document may not paint as bright a picture as you may have preferred, rest assured that underwriters and investors are accustomed to the tone of the typical prospectus and are adept at extracting the salient messages.

Content of a Registration Statement

The SEC has established the informational content as well as a generally standardized sequence and form for IPO registration statements. Information requirements vary, depending on the nature of the securities being registered, the size of the offering, and the type of company issuing the securities (industry, size, etc.).

Small companies that meet certain size tests under Regulation S-B are allowed to omit certain disclosures in their registration statements that are otherwise required for larger companies that are subject to Regulations S-K and S-X. For small businesses that qualify, the Regulation S-B rules simplify both the initial and the ongoing disclosure and filing requirements. (To file a registration statement under Regulation S-B, your company must meet the eligibility criteria described in Appendix E.)

A registration statement requires a considerable period of time to prepare. The document must contain all disclosures, both favorable and unfavorable, necessary to enable investors to make well-informed decisions, and it must not include any materially misleading statements.

A registration statement consists of two parts:

- Part I is the prospectus, which is widely distributed to underwriters and prospective investors.
- Part II contains additional information that is required by, and provided to, the SEC.

The entire registration statement is filed electronically with the SEC and becomes part of the public record. The SEC requirements are highly technical and everchanging, so most companies rely on their auditors and attorneys to help them interpret and apply the requirements.

The following is a summary of the content of a typical IPO registration statement.

Part I—The Prospectus

The prospectus must comply with the SEC's "plain English" rules.[3] That means the entire prospectus, including the cover and the back pages, the prospectus summary, and risk factors must be written using plain-English principles and must be clear, concise, and understandable. The rules require you to:

- Use short sentences, bullet lists, descriptive headings, and subheadings whenever possible.
- Avoid glossaries, defined terms, and legal and highly technical business terms.
- Avoid legalistic, overly complex presentations, vague boilerplate, excerpts from legal documents, and repetition.

The rules encourage you to use pictures and logos in designing the prospectus. You should also use charts, graphs, tables and schedules to present financial data. But graphs and charts must be drawn to scale and should not be misleading.

Outside front cover page. Shows key facts about the offering, including the name of the company; the title, the amount, and a brief description of the securities offered; a table showing the offering price, the underwriting discounts and commissions, and the proceeds to the company; and the date of the prospectus. The cover page also must include a cross reference to the risk factors section, including the page number where

---

[3]Rules 421(b) and (c) of Regulation C under the 1933 Act.

it appears in the prospectus. A sentence that says that the SEC has not approved or disapproved the securities being offered must appear on the cover page. If the offering is a secondary or partial secondary offering, a statement to that effect is included, and the proceeds to selling shareholders are shown. Generally, the managing underwriter's name is shown as well.

If the offering is not to be made on a firm commitment basis, the cover page must include a clear, concise description of the underwriting arrangements. (See Exhibit 8.3 for an illustrative example of an IPO prospectus cover page.)

Inside front and outside back cover of prospectus. Includes a table of contents, information about price stabilization, and a statement on dealers' delivery requirements for the prospectus.

Prospectus summary. May include an overview of the company and its business, a brief description of the security offered, estimated net proceeds and use of those proceeds, and selected financial data.

The company. Provides more detailed background information on the company, including where and when it was incorporated, the location of its principal offices, and a brief description of its primary business activities.

Risk factors. Highlights any factors that make the offering risky or speculative. Examples include dependence on a single supplier or a few customers, existing contractual restrictions on the company, an unproven market for its product, lack of business experience or earnings history, existence of plans put in place by the company to deter unwanted takeovers, material dilution to public investors as a result of the offering, or potential dilution that may result from the exercise of any outstanding stock options or warrants.

Use of proceeds. Discloses the principal intended use of the net proceeds of the offering, including specified details if the offering is to reduce debt or acquire a new business. If there is no specific plan for the proceeds, the reason for the offering must be disclosed.

Dilution. Describes, generally in tabular form, any material dilution of the prospective purchasers' equity interest caused by a disparity between the public offering price and tangible book value of the shares imme-

EXHIBIT 8.3. Example of an IPO prospectus cover.

Initial Public Offering Prospectus

Diversified Industries Incorporated

10,000,000 Shares of Common Stock

$5.25 per Share

Diversified Industries, Incorporated
1250 Elm Street
Anytown, Anystate 90210

We sell widgets to retailers in the United States and Canada.

The Offering

	Per Share	Total	
Public price	$5.25	$52,500,000	This is our initial public offering, and no public market currently exists for our shares. The offering price may not reflect the market price of our shares after the offering.
Underwriting discounts	$0.525	$ 5,250,000	
Proceeds to DII	$4.725	$47,250,000	

Proposed Trading Symbols:

The Nasdaq SmallCap Market[SM]—DII

This investment involves a high degree of risk. You should purchase shares only if you can afford a complete loss. See "Risk Factors" beginning on page 5.

Neither the Securities and Exchange Commission nor any state securities commission has approved or disapproved these securities or determined if this Prospectus is truthful or complete. Any representation to the contrary is a criminal offense.

LEAD UNDERWRITERS, INC.

CO-UNDERWRITERS, INC.

September 15, 2000

diately preceding the offering. Because existing shareholders often will have acquired their shares at a significantly lower cost than the offering price (e.g., through being a company founder or through employee stock option or award plans), material dilution often does occur for new purchasers.

Dividend policy. Discloses the company's dividend history and present dividend policy. Any restrictions on the payment of dividends also must be disclosed. If you do not intend to pay dividends in the near future, that fact must be disclosed.

Capitalization. Discloses the company's debt and equity capital structure, both before and after the offering. The pro forma capital structure after the offering is adjusted to reflect the securities issued and the intended use of the proceeds.

Selected financial data. Summarizes financial information for each of the past five years and for any interim periods that are included in the financial statements. This data generally includes net sales or operating revenue; income (or loss) from continuing operations, both in total and in per share amounts; total assets; long-term debt; capital leases; redeemable preferred stock; and cash dividends per share. Companies also may include additional data that would enhance an understanding of, or highlight trends in, their financial condition and results of operations. (Small business issuers are not required to furnish selected financial data.)

Management's discussion and analysis (MD&A) of financial condition and results of operations. Answers the question "why" for the financial condition and results of operations presented in the financial statements. This section of the prospectus provides investors with management's assessment of historical financial information as well as forward-looking information about expectations for the future. MD&A highlights trends, known events, and uncertainties that either have already had or are likely to have a material impact on continuing operations. The section includes a discussion of management's plans and commitments for capital expenditures and the sources for funding them, as well as significant items that have affected or will affect working capital. MD&A also includes a qualitative discussion of the reasons for significant changes in financial statement line items from year to year.

MD&A disclosures are particularly important in IPOs because they provide valuable insight into the company.[4] The general purpose of the MD&A requirements is "to give investors an opportunity to look at the registrant through the eyes of management by providing an historical and prospective analysis of the registrant's financial condition and results of operations, with particular emphasis on the registrant's prospects for the future."[5]

Quantitative and qualitative disclosures about market risks. Provides information about derivatives and exposures to market risk (e.g., interest rate risk, foreign currency exchange rate risk, commodity price risk, equity price risk) from derivative financial instruments, from other financial instruments (e.g., long-term debt, investment securities), and from certain derivative commodity instruments. The disclosure must include detailed quantitative information about the company's primary market risk exposures, together with qualitative information about the company's objectives for managing those exposures, strategies for achieving those objectives, and the context needed to understand those objectives and strategies.[6] These disclosures are not required for small business issuers.

Description of business. Provides investors with detailed information about your company's business operations. Items addressed in this section include:

- General development of the company and the business during the past five years.
- Future operating plans if the company has not had revenue from operations in each of the last three years.
- Segment information.
- Principal products or services.
- Principal markets and methods of distribution.
- Status of any publicly announced new products under development.
- Sources and availabiiity of raw materials.
- Patents, trademarks, licenses, franchises, and concessions held.
- Extent to which business is or may be seasonal.

---

[4]The specific requirements for MD&A are set forth in Item 303 of Regulation S-K and in FRR 36. For small business issuers, the applicable requirements are set forth in Item 303 of Regulation S-B.
[5]Financial Reporting Release 36 (FRR 36).
[6]The requirements are contained in Item 305 of Regulation S-K.

- Practices with respect to working capital items (e.g., if you are required to carry significant amounts of inventory to meet rapid customer delivery requirements).
- Dependence on one or a few customers.
- Firm backlog of orders.
- Government contracts, including whether they are potentially subject to termination or renegotiation.
- Competitive conditions.
- Research and development expenditures for the past three years, including amounts funded by others.
- Environmental matters.
- Number of employees.

Properties.   Discloses the location and a brief description of the major plants, mines, and other important physical properties owned or leased.

Legal proceedings.   Describes any material pending legal proceedings, other than ordinary routine litigation incidental to the business.

Management and certain security holders.   Provides certain key information on the business experience and compensation of management and on major shareholders. These disclosure requirements often give rise to objections from management because they now must publicly disclose the following information, much of which is generally considered strictly confidential by a private company:

- The names, ages, and business experience (and any involvement in specified legal proceedings) of all current or nominated directors and executive officers and other key employees.
- The compensation, both direct and indirect (including stock options and other benefits), current and proposed, for directors and certain executives.
- Loans to management and directors (and their immediate families) and certain transactions with management, directors, and major shareholders (and their immediate families).
- Transactions with promoters, if the company has been in existence for less than five years.
- Certain compensatory arrangements with officers and directors contingent on their resignation or termination or on a change in control of the company (e.g., employment, severance, or "golden parachute" agreements).

- The shareholdings of all officers and directors and of those shareholders who beneficially own more than 5 percent of any class of shares.

Description of securities to be registered. Describes the particular securities being offered, including the title of the security, par or stated values, dividend rights, conversion and voting rights, liquidation rights, and the transferability of each class of stock. The terms of any warrants or rights offered also are described.

Underwriting. Describes the underwriting and plan of distribution for the securities offered, including the names of the principal underwriters in the syndicate, the number of shares to be purchased by each, the method of underwriting, and any material relationships between the company and the underwriters. The underwriters' compensation, board representation, and indemnification also are disclosed.

If the underwriting agreement provides an overallotment, or "green shoe," option[7] or if the underwriters plan to engage in price stabilization transactions[8] immediately following the closing of your offering, the prospectus must include a statement similar to the following to alert potential investors to these matters:

> In connection with this offering, the underwriters may overallot or effect transactions that stabilize or maintain the market price of the common stock of the company at a level above that which might otherwise prevail in the open market. Such stabilizing, if commenced, may be discontinued at any time.

Price stabilization is a very technical practice that is allowed only if certain conditions are met. The SEC's rules require very detailed reports about stabilizing transactions.

Legal matters, experts, and additional information. Briefly identifies the attorneys, states whether they hold any securities of the company, and includes their opinion on the validity of the securities offered. This section also identifies any experts on whom you have relied in the preparation of the registration statement.

---

[7]An option the company sometimes gives the underwriters to purchase additional shares at the IPO price to cover overallotment. Named for the Green Shoe Company.
[8]See Price Stabilization and Overallotments later in the section "After the Offering."

Changes in and disagreements with independent auditors. Discloses circumstances surrounding changes in auditors during the past two fiscal years, including whether there were any disagreements between management and the former auditors or other reportable events on accounting, auditing, or financial reporting matters.

Financial statements. Contains the company's financial statements and the independent auditors' report for the requisite periods.[9] In addition to the company's financial statements, additional financial statements also may be necessary for:

- Recently completed or probable business acquisitions. (S-X Rule 3-05)
- Equity method investees. (S-X Rule 3-09)
- Subsidiaries that have guaranteed public debt of the company or whose stock is pledged as collateral for public debt of the company. (S-X Rule 3-10)
- Recently acquired real estate operating properties. (S-X Rule 3-14)

The SEC rules regarding when these additional financial statements are required are described in Appendix D.

Pro forma information. In certain circumstances, pro forma financial information (S-X Article 11) also may be required to reflect the effects of transactions (e.g., business combinations, dispositions, reorganizations) "as if" they had occurred at an earlier date.

Part II—Additional Information

The second part of the registration statement is not included in the printed prospectus provided to prospective investors. However, this information is filed electronically with the SEC and becomes publicly available. The following information is typically provided in Part II:

- Summary of expenses incurred by the company in connection with the issuance and distribution of the securities.
- Indemnification or insurance for liability of directors and officers acting for the company.
- Sales of unregistered securities in the past three years.

[9]Described in Chapter 7.

- Various financial statement schedules (not required for small business issuers under Regulation S-B).
- Various exhibits, including a list of all subsidiaries, the underwriting agreement, the corporate charter and bylaws, stock option plans, pension plans, and material contracts (e.g., employment agreements, leases, mortgage and debt agreements, key customer and supply contracts). This section also includes consents of any experts who prepared or certified any of the material included in the registration statement.

Some companies request confidential treatment of sensitive terms and provisions of certain contracts. If confidential treatment is granted by the SEC, the sensitive portions of the contracts are omitted from the exhibits. However, obtaining confidential treatment is not automatic, and such requests may take time that could significantly lengthen the registration process.

Review and Approvals

After the registration statement has been drafted and circulated, the working group meets to review and amend the document. The draft is modified as needed until all members of the working group are satisfied. Then a printer's proof is produced that goes through the same circulation, comment, and revision process. When the working group is satisfied with the document, it is distributed to the board of directors and all company executives who will sign the registration statement for review and approval before it is filed with the SEC and any appropriate state agencies.

Preparing a registration statement that is acceptable to all the parties is extremely difficult and often involves a series of compromises. For example, underwriters' counsel may insist on disclosures about the company that management is initially reluctant to make. These discussions, when coupled with severe time pressures and changing market conditions, can result in frazzled nerves and frayed tempers, particularly as the proposed offering date approaches.

Prefiling Communications with the SEC

When the registration statement has been drafted, but before it is initially filed with the SEC, some companies take advantage of the SEC's willingness to entertain prefiling communication with a registrant and its representatives. Most issues can be expediently resolved by preparing written prefiling submissions to the SEC staff. Prefiling communications with the SEC enable companies to discuss any important accounting or disclosure matters in advance, minimizing the number of costly and time-consuming revisions that may be necessitated by the SEC's formal review. Companies should consider the following when planning a meeting with the SEC staff:

• The company's officers should be prepared to explain and support the company's position because the SEC staff prefers to hear the company's position directly. This also ensures that the company's position is correctly and appropriately stated. The company's independent accountants should accompany the officers in this meeting. The company's legal counsel also may attend.

• Before attending a conference with the SEC staff, necessary documentation should be accumulated, and the material should be sent *in advance* to the SEC staff for consideration. Such material should include drafts of financial statements, as well as statements of the company's positions.

• The company should document in a memorandum all nonwritten communications with the SEC staff (i.e., telephone calls and meetings).

• It may be desirable for the registrant to send a letter to the SEC staff summarizing the subjects discussed at a prefiling conference and setting forth its understanding of the conclusions reached on accounting matters. This is particularly the case for complex issues where it is important to ensure that all parties clearly understand the conclusions reached. The person addressed is requested to review the letter and advise the registrant if the SEC staff has any comments. Such a letter serves to minimize future differences of opinion as to the conclusions reached. It is not customary to write to the SEC staff to confirm a telephone discussion; however, this may be desirable in some cases.

In 1997, the American Institute of Certified Public Accountants (AICPA) developed a summary of best practices for dealing with the SEC staff. Among other things, the AICPA's report, *Best Practices—Accounting Consultations, Communications with Board of Directors/Audit Committees, and*

Communications with the SEC Staff, focuses on helping registrants work more effectively to resolve accounting and compliance issues with the SEC staff. The report contains numerous helpful tips for handling SEC staff inquiries; for soliciting the staff's views; for prefiling resolution of issues; for resolution of SEC comment letters, conference calls or meetings with the staff; and for resolution of dissents or appeals of SEC staff positions. (You can get the report from the AICPA's web site at www.aicpa.org.)

Filing the Registration Statement

When outstanding issues have been resolved to the satisfaction of all concerned and the registration statement has been signed by specified company officers and a majority of the board of directors, it is electronically filed with the SEC on the EDGAR system, together with a transmittal letter and any applicable filing fee. (Although it is not appropriate to file paper copies with the SEC, the SEC staff may ask to see certain portions of the prospectus so they can determine whether you have complied with the page layout and formatting suggestions in the "plain English" rules.) At this stage, the registration statement is incomplete only with respect to certain information that is not finalized until the day before, or the morning of, the effective date. This information includes the price and related terms at which the securities will be offered, the underwriting syndicate, the underwriters' and dealers' commissions, and the net proceeds.

In addition to filing with the SEC, the registration statement will be filed with any state in which the securities will be offered and with the National Association of Securities Dealers (NASD). The SEC review is designed only to assess compliance with its requirements, including the adequacy of disclosures about the company, without addressing the merits of the offering. In addition to reviewing the adequacy of the disclosures, some states also consider the merits of the offering under their Blue Sky laws (i.e., whether the offering is "fair, just, and equitable").[10] Some states perform in-depth reviews, while others perform cursory reviews. The primary purpose of the NASD's review is to determine whether the underwriters' compensation is excessive.

---

[10]See "State Securities Laws" on p. 167.

SEC Staff Review

The review of registration statements is performed by SEC staff accountants and lawyers in the SEC's Division of Corporation Finance. The purpose of the SEC's review is not to evaluate the quality of an offering, but rather to determine whether they include adequate disclosure in accordance with the SEC's regulations and other pronouncements and to ensure that they comply with the relevant form instructions and regulations. Although the intensity of the Division of Corporation Finance's reviews varies, IPOs receive a thorough review.

When the SEC staff completes its review of the initial filing (usually within 30 days, but sometimes longer), it will issue a comment letter. The SEC staff's comment letter describes any deficiencies it has identified. The letter may also include requests for supplemental information if the disclosure is unclear or if the staff suspects that one or more requirements have not been satisfied. Comment letters often focus on the specific uses of the proceeds (including the adequacy of the proceeds for the designated purposes), whether the MD&A is complete and fully responsive to the SEC's requirements, and disclosures about risk factors.

The letter is usually divided into two parts: one part that contains comments and questions on the nonfinancial portions of the registration statement (sometimes referred to as the "legal comments"); and a second part that contains comments on the financial statements (the "accounting comments"). The accounting comments may question such matters as accounting policies and practices, related-party transactions, unusual compensation arrangements, off-balance-sheet financing methods, or numerous other issues related to the financial statements and whether they comply with GAAP and the SEC's accounting and disclosure rules.

The SEC staff may require you to disclose risk factors, adverse business conditions, or other weaknesses in the offering more prominently than you think is necessary, either by including cross-references to certain disclosures on the cover page (risk factors must be referenced on the cover page in any event), by supplying more information, or simply by moving the relevant disclosures closer to the front of the prospectus. They may ask you to support certain claims or statements made in the prospectus—and to remove them if they consider the support inadequate. They also may take issue with a particular choice of accounting policy, or they may request additional disclosures in the financial statements.

The experience of your professional advisors in identifying sensitive areas and anticipating potential accounting and disclosure issues should minimize the number of comments you receive on the initial filing.

However, rarely do first-time registration statements go through the SEC staff review process without any comments. In fact, some comment letters are quite lengthy—containing well over a hundred comments!

Amending the Registration Statement

Your attorneys and auditors will help you address and rectify any deficiencies noted by the SEC staff. If the changes required by the SEC staff's comments are not significant, you may be able to send the SEC staff a letter outlining the proposed changes or a printer's proof of the prospectus showing the proposed changes. You may be able to get the staff's agreement on minor changes by telephone, but this is rare. On the other hand, if the required changes to the initial filing are significant—and they usually are—you will need to file an amendment (a pre-effective amendment) with the SEC and submit a written response to the SEC's comment letter.

At this stage, the pace of the working group picks up dramatically. The underwriters are usually preparing for the road show, and they can't begin selling efforts until the preliminary prospectus (the red herring) is available. Members of the working group will often work around the clock at the financial printer to prepare the company's response to the SEC comment letter and draft any necessary changes to the initial filing.

A draft of the company's response to the SEC's comment letter and the pre-effective amendment is distributed to the working group for review. When all necessary changes are made (which may include updating the financial statements) and everyone is satisfied with the company's response to the SEC comment letter, an amended registration statement and the company's written letter of response to SEC staff comments is filed electronically with the SEC. A copy of the written response also is faxed to the SEC staff reviewer to expedite the review.

At this point, some companies choose to go ahead and print red herrings. However, most companies will wait until they have received the SEC staff's response to the changes before printing red herrings. (This reduces the possibility of having to recirculate the preliminary prospectus to each potential investor, which could be required if further changes are necessitated by the SEC's follow-up review.) A full recirculation to all investors will not only substantially increase your printing costs, but it will also confuse investors and cause credibility problems for you and your underwriters.

The SEC staff will usually notify the company within a few days (e.g., five business days) about whether they agree with the company's responses and proposed amendments or (as is often the case) whether the staff has continuing concerns or new questions. This process sometimes becomes iterative, and some companies go through several rounds of comment letters, responses, and pre-effective amendments before the SEC staff is completely satisfied. When the company receives the "all clear" signal from the SEC staff, it is usually safe to print red herrings and to begin the selling phase of the IPO event. (See the description and recommendations for the road show later in this chapter.)

Listing Your Company on a Stock Exchange

Some companies decide to register with a stock exchange. Others decide, instead, to take their securities over-the-counter (OTC) through a large network of securities brokers and dealers. Selecting an exchange or deciding to go with OTC trading is a very important decision. (See Appendix B for an overview of factors you will need to consider when you make this decision, including an overview of the initial listing requirements for the Nasdaq National Market [NNM], the Nasdaq SmallCap Market, and the New York Stock Exchange.)

If you do decide to list your securities on a stock exchange, you can choose among a number of different markets. The New York Stock Exchange (NYSE) is probably the most widely recognized stock exchange, but in recent years more and more companies have turned to the National Association of Securities Dealers and Automated Quotations (Nasdaq) Stock Market for initial listings. There are also a number of regional exchanges located across the country.

In general, the NYSE's listing requirements are the most stringent, followed by Nasdaq's National and SmallCap markets. These requirements are frequently revised, so you will need to obtain current information about them. A good place to look is on the Internet (see www.nasdaq-amex.com, www.nyse.com, or sites for any other exchange that interests you).

The exchange listing applications will need to be prepared and accepted by the exchange before the effective date of the registration statement. Your legal counsel and the underwriters' legal counsel will usually help you complete the listing applications.

State Securities Laws

In addition to filing a registration statement with the SEC and otherwise satisfying federal securities laws, you also must comply with state securities laws in all states in which your securities will be offered. The impact of state securities laws can range from a simple notification requirement to a prohibition on selling your securities in the state, even if your registration statement has been reviewed by the SEC and is effective. Therefore, the various reporting, filing, and qualification requirements of the states in which you intend to offer your securities should be addressed early in the registration process.

State securities laws are known as Blue Sky laws. *Blue Sky* refers to various fraudulent schemes common in the early 1900s that were characterized as selling building lots in the "blue sky." In response to these schemes and to protect investors, many states enacted securities legislation. Unlike federal securities regulation, which is limited to ensuring the adequacy of disclosure, many Blue Sky laws address the merit of offerings and disallow offerings they do not consider to be "fair, just, or equitable." The particular issues that some states consider in evaluating the merit of your offering include the price-earnings ratio; dilution to new shareholders; amount and terms of loans to existing shareholders, directors, and employees; and the voting rights of the offered shares. Many states do not allow you to circulate a red herring until you have filed their Blue Sky applications, so this must be taken care of as soon as the registration statement is filed with the SEC.

The North American Securities Administrators' Association (NASAA) has developed guidelines for securities legislation that are designed to make the state registration process more uniform. However, because some states make their own evaluation of the merits of the offering, there will continue to be some lack of uniformity. NASAA "cheap stock" guidelines, as adopted by many of the states, require shares sold to promoters for less than the proposed offering price within the preceding three years to be held in escrow for several years. This escrow is subject to the success of the issuer's earnings and to the performance of its stock in the public market.

Generally, once you have decided in which states your offering will be registered, the attorneys will prepare a Blue Sky Memorandum setting forth the various provisions and restrictions applicable to each of those states. This gives you time to plan how to deal with the relevant provisions and to decide whether any states should be excluded from the offering. The mechanics of complying with state Blue Sky laws—filing notices, copies of the registration statements, or other information as required—generally will be handled by your underwriters' attorneys.

NASD Clearance

Before an offering becomes effective, it also must be cleared by the NASD. The purpose of the NASD review is to determine whether the underwriting agreement is fair and reasonable. The NASD examines both direct compensation (discount or commission) and indirect compensation (underwriter warrants or stock options and expense reimbursements) and also regulates certain other aspects of the underwriters' arrangements. To avoid delays in the registration process, underwriters' counsel will usually apply for NASD review as soon as possible after the initial filing of the registration statement.

Circulation

To get the selling phase started, copies of the red herring are provided to potential members of the underwriting syndicate[11] and are distributed to prospective investors. The red herring is easily distinguishable from the final prospectus (discussed later) because it includes a statement similar to the following on the front cover, printed in red ink:

> The information in this prospectus is not complete and may be changed. We may not sell these securities until the registration statement filed with the Securities and Exchange Commission is effective. This prospectus is not an offer to sell these securities, and it is not soliciting an offer to buy these securities in any state where the offer or sale is not permitted.

The red herring includes substantially all the information that is required in the prospectus, but certain information is missing because it is not yet known. For example, the red herring does not include the final offering price, but rather it discloses an expected price range. Similarly, it will not include specific information about the underwriting agreement

[11]See next subsection "Forming the Underwriting Syndicate."

(because the agreement will not be finalized until just before the registration statement is declared effective). It also does not include certain other information that is driven by the price range and the offering costs, such as pro forma capitalization, dilution, and net proceeds of the offering.

Forming the Underwriting Syndicate

As soon as the preliminary prospectus is filed with the SEC, your managing underwriters will begin to assemble an underwriting syndicate to sell your securities. They will invite various firms to join the syndicate, based on your particular offering and the objectives established for it. Depending on the size of the offering, the syndicate could include more than 50 underwriters. Their selection will reflect the geographic distribution targeted for your offering and the anticipated or desired mix of institutional and retail investors.

Each of the underwriters in the syndicate will agree to underwrite a certain number of your shares and will then begin to approach its customers to determine the degree of interest in your offering. A copy of the red herring is provided to each prospective investor, who may then "express interest" in your securities based on the expected price range. However, you are not permitted to make any sales or to accept any offers to buy prior to the effective date of the offering.

Based on the success of each member of the underwriting syndicate in selling your shares, they may ultimately take delivery of more or fewer shares than the number for which they originally subscribed. Allocation of the underwriting commission is first made to the managing underwriters as compensation for managing the offering, with the balance allocated to the underwriting syndicate in proportion to both the number of shares underwritten and the number of shares ultimately accepted for sale to investors.

Limitations on Selling Efforts—The Quiet Period

The SEC places various restrictions on what you may and may not do while your company is "in registration." These restrictions apply during the "quiet period"—from the date you reach an understanding with your managing underwriters to handle your offering until 25 days after the securities are offered to the public (90 days for securities not listed on a national exchange or quoted on Nasdaq[12]). During the quiet period, any publicity release can raise questions or concerns about whether the publicity is part of the selling efforts—even if the publicity does not specifically mention the public offering.

During the period prior to initial filing of the registration statement, the 1933 Act prohibits you from "offering" the security. The SEC has broadly interpreted this phrase to include "the publication of information and statements, and publicity efforts, made in advance of a proposed financing that have the effect of conditioning the public mind or arousing public interest in the issuer or in its securities."

However, this does not preclude the normal ongoing disclosure of factual information[13] about the company. The SEC encourages companies to continue product advertising campaigns, periodic reporting to shareholders, and press announcements on factual business and financial developments, such as new contracts and plant openings. However, you may not initiate new publicity or issue forecasts or projections of revenue, income, or earnings per share. To avoid the potentially serious consequences of violating the SEC rules, you should clear any press releases or public statements with your attorneys in advance.

Specific guidelines also have been established with respect to the period after filing the registration statement. As already noted, the red herring prospectus may now be widely distributed to underwriters and to the investing public. Under the current rules, no other written sales literature is allowed during the "waiting period" between the filing date of the registration statement and the completion of the offering.[14] You may, however, publish a limited notice of the offering, including the amount of the offering, the name of the company, a description of the security,

---

[12]In November 1998, the SEC proposed changes to these restrictions. The proposal (SEC Release No. 7606A, sometimes referred to as the "Aircraft Carrier") would establish a new *bright line safe harbor* that would permit communications made more than 30 days before an IPO registration statement is filed. Such communications would not be deemed "offers" in violation of the "gun jumping" prohibitions of the 1933 Act.

[13]The Aircraft Carrier proposal would make it clear that factual business communications are exempt from all communications restrictions.

[14]The Aircraft Carrier proposal would also relax the restrictions on the use of supplemental sales materials, referred to as "free writing" materials, during the waiting period, provided the company circulates red herrings and electronically files all the "free writing" materials used during the waiting period.

the offering price, and the names of the underwriters. Known as "tomb-stone ads" because of their stark appearance, these notices are typically published in newspapers shortly after the initial filing of the registration statement and are not considered sales literature. Exhibit 8.4 shows a hypothetical tombstone ad for a company's IPO.

EXHIBIT 8.4.   Example of a "tombstone ad."

This announcement is neither an offer to sell nor
a solicitation to buy these securities.
The offer is made only by the Prospectus.

New Issue   **November 15, 2000**

10,000,000 Shares

Diversified Industries, Incorporated

Common Stock

Price $5.25 per Share

Copies of the Prospectus may be obtained in any State in which this announcement is circulated from only such of the undersigned or other dealers or brokers as may lawfully offer these securities in such State.

Lead Underwriters, Inc.

Co-Underwriters, Inc.

More Underwriters	More Underwriters	More Underwriters
More Underwriters	More Underwriters	More Underwriters
More Underwriters	More Underwriters	More Underwriters
More Underwriters	More Underwriters	More Underwriters
More Underwriters	More Underwriters	More Underwriters

Pricing the Stock and Completing the Underwriting Agreement

The pricing meeting with your underwriters takes place after you have completed the road show. The price depends on many elements, among them the so-called "book," a spread sheet of buyers' input (referred to as indications of interest.) At this point in the IPO event, you will find that the investment banker who has been your advisor and advocate is suddenly at the opposite side of the table. Your investment bankers are actually taking the risk of buying your stock for a very short period of time and then selling the stock in the public markets. Thus, the pricing is in itself a negotiated transaction.

The final pricing decision is not made until just before the underwriting agreement is signed—generally just before the effective date of the registration statement. But the background research, comparisons, analysis, and discussions will have begun well in advance of that date.

Offering prices of shares of common stock are often compared on the basis of price-earnings ratios. A variety of other factors also affect the price of your shares, among them the projected impact on earnings resulting from the proposed use of the new funds, the past and projected rate of growth, and the quality of past earnings (for example, whether they include extraordinary or nonrecurring gains or losses). Another factor is the dilution issue—the possibility that the value of ownership will be reduced if other shareholders are given an opportunity to exercise outstanding warrants. Your share price will also be affected by your company's vulnerability to competition, by relative management strength, by planned acquisitions, by the size of the offering, and by possible status as a "glamor" or a "hot" industry.

In short, pricing your stock is more of an art than a science. Your underwriters' experience qualifies them to advise you on an appropriate price. Although it is tempting to set as high a price as possible— particularly if a secondary offering of existing shareholders' stock is included—overpricing should be avoided. Underwriters typically advise a company to set a price that will produce an active aftermarket in the shares. Overpricing tends to destroy investor confidence, possibly creating a downward spiral in the share price. By pricing to allow for a modest price rise in the immediate aftermarket, you can stimulate public interest.

When new issues realize substantial price increases in the early weeks of the aftermarket, some owners conclude that the offering price was seriously understated. In most cases, however, the price increase is more reflective of undue public optimism than of underwriting error; within a relatively short time, the stock price will generally return to the more realistic levels that the underwriter had anticipated.

The formal underwriting agreement is executed on the last day (or on the morning) before the registration statement becomes effective. At this stage, the offering price and the number of shares (or amount of debt) to be offered are finalized.

Changed market conditions and feedback from the underwriting syndicate may necessitate changes in the offering price or in the size of the offering. If the market has surged, you may find that you are able to increase the price or the size of the offering. If market conditions have taken an unfavorable turn since the filing date, and if the order book has taken a turn for the worse, your underwriters may recommend a reduction in price or in the number of shares offered. In extreme cases, they may even advise a postponement of the offering.

Declaring the Registration Statement "Effective"

After all the parties involved are satisfied with the technical and disclosure aspects of the registration statement, the pricing amendment is filed. The pricing amendment discloses the offering price, the underwriters' commission, and the net proceeds to the company.

When all deficiencies have been dealt with to the satisfaction of the SEC staff, and when your company and professional advisors are satisfied that there have not been any additional material developments in the period since the registration statement was filed, you can ask the SEC staff to declare the registration statement "effective."

Although technically there is a 20-day waiting period after the final registration statement is filed before it becomes effective, an "acceleration request" is usually filed concurrently with the pricing amendment. The request asks the SEC to waive the 20-day waiting period and to declare the registration statement effective immediately. The SEC usually approves acceleration requests, provided you have appropriately circulated red herrings.

After the registration statement becomes effective, the final prospectus is printed and distributed to everyone who received a copy of the red herring and to others who expressed an interest in purchasing the stock.

Registrars and Transfer Agents

If your stock will be traded over the counter rather than listed on a stock exchange, you are not required to have an independent registrar and transfer agent. Your corporate secretary can maintain the company's shareholder records. But you will probably have a much larger number of shareholders and a much greater trading volume. This can be a tremendous administrative burden. In addition, security ownership records must be maintained accurately—there is no margin for error. Any mistakes can lead to claims against the company and possible financial liability. Independent agents can assume responsibility for making sure that mistakes in stock transfers do not occur. And, as a practical matter, your underwriting agreement will probably require you to have an independent stock registrar and a transfer agent.

You should appoint a registrar and a transfer agent before the closing of your offering. Many commercial banks and trust companies provide stock registration and transfer services. The same company can provide both services.

The transfer agent's primary responsibilities are to handle the transfer of shares from one person to another and to maintain the official shareholder records. Transfer agents also may pay cash dividends, mail annual reports and proxies, distribute stock dividends, and maintain custody of any unissued stock certificates.

Independent registrars make sure that your stock is not overissued. They countersign all stock certificates to make sure the number of shares issued is not greater than the number surrendered for cancellation, and they keep active records of all the shares that are outstanding. Registrars keep records of the certificates that have been canceled, lost, or destroyed as well as those that have been issued, so that at any given moment they have an exact record of shares outstanding.

The Closing

The registration process culminates with the company issuing the securities to the underwriters and receiving the proceeds (net of the underwriters' compensation) from the offering. The closing for firm-commitment underwritings generally occurs five to seven business days after the registration statement becomes effective. This gives the company and the underwriters a final chance to consider any last-minute material adverse events and to withdraw the offering if necessary (although this rarely occurs). The closing for best-efforts underwritings generally is 60 to 120 days after the effective date, provided the underwriters have sold at least the minimum number of shares specified in the registration statement.

At closing, documents are executed and exchanged (e.g., stock certificates, wire transfers or cashier's checks, receipts). Usually, the company's appointed representative, company counsel, the managing underwriter and its counsel, the stock registrar, and the transfer agent attend the closing. The company's independent auditor will ordinarily deliver an updated comfort letter, sometimes referred to as a "bring-down" letter, to the underwriters on the closing date. Under the SEC's "T+3" rules, sales of your stock through broker-dealers must be settled within three business days of the transaction. The rules also require that a final prospectus be delivered to all purchasers of your stock, together with the confirmation of sale.[15]

THE ROAD SHOW

After your registration statement has been filed, your underwriters generally will take representatives of your company on a traveling road show, also referred to as a "dog-and-pony show." These meetings give prospective members of the underwriting syndicate, institutional investors, and industry analysts an opportunity to meet your company's management team and to ask questions about your offering and your company.

The participants probably will be the company's CEO and the CFO (chief financial officer), whose major task will be to woo the investors, and the investment bankers, who will manage the tour and monitor the book, or computerized log of orders. Typically, the road show consists of between five and seven back-to-back meetings every day for two weeks. It can be a grueling marathon—covering many cities and, in today's global marketplace, foreign countries as well.

Each day you will go through the same slide presentation many times. Remember that the presentation does not end with the last slide. The question-and-answer period is equally important, and, as we have sug-

[15]The SEC's November 1988 Aircraft Carrier proposal would eliminate the requirement to deliver a final prospectus to purchasers unless they request one. The final prospectus would still be filed on EDGAR.

gested, it requires extensive preparation. If you anticipate the most challenging questions and welcome them, you will have a chance to turn what might have been an issue into a nonissue.

The following tips may help you make your road show more effective:

• *Prepare and rehearse.*   As we have noted, it is important that you anticipate and practice answering tough questions. Make sure to rehearse a few times before you make your first presentation.

• *Choreograph your presentation, and use visual aids and product demonstrations.*   Make sure you know who is operating the slide projector, and test it periodically to be sure it works. Any visual aids or demonstrations should be well rehearsed. Use these devices to vary your presentation and to get attention. There is truth in the adage "A picture is worth 1,000 words."

• *Understand each audience.*   Find out from your investment bankers whether each participant is a generalist or a specialist in your industry or sector. Find out their investment criteria. This will help you position your story and decide whether or not you need to explain your industry sector.

• *Develop rapport.* Begin building the relationship on a positive note by immediately assuming the attitude that they will invest in your company. After summarizing your strategy, ask the audience if there are any questions you have failed to address. Schedule a follow-up visit, and ask how frequently they wish to be in touch.

• *Be consistent and enthusiastic.*   You may have seven meetings a day, and sometimes you will have trouble remembering what you have covered. That is why it is best to maintain the same order, approach, and materials in all your presentations. Most important of all, be sure to sustain your enthusiasm and to act as if each meeting is your first.

• *Keep your finger on the pulse.*   The audience will remember what they said to you. Jog your memory of the meeting by taking time to jot down what people said. When each meeting is over, get feedback, and review it at the end of each day. What didn't go well? It is important to keep improving your presentation.

AFTER THE OFFERING

Going public will subject your company and its shareholders, directors, and executives to a variety of new responsibilities. Some of these relate to the requirements of the securities laws, and others relate to the way you must now conduct your company's affairs. Some of the laws to which you are now subject are extremely technical and complex, and your attorneys and auditors will advise and assist you in complying with those provisions. The following is a brief overview of some of new issues, responsibilities, and concerns you will face in the near term after your public offering.

Price Stabilization and Overallotments

Immediately after the offering closes, your shares begin trading on whatever market or exchange you selected. As part of your underwriters' services (which are spelled out in the underwriting agreement), they will normally be the principal market makers for your stock.

During the critical period of initial trading, your underwriters may engage in certain *stabilizing* transactions. Stabilizing transactions are intended to guard against sudden downward pressure on your stock price caused by speculators who purchased shares of your stock in the IPO with a view to holding them only for a few days, and then selling them at the sign of the first run-up. When this type of short-term profit-taking occurs, it could adversely affect your stock price—even forcing it below the IPO price. To stabilize the market, your managing underwriter is allowed to enter bids to buy the stock, but the bids cannot be higher than the offering price and cannot begin at a price above the current bid price.

Your underwriters may offer and sell more shares than they are otherwise obligated to purchase under the underwriting agreement. This activity, known as *overallotment*, immediately creates a "short" position—the underwriters have sold more shares than they own. To cover the short position, they must purchase enough shares in the open market to satisfy their overallotments. They may use some of the shares sold by early profit takers to cover their short position. Alternatively, your underwriting agreement may have given the underwriters a green shoe option to purchase additional shares to cover the overallotments.

Periodic Reporting under the 1934 Act

As a newly public company that has filed a 1933 Act registration statement, you are immediately subject to the periodic reporting requirements of the 1934 Act. Your ongoing reporting obligations will differ depending on whether your securities were registered under Section 15 or Section 12 of the 1934 Act, or both.

Your attorneys will help you navigate the complexities of the securities laws. Generally speaking, if your securities are listed on a national securities exchange, you will be a registrant under Section 12 of the 1934 Act. You may be listed only under Section 15 if your securities are not listed on a national exchange.

If your shares are to be traded on a national securities exchange or on Nasdaq or if (at the end of the year) you have more than 500 shareholders of any class of your shares and more than $10 million in assets, you will need to file Form 8-A to register your securities under Sections 12(b) or 12(g) of the 1934 Act. Form 8-A incorporates information from your IPO registration statements as well as any future periodic reports to the SEC. A registration on Form 8-A will usually become effective after the national securities exchange approves the listing application and notifies the SEC.[16]

Although you will be required to file periodic reports under the 1934 Act for your first fiscal year as a public company, your continuing obligation to file those reports may be suspended after the first fiscal year-end if, with respect to the class of securities registered, there are fewer than 300 shareholders. It will also be suspended if, after the first two fiscal years following the offering, there are fewer than 500 shareholders and the company reported less than $10 million in assets on the last day of each of the previous three years.

The reporting suspension becomes effective immediately on filing of Form 15 with the SEC. If your company's securities are listed on a national securities exchange or on Nasdaq, however, you will be subject to the periodic reporting requirements regardless of the number of shareholders.

The importance of complying with the periodic reporting requirements cannot be overemphasized. Periodic reports represent a primary form of communication with your shareholders and the financial community in general. Poorly prepared, incomplete, or late reports may adversely affect

---

[16]The SEC's Aircraft Carrier proposal, if adopted, would eliminate the need to file Form 8-A.

your relationship with investors and the public. You also run the risk of SEC sanctions or at least the risk of creating ill will toward your company by the SEC staff. You could also be precluded from using a more streamlined simplified registration form for future registrations.

Form 10-K

This is the primary report used annually to update much of the information that is contained in your original registration statement. The specific disclosure requirements are similar to those found in your IPO registration statement. As with the registration statement, the form itself is merely a guide, not a blank form to be filled in. Form 10-K is due within 90 days after the end of the fiscal year.

Much of the information required in Form 10-K is also required in various other SEC filings or in the annual report to shareholders prescribed by the SEC's proxy requirements (discussed later under Proxy Solicitation). Instead of including information from a previous SEC filing or report in Form 10-K, you may incorporate a lot of the information into the Form 10-K by reference to the previously filed document or report. For example, a company may include as an exhibit to the Form 10-K a copy of the annual report to shareholders containing the audited financial statements in lieu of reproducing the same financial statements in the 10-K.

Form 10-Q

The Form 10-Q quarterly report is a summarized report containing quarterly unaudited financial statements and MD&A. Additionally, certain specified events (e.g., legal proceedings, changes in the terms of securities, certain defaults, and matters submitted to a shareholders' vote) need to be disclosed in the 10-Q. Form 10-Q must be filed within 45 days after the end of each of the first three fiscal quarters (no quarterly report is required for the fourth quarter of your fiscal year).

Form 8-K

This report is required to be filed after specified significant events, including a change in control, significant acquisitions or dispositions of assets, bankruptcy or receivership, change in independent auditors, resignation of a director, or any other event considered of importance to shareholders. The form must be filed within 15 days of the reportable event, except in the case of a change in independent auditors or the resignation of a director (under certain circumstances), which must be reported within five business days. The form specifies certain minimum disclosures about each event.[17]

Periodic Reporting under the Small Business Disclosure System

Small business issuers[18] may elect to fulfill their quarterly and annual financial reporting requirements by filing Form 10-QSB and Form 10-KSB, respectively. These reports require somewhat less extensive disclosures than Forms 10-Q or 10-K, but they are very similar and are intended to accomplish the same purpose—to keep the market generally informed about your company, its business, and your financial and operating performance. (See Appendix E for additional information about stream-lined registration and periodic reporting under the small business disclosure system.)

Your First Periodic Reports after the IPO (under the 1934 Act)

Depending on when your registration statement is declared effective, your first report under the 1934 Act could be either a Form 10-Q or a Form 10-K.[19] If you are registered only under Section 15d of the 1934 Act and if your first report is a Form 10-Q or 10-QSB, the report must be filed within 45 days of the effective date of your IPO registration statement or on or before the date the report would have been due if you had been a registrant—whichever is later.

---

[17]The SEC's Aircraft Carrier proposal would expand the types of current events that are required to be reported on Form 8-K and would accelerate the due dates for reporting most events to one or five days after the event occurs. The proposal would also require a Form 8-K to be filed within 30 days after the end of the first three quarters or within 60 days after the end of the fiscal year to report earnings and other selected financial data. Access www.ey.com for updates related to the SEC's Aircraft Carrier rule proposal.
[18]Generally a U.S. or Canadian company that has less than $25 million in revenues and public float for each of the past two years.
[19]Form 10-QSB or 10-KSB for small business issuers.

For example, an IPO for a calendar year registrant that is declared effective on July 15 ordinarily will include unaudited interim financial statements for the quarter ended March 31. In this circumstance, the new registrant's first Form 10-Q, covering the three- and six-month periods ended June 30, would be due August 29 (the 45th day following the effective date of the registration statement). On the other hand, if your company is registered under Section 12 of the 1934 Act, your first Form 10-Q or 10-QSB will be due by its normal due date (i.e., within 45 days of the end of the quarter). The content of this first report is unaffected by its due date.

On the other hand, if the first report to be filed after the IPO is a Form 10-K (or 10-KSB), the content of that report will be affected by whether your securities are registered under Section 12 or Section 15 of the 1934 Act:

• Registrants filing periodic reports under Section 12 of the 1934 Act must file their complete Form 10-K with the SEC within 90 days of their year end (Rule 13a-1 under the 1934 Act).

• Registrants filing periodic reports only under Section 15 of the 1934 Act—whose IPO registration statement did not contain financial statements for the registrant's last full fiscal year (or life of the registrant if less than a full fiscal year) preceding the fiscal year in which the registration statement became effective—may be eligible to file a "special report" within 90 days after the effective date of the registration statement. This special report contains only financial statements for the latest fiscal year (i.e., there is no requirement to provide most of the nonfinancial disclosures that are otherwise required by Regulation S-K)[20]. However, if your stock is listed on a national securities exchange (i.e., you filed a Form 8-A to register a class of listed securities under the 1934 Act), you will not be permitted to file a special report, and your 10-K (or 10-KSB) must be filed within 90 days of your fiscal year-end, regardless of when the registration statement became effective.

Proxy Solicitation

Because the shareholders of most public companies are widely dispersed and because few attend shareholders' meetings, management of public

---

[20]Exchange Act Rule 15d 2-1.

companies usually solicits proxies[21] from shareholders before the annual shareholders' meeting. Proxies typically account for the majority of votes cast at shareholders' meetings.

The SEC requires that, before proxies may be solicited, a proxy statement must first be provided to shareholders. The content of the proxy statement is specified in the SEC regulations and varies according to the matters on which there will be a vote. If directors are to be elected, an annual report including financial statements must also be provided. Even if management does not solicit proxies, an information statement similar in content to a proxy statement must be furnished to shareholders.

The proxy rules apply only to companies that are subject to the 1934 Act because they are listed on a national exchange or because they have more than 500 shareholders and $10 million in assets (i.e., companies reporting under Section 12). The proxy rules do not apply to unlisted companies that do not meet the size test (companies that are reporting under Section 15(d)). Many public companies that have only registered debt securities (and thus are registered only under Section 15(d)) are not subject to the SEC's proxy rules.

Tender Offers and Reports by Shareholders with Five Percent Ownership

The SEC regulates both the mechanics for making tender offers and the procedures for management's resisting tender offers. Additionally, shareholders or groups of shareholders acting together who acquire 5 percent or more of your company's shares or who make a tender offer that would result in 5 percent or more ownership are subject to specified disclosure requirements. Reports must be filed with the SEC and provided to your company and any stock exchanges on which the shares are listed.

The reports must provide specified information, generally including the identity and background of the purchaser(s), the source and amount of funds used in the purchase, the purpose of the transaction, and the number of shares owned. As with the proxy solicitation rules, the tender offer rules do not apply to unlisted companies that do not meet the size test (companies that are reporting under Section 15(d)).

---

[21]A proxy gives management the authority to vote a shareholder's shares at the annual meeting in the manner described in the proxy statement.

Insider Trading and Short-Swing Profits

All directors and officers, as well as shareholders with 10 percent or more of your company's shares, are subject to the SEC's insider trading and short-swing profits rules (see the discussion in Chapter 7). If you have not already addressed these new requirements, now is the time to take appropriate measures to provide reasonable assurance that controls are in place to protect the confidentiality of sensitive information and that anyone who must become privy to insider information is made aware of the proscription on trading on or conveying such information. It is also advisable to coordinate all press statements and communications with analysts, reporters, and other public communications through a single individual and to have such statements reviewed by counsel before they are released. Now is also the time to educate your corporate insiders and any other persons subject to these rules about the short-swing profit and beneficial interest reporting rules.

Sale of Restricted and Control Stock—Rule 144

Because of underwriting concerns, it is unusual for all of a company's outstanding shares to be registered immediately after the IPO. Only the shares covered (i.e., listed on the front cover) by the 1933 Act registration statement are publicly tradable free and clear of all restrictions. This means that some of your shareholders will not be able to sell their shares in the public markets at will. Instead, if they desire to liquidate their holdings, they can do so only through a registered secondary offering or by relying on a specified exemption. Similarly, shares acquired in most private placements (e.g., Regulation D offerings, discussed in Appendix C) are considered "restricted stock" and are subject to resale restrictions intended to ensure that the private placement was not simply one step in a broader public distribution.

Securities Act Rule 144 provides a safe harbor for sales of restricted and control stock by affiliates (i.e., officers, directors, or 10 percent shareholders) and nonaffiliates of the registrant. Essentially, it allows controlling shareholders and holders of restricted stock who have held the stock for specified periods of time (from one to three years) after it was fully paid to resell their securities without registering under the 1933 Act if they meet certain conditions. (Note, however, that the SEC has interpreted *payment in full* to exclude, for example, certain notes accepted in payment under stock option or stock purchase plans.)

Under Rule 144, any person may resell *limited* amounts of restricted securities after a one-year holding period. The limitations currently allow holders to sell up to the greater of the following two conditions in any three-month period (see discussion of proposed changes in footnote 22):

1. One percent of the securities of that class outstanding.
2. The average weekly trading volume on the stock exchange or Nasdaq during the four weeks preceding the sale.

Under the rules, nonaffiliates of the registrant may resell *unlimited* amounts of unregistered securities after a two-year holding period. Restricted stock held by controlling shareholders becomes free of most resale restrictions after a three-year holding period. However, insiders (e.g., officers, directors, and 10 percent shareholders) are limited to certain trading windows whenever they buy or sell securities, regardless of whether the stock is registered or unregistered.

Other provisions of Rule 144 relate to combining sales of certain affiliated persons for purposes of the rule, to limitations on brokerage commissions, and to SEC notification requirements for sales in excess of 500 shares or $10,000 in a three-month period. Because the provisions of Rule 144 are complex, you should consult your attorneys with respect to any proposed sales under the rule.[22]

[22]In February 1997, the SEC proposed amendments (not adopted as of this writing) to simplify Rule 144 (Release No. 33-7391). The SEC also is reportedly considering changes to Rule 144, including revisions to the specified holding periods and elimination of the resale limitations based on trading volumes in favor of a single limitation based on 1 percent of the outstanding securities. Again, you will need to consult your legal counsel to make sure that any shareholders who hold restricted stock fully understand the trading restrictions applicable to their unregistered shares and the current status of these complicated rules.

9

DELIVER THE VALUE

Going public is like having a baby.
Initially, you focus on the birth, but
the real challenge is raising the child.

Margo L. Vignola, First Vice President and Co-Director,
U.S. Fundamental Equity Research, Merrill Lynch & Company

Throughout this book, we have emphasized the Ernst & Young view that the IPO is a journey that goes far beyond the event itself. We have stressed the importance of preparation, noting that the company that thoroughly prepares itself for the IPO is much more likely to succeed. However, when all the fanfare of the IPO and the road show becomes history, the CEO's challenges continue unabated.

The opening analogy of having a child is particularly apt. Your "child," the public company, has entered the world. Now your responsibilities, like those of a new parent, are just beginning. As CEO of a public company, you are now managing in a completely different arena. You are living in a fishbowl. From Wall Street analysts to your next door neighbors— it seems that everyone is watching what you do and listening more attentively to what you say.

Most important, everyone has expectations, and as soon as you disappoint your stakeholders, the repercussions can be enormous. The public market is not a forgiving place; the market is saturated, and investors are very well informed and always looking for the best deal. If you miss your earnings projections even by a very small amount, your stock price can drop 10 percent or more the next day. It has been said that it can take six quarters of on-target performance to win the market back.

Clearly, your challenge after the IPO is to deliver the value that you promised to deliver in your business plan and your offering memorandum. Delivering the value is a balancing act that involves meeting and exceeding the expectations of the market and all your stakeholders while implementing your strategic initiatives on time and on budget.

KEEPING YOUR PROMISES

As the CEO of a public company, your credibility is supremely important, and your word is your bond. Yet there are many elements that you cannot control, such as the fluctuations of your industry, of the stock market, and of the national and world economies. Nevertheless, you can continue to provide strong leadership by delivering the growth that you promised and by communicating with all your stakeholders openly, constantly, and consistently.

Balancing Short-Term Profits and Long-Term Growth

One of the most discussed issues facing public companies is the pressure to maintain short-term earnings growth. The financial markets generally react adversely to reports of reduced earnings, even if the long-term strategic decisions from which they result are sound. Consequently, companies are often tempted to maintain share prices by sacrificing long-term profitability and growth for short-term earnings. There is a popular misconception that this unfortunate dilemma implies that investors are shortsighted. Actually, investors' emphasis on the short term reflects the realities of the financial markets and reinforces the need for a strong investor relations program.

John Maynard Keynes, the noted economist, likened professional investment decisions to old-time newspaper beauty contests:

> The competitors have to pick out the six prettiest faces from a hundred photographs, the prize being awarded to the competitor whose choice most nearly corresponds to the average preferences of the competitors as a whole; so that each competitor has to pick, not those faces which he himself finds prettiest, but those which he thinks likeliest to catch the fancy of the other competitors, all of whom are looking at the problem from the same point of view.
> It is not a case of choosing those which, to the best of one's

judgment, are really the prettiest, nor even those which average opinion genuinely thinks the prettiest . . . [We] have reached the third degree where we devote our intelligence to anticipating what average opinion expects the average opinion to be.

There is no easy solution for the CEO of a public company. Our best advice is that you strive to adopt a sound business strategy that is balanced between short- and long-term needs and that you communicate that strategy to shareholders and the financial community.

Completing Initiatives on Time and on Budget

It is natural to focus on managing the expectations of your various stakeholders now that you are a public company. Huge capital inflows, customers and vendors with intensified interest, and high expectations all around can make you feel as if you were on a perpetual road show. That is only half of the truth.

Fundamentally, you still have to manage the strategies and the operations of the company as you did before the IPO. In your strategic plan and other documents, you have targeted certain initiatives that will move the company forward to its next stage of growth. These are the initiatives that are critical to your long-term success.

When companies enter into periods of rapid investment, they often experience growing pains. One exercise we recommend is asking yourself what growing pains you would experience if your sales doubled tomorrow. Would you need to strengthen your systems? Your technologies? Your human resources? This is the time to begin expanding your capacities in readiness for future growth.

Meeting and Exceeding Market Expectations

It is worth repeating that the best way to manage the expectations of the market is to *underpromise* and *overdeliver*, no matter who is pressuring you to promise more. If you ever do overpromise, you will get caught and the consequences will be dire.

Coping with Fluctuations.   Despite your best efforts, however, the stock market is not always rational. Your stock may languish even when you have done everything humanly possible to buoy it up. The best solution to this situation is not to obsess. There will always be hot streaks and cold streaks and times when your stock is in favor or out of favor.

Your ultimate responsibility is to stay focused by continuing to manage the business diligently. The quality of your management is what brought you the success you already have achieved. Consult your strategic plan, implement it, and update it when necessary. Continue to manage the company and produce the numbers—the stock will surely follow. That's truly the bottom line for delivering shareholder value.

On Projecting Earnings.   Projections are a critical part of investor relations. They are also a very sensitive area in which you must exercise extreme caution. Investors in newly public companies are looking for growth. If you can tell a cogent story to investors about how you can move forward with relative consistency, they will buy the stock and stay with your company. Growth always sells in every market.

Beware of using the term *earnings forecast*. It is safer to talk about a *targeted growth range*, but don't even make promises about a growth range or use the word *comfortable*. If analysts pressure you for an earnings forecast, you can respond by saying, "I'd like to do that for you, but my lawyers won't let me."

Legal Protections and Liabilities Concerning "Forward-Looking Disclosures."   The Securities and Exchange Commission (SEC) rules require registrants to disclose known trends and uncertainties if they are reasonably likely to have a material effect on the company's financial performance. These rules also encourage voluntary "forward-looking disclosures" such as estimates and projections. Until recently, most registrants steered clear of forward-looking disclosures for fear of a securities class-action suit.

Fortunately, however, the 1995 Private Securities Litigation Reform Act (PSLRA) added a safe harbor protecting public companies from liability stemming from estimates and projections *when the company includes appropriate cautionary language in the forward-looking statement.* The new law does not apply to an IPO. It does apply to oral statements at meetings with analysts, as well as to written statements in press releases and in your periodic reports to the SEC after your IPO.

To qualify for protection under the PSLRA, your forward-looking statement has to be made in "good faith" and with a "reasonable basis." It has to include "meaningful cautionary language," and it must provide substantive information about risk factors that could affect your forward-looking statement. The cautionary language cannot be boilerplate; it must be tailored to the circumstances. It also must be prominently disclosed.

If your disclosure complies with these requirements, the courts are likely to dismiss any private lawsuit. For a lawsuit to be viable, plaintiffs will have to prove that the person who made the statement knew that it was false or misleading.

Useful Tips on Investor Relations

At first, newly public companies often enjoy high share prices fueled, in part, by investors' interest in IPOs and by the press coverage that often attends a company's going public. However, unless you sustain the market's interest in your company after the IPO, the initial euphoria will disappear and the value of your company's shares will decline.

Now that you are a public company, dealing with your company's owner no longer consists of gazing in the mirror or walking into the corner office. You have acquired a group of shareholders, each of whom has a valid and vital interest in the company's success. Your responsibility to your shareholders has far-reaching implications for the way you conduct your company's business. You will have to keep them informed of corporate developments in a variety of disclosure vehicles—including annual and quarterly reports, proxy statements, press releases, direct mailings, and shareholders' meetings.

Shareholders, analysts, and the financial press will be focusing their attention on your share price. Either directly or by relying on securities analysts and the financial press, they also will critically evaluate your management's performance. That is why investor relations are of such prime importance, particularly to a company that has recently gone public. Maintaining your company's positive image with the financial community, and maintaining the market's interest in your shares, requires a conscientious, intelligently planned, and well-coordinated effort.

Create and Execute a Strong Communication Strategy.   To maintain the market's interest in your stock, you should direct your efforts not only at your current shareholders, but also at potential investors. A strategic, well-coordinated public relations program is an essential part of life in the fishbowl of the public marketplace. You can use various media to reach this community effectively—web pages, advertising, special events, and many more.

Most companies have found that it pays to engage experienced professionals to formulate and to execute their investor relations programs. This is an area in which you should not try to skimp. You need credible, experienced professionals with excellent communication skills and an executive presence. They must have a true understanding of your business and its issues, and they must be highly organized and responsive.

A public company is required to disclose any significant events or developments promptly, whether those events are positive or negative. Particular care should be taken that the information is disclosed publicly—not leaked, whether intentionally or inadvertently.

Take an offensive stance, not a defensive one. It is likely that you are your company's best spokesperson. You should be explaining the dynamics of your market—what is happening with your competitors as well as with your own company. You will build credibility, especially with analysts, if you can compare and contrast your company's strategy and operations with those of your peers and competitors.

Try not to get caught in a reactive mode. Be out there in front of various audiences—including key players like analysts and major shareholders—and in front of the news. If necessary, tell them bad news, but give them your side of the story before they hear it from somebody else.

Be sure to be clear about who in your company is authorized to talk in public and what they are authorized to say. Limit the number of people who can speak for the company, and coordinate the information they disclose so that your investors receive a consistent message.

As part of their public relations effort, many companies prepare a corporate brochure and update it regularly. Such a brochure may include a description of the company and its products or services, a brief history of the company, information on its management team, selected financial data, and any other information that you consider to be relevant. Some companies update their brochures frequently to include updated analysts' reports on their company and their industry. Many companies publish corporate profiles on their Internet site.

In addition to a corporate brochure, many companies are finding that a presence on the World Wide Web is becoming a necessity as the number of Internet users continues to mushroom. Web sites can range from very simple information sources to highly sophisticated, interactive sites that can handle large volumes of transactions and are a major profit center for the company.

Whether you have a strong Web presence or none at all, maintaining a strong, positive corporate image will serve your company well. In addition to reinforcing your relationship with shareholders and potential investors, a positive image will help attract and retain employees, will influence consumers' purchase decisions, and will create goodwill that can benefit your company indirectly in numerous ways.

Build Long-Term Relationships.   The essence of investor relations is credibility. You earn your credibility by working hard at developing strong long-term relationships with analysts and major shareholders. These bonds are a critical element in creating perceived shareholder value and making sure your stock trades well.

Possibly the most important relationships you can cultivate are with securities analysts because they play such a vital role in the financial community. They are often part of the research departments of brokerage houses and investment banking firms. Their assessments of your company will influence the investment advice they provide to their investor clients.

Securities analysts not only will analyze your annual reports and other published information, but also will conduct interviews with your company's management to gain insight into your operations, plans, and prospects. Your company's management should welcome such interviews and even initiate them when they can. As part of building your relationships with analysts, you should invite them to your facility to see your equipment, to experience the excitement of your corporate culture, and to learn about new things you are doing.

Many cities have local societies or groups of securities analysts who meet regularly to hear presentations that are delivered by CEOs or other senior executives of public companies. These forums allow management to promote the company, to disseminate information on their plans, and to respond to analysts' questions. You should welcome any opportunities to appear before these groups.

Because credibility is the basis for a strong relationship with analysts, you have to be thoroughly prepared whenever you speak with them. Become familiar with the financial drivers that are important to analysts in your industry. Speak from notes and be totally honest, staying with the fundamentals of the business. Rather than fudge or backtrack to an earlier statement, it is better to say "I don't know."

Analysts are paid to be skeptical and sometimes can be aggressively so. The best ones often ask the toughest questions. If you need assistance in communicating with them, ask an analyst for guidance. Remember that your press release is not the only source they will consult about your company. You have to be prepared to respond to ideas that come from a variety of external sources.

Pay Attention to Tactics and Execution. Being a public company makes you subject to many new rules about your disclosures. Be sure you keep up with all of them—particularly the stock exchange and SEC rules. Outline a process for your disclosures, and follow that process every time. Make sure you review your disclosures with your attorneys and accountants. Also review them with the board, and do it early. If you have a strong board, their advice can usually be helpful.

Whether it's a shareholder report or a quarterly conference call, you should script every disclosure and tie it to a theme or message for the year. Anticipate as many questions as possible and have answers ready. Prepare similarly for your annual meeting with shareholders, complete with a script and answers to probable questions.

Your investor relations program should be an organized effort, supported by appropriate databases and careful attention to details. Maintain a single consistent channel of information, and refer all calls to that source. Make sure that you respond to inquiries in a timely manner, within 24 hours. We have heard tales about investors who felt ignored by management and actually sold their stock because mail clerks and receptionists failed to transmit their messages. That level of attention to detail really can make a difference.

Carefully Orchestrate Your Quarterly Conference Calls. When public companies release their quarterly earnings, they customarily arrange a conference call and invite all the analysts who follow the stock to participate. You should release your earnings on a regular basis, specifying the number of days after the end of the quarter. Most companies will have released the information three or four weeks after the end of the quarter.

Send out an invitation setting the time for the conference call and inviting the analysts to R.S.V.P. Then you arrange the conference call with a company that specializes in conference calls and investor relations.

On the day of the release, there is a need to follow an approval process that includes faxing the press release to the stock exchange. The release then goes out on the newswire, and you receive confirmation of that process. Finally, you mass-distribute the fax to investors and analysts. Give the people about an 30 to 60 minutes to read the release before the start of the conference call.

The call itself begins with 15 or 20 minutes of prepared comment by the company. The CEO or the CFO generally presents the information, aided by a script. Then you open up for questions and answers, for which you should thoroughly prepare yourself in advance.

No Surprises, No Surprises, No Surprises. This is the mantra of investor relations. As with any mantra, repeat it often and keep it in mind at all times.

Managing Internal Investors: Blackout Periods

One constituency within your investor group is the internal investors—your officers and directors. Be sure they are thoroughly informed about insider trading rules and about your policies for handling these rules. Your law firm will create blackout periods when officers and directors are not permitted to buy or to sell the company's stock. These blackout periods include quarterly periods during which your earnings are being released. There also will be blackout periods when insiders are aware of a pending transaction or any other event that might materially affect the share price.

Legally, the blackout periods extend between the time that the information is released internally until about 24 hours after the disclosure. However, most companies establish a longer period.

RENEW AND RECREATE

Nothing stays the same. We are living in a world of constant and ever-accelerating change. Business conditions are changing so fast that your challenge is to stay ahead of the curve, constantly seeing what is next and reconsidering your strategy.

Not unlike any life phase, the Value Journey is cyclical. From time to time, you will go back and start at the beginning. Each time you start again, you will approach the process from a more sophisticated perspective. Generally, the first step—define *success*—is the best place to begin.

After your public offering, you are accountable for many new definitions of success: those of shareholders, the board, customers, your management team, Wall Street analysts and financeers, and the press. You can now add the new definitions to your original set and become a portfolio manager for all these varying steps to success. Your ongoing challenge as CEO of a public company is to juggle all these interests—satisfying the needs of all your stakeholders—while at the same time driving your company ahead.

Go back to the strategic plan and the implementation plans you created long before your IPO. Now is the time that you should move forward aggressively, bearing in mind that revisions may be necessary as you go. You may want to consider new strategic transactions. Both personal wealth plans and employee compensation plans should be updated and upgraded. As a private company, your stock option plan rewarded employees with low-priced shares. Now that the share price has risen, it is time to revisit the plan and, perhaps, to place greater emphasis on cash payments.

These are merely examples. Your general goal at this point is to keep the momentum up, continuing to build your organization by focusing on the following core drivers:

- *Intellectual capital.* Can you minimize your time to market? Can you create innovative solutions to tomorrow's market needs and sustain the quality of your product?
- *Talent capital.* Are you continuously focused on recruiting, attracting, and retaining the right people, while leveraging their talent and expertise?
- *Value-chain capital.* The value chain refers to the operational elements of your business. Can you find new ways to anticipate customers' needs? Can you develop better sales and distribution strategies? How can you improve customer service and customer support? Are your business processes supporting your operations?
- *Financial capital.* How can your company grow and continue to produce strong earnings? Do you need to consider new financing strategies?

CONCLUSION

We return to the analogy between the new public company and the newborn child. Like raising a child, managing a public company is a challenging and deeply rewarding task—nurturing the company, watching it grow, financing its needs, providing discipline when necessary. With the proper balance between caring attention, intelligent thought, informed advice, and good luck, your company will mature into an entity that is healthy, strong, and prosperous.

OUTLINE FOR A BUSINESS PLAN

The following is an outline of suggested topics for inclusion in a business plan and certain other suggestions on writing an effective business plan:

I. EXECUTIVE SUMMARY

The Executive Summary should be a clear, concise overview of the key issues and strategies of the business plan, not just a mere listing of topics. A critical point that must be communicated in the Executive Summary is your company's distinctive competence—the factors that will make your business successful in a competitive market. The main purpose of the Executive Summary is to catch the reader's interest, so make it worth their while to carefully study the details about your plan that follows.

A. Market Analysis

1. The characteristics of your target market (demographic, geographic, etc.).

2. The size of your target market.

B. The Company

1. The needs your company will satisfy.

2. The products or the services you will offer to satisfy those needs.

C. Marketing and Sales Strategies

1. Marketing strategy.

2. Sales strategy.

3. Keys to success in your competitive environment.

D. Products and Services

1. Major milestones.

2. Ongoing efforts.

E. Operating Techniques and Strategies

1. Production and service-delivery capabilities.

2. Competitive advantages.

F. Management and Ownership

1. Key managers and owners.

2. Key operations employees.

G. Financing Requirements

1. Current and near-term funding needs.

2. Use of proceeds.

3. Long-range financing plans.

H. Financial Information

1. Historical financial summary.

2. Prospective financial summary (including a brief justi-
fication for your forecasted sales levels).

If your company is new, you could be sending your business plan to potential investors who review hundreds of them each year. More often than not, these individuals do not get past the Executive Summary of the plans they receive. Your Executive Summary must therefore give the reader a useful understanding of your business and make the point of most interest to them, "What is in it for the investor?"

In total, your Executive Summary should be less than three pages in length and provide the reader with a succinct overview of your entire business plan.

The Executive Summary should be followed by a brief Table of Contents designed to assist readers in locating specific sections in the plan. Detailed descriptions of the plan's contents should be avoided in the Table of Contents.

II. MARKET ANALYSIS

The Market Analysis section should reflect your knowledge of your industry and present highlights and analysis of your market research. Detailed market research studies, however, should be presented as appendices to your plan.

A. Industry Description and Outlook

1. Description of your primary industry.
2. Size of the industry.
   a. Historically.
   b. Currently.
   c. In five years.
   a In ten years.
3. Industry characteristics and trends. (Where is it in its life cycle?)
   a. Historically.
   b. Currently.
   b In the future.
4. Major customer groups.
   a. Businesses.
   b. Governments.
   c. Consumers.

B. Target Markets

1. Distinguishing characteristics of your primary target markets and market segments. (Narrow your target markets to a manageable size. Efforts to penetrate target markets that are too broad are often ineffective.)
   a. Critical needs.
   b. Extent to which those needs are currently being met.
   c. Demographics.
   d. Geographic location.
   e. Purchase decision makers and influencers.
   f. Seasonal/cyclical trends.
2. Primary target market size.
   a. Number of prospective customers.
   b. Annual purchases of products or services meeting the same or similar needs as your products or services.
   c. Geographic area.
   d. Anticipated market growth.
3. Market penetration. (Indicates the extent to which you

anticipate penetrating your market and demonstrates why you feel that level of penetration is achievable based on your market research.)

   a. Market share.

   b. Number of customers.

   c. Geographic coverage.

   d. Rationale for market-penetration estimates.

4. Pricing/gross margin targets.

   a. Price levels.

   b. Gross margin levels.

   c. Discount structure (volume, prompt payment, etc.).

5. Methods by which specific members of your target market can be identified.

   a. Directories.

   b. Trade association publications.

   c. Government documents.

6. Media through which you can communicate with specific members of your target market.

   a. Publications.

   b. Radio/television broadcasts.

   c. Sources of influence/advice.

7. Purchasing cycle of potential customers.

   a. Need for identification.

   b. Research for solutions to needs.

   c. Solution evaluation process.

   d. Final solution selection responsibility and authority (executives, purchasing agents, engineers, etc.).

8. Key trends and anticipated changes within your primary target markets.

9. Secondary target markets and key attributes.

   a. Needs.

   b. Demographics.

   c. Significant future trends.

C. Market Test Results

1. Potential customers contacted.

2. Information/demonstrations given to potential customers.

3. Reaction of potential customers.

4. Importance of satisfaction of targeted needs.

5. Test group's willingness to purchase products/services at various price levels.

D. Lead Times (amount of time between customer order placement and product/service delivery)

1. Initial orders.

2. Reorders.

3. Volume purchases.

E. Competition

1. Identification (by product line or service and market segment).

   a. Existing.

   b. Market share.

   c. Potential (How long will your window of opportunity be open before your initial success breeds new competition? Who will your new competitors likely be?).

   d. Direct.

   e. Indirect.

2. Strengths (competitive advantages).

   a. Ability to satisfy customer needs.

   b. Market penetration.

   c. Track record and reputation.

   d. Staying power (financial resources).

   e. Key personnel.

3. Weaknesses (competitive disadvantages).

   a. Ability to satisfy customer needs.

   b. Market penetration.

   c. Track record and reputation.

   d. Staying power (financial resources).

   e. Key personnel.

4. Importance of your target market to your competition.

    5. Barriers to entry into the market.
       a. Cost (investment).
       b. Time.
       c. Technology.
       d. Key personnel.
       e. Customer inertia (brand loyalty, existing relation-
          ships, etc.).
       f. Existing patents and trademarks.

F. Regulatory Restrictions
    1. Customer or governmental regulatory requirements.
       a. Methods for meeting the requirements.
       b. Timing involved.
       c. Cost.
    2. Anticipated changes in regulatory requirements.

Because your market analysis provides the only basis for your fore-casted sales and pricing estimates, make sure that this section clearly demonstrates that there is a market need for your product or service, that you as owner not only understand this need but can meet it, and that you can sell at a profit. This section should also include an estimate of your market penetration annually for the next five years.

III. COMPANY DESCRIPTION

The Company Description section must provide an overview of how all of the elements of your company fit together. This can be done without going into detail because most of the subjects will be covered in depth elsewhere in the plan.

A. Nature of Your Business
    1. Marketplace needs to be satisfied.
    2. Method(s) of need satisfaction (products and services).
    3. Individuals/organizations with the needs.

B. Your Distinctive Competencies (primary factors that will lead to your success)
    1. Superior customer-need satisfaction.
    2. Production/service delivery efficiencies.
    3. Personnel.
    4. Geographic location.

Writing this section is the first real test of your ability to communicate the essence of your business. Because the lack of a clear description of the key concepts of your company will indicate to the reader that you have not yet clearly defined it in your own mind, you must be certain that this section concisely and accurately describes the substance of your new business.

IV. MARKETING AND SALES STRATEGIES

Both general and specific information must be included in this part of your plan. Your objective is to describe the activities that will allow you to meet the sales and margin levels indicated in your forecast.

    A. Overall Marketing Strategy
1. Marketing penetration strategy.
2. Growth strategy.
   a. Internal.
   b. Acquisition.
   c. Franchise.
   d. Horizontal (providing similar products to different users).
   e. Vertical (providing the products at different levels of the distribution chain).
3. Distribution channels (include discount/profitability levels at each stage).
   a. Original equipment manufacturers.
   b. Internal sales force.
   c. Distributors.
   d. Retailers.
4. Communication.
   a. Promotion.
   b. Advertising.
   c. Public relations.
   d. Personal selling.
   e. Printed materials (catalogues, brochures, etc.).

    B. Sales Strategies
1. Sales force.

      a. Internal representatives versus independent representatives (advantages and disadvantages of your strategy).

      b. Size.

      c. Recruitment and training.

      d. Compensation.

  2. Sales activities.

      a. Identifying prospects.

      b. Prioritizing prospects.

      c. Number of sales calls made per period.

      d. Average number of sales calls per sale.

      e. Average dollar size per sale.

      f. Average dollar size per reorder.

Do not underestimate the importance of presenting a well-conceived sales strategy here. Without an efficient approach to beating a path to the doors of potential customers, companies with very good products and services often fail.

V. PRODUCTS AND SERVICES

Special attention should be paid to the users of your business plan as you develop this section. Too much detail will have a negative impact on most external users of the plan. Avoid turning this section of your business plan into a policies and procedures manual for your employees.

  A. Detailed Product/Service Description (from the user's perspective)

    1. Specific benefits of product/service.

    2. Ability to meet needs.

    3. Competitive advantages.

    4. Present state (idea, prototype, small production runs, etc.).

  B. Product Life Cycle

    1. Description of the current position of the product/service within its life cycle.

    2. Factors that might change the anticipated life cycle.

      a. Lengthen it.

      b. Shorten it.

C. Copyrights, Patents, and Trade Secrets

1. Existing or pending copyrights or patents.
2. Anticipated copyright and patent filings.
3. Key aspects of your products or services that cannot be patented or copyrighted.
4. Key aspects of your products or services that qualify as trade secrets.
5. Existing legal agreements with owners and employees.
   a. Nondisclosure agreements.
   b. Noncomplete agreements.

D. Research and Development Activities

1. Activities in process.
2. Future activities (include milestones).
3. Anticipated results of future research and development activities.
   a. New products or services.
   b. New generations of existing products or services.
   c. Complementary products or services.
   d. Replacement products or services.
4. Research and development activities of others in your industry.
   a. Direct competitors.
   b. Indirect competitors.
   c. Suppliers.
   d. Customers.

The emphasis in this section should be on your company's unique ability to satisfy the needs of the marketplace. Avoid criticizing your competition's products too severely in this section because the natural tendency of a reader who is not part of your organization will be to empathize with your competition. Concentrate on the positive aspects of your product's ability to meet existing market needs, and allow your readers to come to their own conclusions about your competition based on the objective information presented here and in the Market Analysis section.

VI. OPERATING TECHNIQUES AND STRATEGIES

Here again, too much detail can detract from the rest of your plan. Be certain that the level of detail included fits the specific needs of the plan's users.

A. Production and Service Delivery

1. Internal.
2. External (subcontractors).

B. Production and Service-Delivery Capability

1. Internal.
2. External (subcontractors).
3. Anticipated increases in capacity.
   a. Investment.
   b. New cost factors (direct and indirect).
   c. Timing.

C. Operating Competitive Advantages

1. Techniques.
2. Experience.
3. Economies of scale.
4. Lower direct costs.

D. Suppliers

1. Identification of the suppliers of critical elements of production.
   a. Primary.
   b. Secondary.
2. Lead-time requirements.
3. Evaluation of the risks of critical element shortages.
4. Description of the existing and anticipated contractual relationships with suppliers.

Because many of the aspects of your new business are still theoretical at this point, special care must be taken to be sure that the specifics of your operations do not conflict with the information included in your forecast. Any inconsistencies between those two areas will result in some unpleasant surprises as your company begins operations.

VII. MANAGEMENT AND OWNERSHIP

Your management team's talents and skills are some of the few truly unique aspects of your company. If you are going to use your plan to attract investors, this section must emphasize the talents and skills of your management team and must indicate why each member is a part of your company's distinctive competence that cannot easily be replicated by your competition. Remember that individuals invest in people, not ideas.

Do not use this section of the plan to negotiate future ownership of the company with potential investors. Simply explain the current ownership.

A. **Management Staff Structure**

  1. Management staff organization chart.

  2. Narrative description of the chart.

B. **Key Managers** (complete resumes for each manager should be presented in an appendix to the business plan)

  1. Names.

  2. Position.

  3. Brief position description, including primary duties.

  4. Primary responsibilities and authority with previous employers.

  5. Unique skills and experiences that add to your company's distinctive competencies.

  6. Compensation basis and levels (be sure they are reasonable—not too high and not too low).

C. **Planned Additions to the Current Management Team**

  1. Position.

  2. Primary responsibilities and authority.

  3. Requisite skills and experience.

  4. Recruitment process.

  5. Timing of employment.

  6. Anticipated contribution to the company's success.

  7. Compensation basis and levels (be sure they are in line with the market).

D. Legal Structure of the Business

1. Corporation.
   a. C corporation.
   b. S corporation.
2. Partnership.
   a. General.
   b. Limited.
3. Proprietorship.

E. Owners

1. Names.
2. Percentage ownership.
3. Extent of involvement with the company.
4. Form of ownership.
   a. Common stock.
   b. Preferred stock.
   c. General partner.
   d. Limited partner.
5. Outstanding equity equivalents.
   a. Options.
   b. Warrants.
   c. Convertible debt.
6. Common stock.
   a. Authorized.
   b. Issued.

F. Board of Directors

1. Names.
2. Position on the board.
3. Extent of involvement with the company.
4. Background.
5. Contribution to the company's success.
   a. Historically.
   b. In the future.

Because your management team is unique, make sure that you stress each person's background and skills and how he or she will contribute to the success of your product/service and business. This is especially important to emphasize when you are looking for financing.

VIII. FINANCING REQUIREMENTS

Any new or additional funding reflected in your forecast should be discussed here. Alternative funding scenarios can be presented if appropriate, and corresponding forecasts are presented in subsequent sections of your plan.

A. Current Funding Requirements
1. Amount.
2. Timing.
3. Type.
   a. Equity.
   b. Debt.
   c. Mezzanine.
4. Terms.

B. Funding Requirements over the Next Five Years
1. Amount.
2. Timing.
3. Type.
   a. Equity.
   b. Debt.
   c. Mezzanine.
4. Terms.

C. Use of Funds
1. Capital expenditures.
2. Working capital.
3. Debt retirement.
4. Acquisitions.

D. Long-Range Financial Strategies (exit strategies)
1. Going public.
2. Leveraged buyout.
3. Acquisition by another company.
4. Debt service levels and timing.
5. Liquidation.

Remember that because the rate of return is their most important consideration—and because the IPO market is sometimes not available—investors will be looking for alternative exit strategies. Therefore, be flexible and creative in developing these opportunities, taking into consideration such recent trends as a merger/acquisition and strategic partnering. Although details can be worked out later, investors need to know that you understand their primary objectives as you develop your overall business strategy.

IX. FINANCIAL DATA

The Financial Data section contains the financial representation of all the information presented in the other sections. Various prospective scenarios can be included, if appropriate.

    A. Historical Financial Data (past three to five years, if applicable)

        1. Annual statements.

            a. Income.

            b. Balance sheet.

            c. Cash flows.

        2. Name of CPA firm and type of report.

            a. Audit.

            b. Review.

            c. Compilation.

    B. Prospective Financial Data (next five years)

        1. Next year (by month or quarter).

            a. Income.

            b. Balance sheet.

            c. Cash flows.

            d. Capital expenditure budget.

        2. Final four years (by quarter and/or year).

            a. Income.

            b. Balance sheet.

            c. Cash flows.

            d. Capital expenditure budget.

        3. Summary of significant assumptions.

    4. Type of prospective financial data.

       a. Forecast (management's best estimate).

       b. Projections (what-if scenarios).

    5. Level of CPA involvement (if any).

       a. Assembly.

       b. Agreed-on procedures.

       c. Review.

       d. Examination.

C. Analysis

    1. Historical financial statements.

       a. Ratio analysis.

       b. Trend analysis with graphic presentation.

       c. Comparison to peers.

    2. Prospective financial statements.

       a. Ratio analysis.

       b. Trend analysis with graphic presentation.

The Financial Data section of your business plan is another area where specialized knowledge can be invaluable. If you do not have someone with sufficient financial expertise on your management team, you will probably need an outside advisor.

X. APPENDICES OR EXHIBITS

Any additional detailed or confidential information that could be useful to the readers of the business plan but that was not appropriate for distribution to everyone receiving the body of the plan can be presented here. Accordingly, appendices and exhibits should be bound separately from the other sections of the plan and provided on an as-needed basis to readers.

    A. Resumes of Key Managers

    B. Pictures of Products

    C. Professional References

    D. Market Studies

    E. Pertinent Published Information

       1. Magazine articles.

      2.   References to books.

F. Patents

G. Significant Contracts

      1.   Leases.

      2.   Sales contracts.

      3.   Purchases contracts.

      4.   Partnership/ownership agreements.

      5.   Stock option agreements.

      6.   Employment/compensation agreements.

      7.   Noncomplete agreements.

      8.   Insurance.

           a.   Product liability.

           b.   Officers' and directors' liability.

           c.   General liability.

In some instances, the thicker the business plan, the less likely a potential investor is to read it thoroughly. However, you do want to be able to demonstrate to potential funding sources that you have done a complete job in preparing your plan and that the comments made within it are well documented. By properly utilizing appendices and exhibits, you can make the size of your business plan palatable to its users and can still have readily available the additional information they may require.

APPENDIX B

SELECTING A STOCK MARKET

Not all stock markets are the same, nor is one stock market appropriate for all types of companies. Markets vary by listing requirements (to begin trading) and maintenance standards (to continue trading), as well as by their rules and regulations governing trading, reporting, and settlement. Stock markets also vary according to market structure and trading mechanisms. The choice of market for a company undergoing its initial public offering (IPO) is a strategic financial decision. Companies should choose a stock market by determining which market will most effectively enhance the attractiveness of their stock to investors. That market should also continue to meet their needs as they take on the role of a public company.

The material in this appendix comes directly from two sources: the National Association of Securities Dealers and Automated Quotations (Nasdaq) Stock Market and the New York Stock Exchange (NYSE). It is our belief that this provides our readers with the best information on which to base their decision. As a convenience, we have also provided a listing of additional markets throughout the United States.

The opinions expressed in these sections do not represent the point of view of the authors of this book; rather, they offer the perspective of the two stock markets. We suggest that you base your choice of a market on objective opinions from your trusted business advisors. To make an educated decision, you should also meet with representatives of both exchanges and with representatives of any other exchanges you may be considering.

GOING PUBLIC ON THE NASDAQ

Since its debut as the world's first electronic stock market in 1970, the Nasdaq Stock Market has used technology to bring millions of investors together with the world's leading companies. It is among the world's best regulated stock markets, employing highly sophisticated surveillance systems and regulatory specialists to protect investors and to provide a fair and competitive trading environment. Today, Nasdaq lists nearly 5,100 companies and trades more shares per day than any other major U.S. market.

In 1998, Nasdaq handled a record nine trading days where volume exceeded one billion shares. Additionally, preliminary figures show that share volume on Nasdaq reached 201.5 billion in 1998, up from 163.9 billion in 1997—a 23 percent increase. At year-end, the market value of the more than 5,100 companies listed on Nasdaq stood at $2.6 trillion, up over 44 percent from year-end 1997.

By providing an efficient environment for raising capital, Nasdaq has helped thousands of companies achieve their desired growth and successfully make the leap into public ownership. Over the past five years, Nasdaq captured 80 percent of all IPO listings on the three primary U.S. stock markets. During that time, Nasdaq helped companies raise a total of $92 billion to fund their growth.

The Nasdaq Stock Market

On October 30, 1998, The National Association of Securities Dealers, Inc. (NASD) and the American Stock Exchange (Amex) officially joined forces. As a result of this combination, two of the world's leading securities markets —the Nasdaq Stock Market and the American Stock Exchange— are now together under one corporate organization. In this new marketplace, Nasdaq and Amex will operate under a single holding company, The Nasdaq-Amex Market Group, with each market continuing to function as an independent subsidiary.[1]

---

[1]Here we have focused exclusively on the benefits of The Nasdaq Stock Market. For more information on the American Stock Exchange or the Nasdaq-Amex Market Group, please see the information listed at the end of this appendix.

Nasdaq's Market Structure

What's the difference between the Nasdaq Stock Market and other major U.S. markets? Primarily, Nasdaq's distinctive market structure. As the world's largest electronic, or screen-based, market, Nasdaq is not limited to a single, physical trading "floor." Rather, trading is executed through an advanced computer and telecommunications network, which can be accessed from desktop computer terminals. Without size limitations or geographical boundaries, Nasdaq's market structure allows a virtually unlimited number of market participants to trade in a company's stock.

Nasdaq Market Participants

Nasdaq market participants are divided into two groups: (1) Market Makers, individual dealers who commit capital and who actively compete with one another for investors' buy and sell orders, and (2) electronic communications networks (ECNs), trading systems that bring additional customer orders into Nasdaq. Both Market Makers and ECNs help to support investor demand for a company's stock while maintaining an orderly market and functioning under tight regulatory controls.

Market Makers

Essential to Nasdaq's market structure, Market Makers are independent dealers who actively compete for investor orders by displaying quotations representing their buy and sell interest, plus customer limit orders, in Nasdaq-listed stocks. Each Market Maker has equal access to Nasdaq's trading system, which broadcasts its quotations simultaneously to all market participants. By standing ready to buy and to sell shares of a company's stock, Market Makers provide Nasdaq-listed companies a unique service. The result of the Market Makers' combined sponsorship helps meet investor demand and creates an environment of immediate and continuous trading. Currently, more than 500 market-making firms provide capital support for Nasdaq-listed stocks. All are required to:

- Disclose their buy-and-sell interest by displaying two-sided quotes for all stocks in which they choose to make a market.

- Display both quotes and orders in Nasdaq, in compliance with the Securities and Exchange Commission's (SEC) order handling rules.
- Honor their quoted prices, and report trading in a timely manner. Failure to do so can lead to disciplinary action.

Electronic Communications Networks

Electronic communication networks (ECNs) are the newest market participants in Nasdaq's inclusive marketplace. These private trading systems were incorporated into the Nasdaq market structure in 1997 when Nasdaq implemented the SEC Order Handling Rules. To trade on Nasdaq, ECNs must be certified with the SEC and registered with Nasdaq and NASD Regulation. As Nasdaq market participants, ECNs display either one-sided or two-sided quotes, which reflect actual orders. Furthermore, they provide institutions and Market Makers with an anonymous way to enter orders for stock into the marketplace. Overall, ECNs foster heightened competition among Market Makers and enhance the market's liquidity.

Trading Impetus

Until recently, trading activity on the Nasdaq Stock Market was quotation-driven: Nasdaq Market Makers competed for investor orders by displaying their quotations—offers to buy and to sell stock— on screen. In 1997, Nasdaq's implementation of the new SEC order-handling rules allowed customer limit orders to be displayed in both Market Maker and ECN quotes. As a result, Nasdaq is now both quotation- and order-driven and is sometimes referred to as a "hybrid" market.

Nasdaq Market Characteristics

In much the same way that multiple distributors help meet increased demand for a company's product, Nasdaq market participants help create increased opportunities for a company's stock to be bought and sold in an orderly fashion. Through both Market Makers and ECNs, a company's stock is ensured greater access to available capital, increased visibility in the marketplace, and market characteristics that are conducive to immediate and continuous trading, such a the following:

- *Visibility.* On Nasdaq, Market Makers commit capital and resources to make a market in a company's stock. This combined sponsorship provides a company's stock with increased visibility and immediate, continuous trading. In addition, many Market Maker firms offer a full range of services to investors. These services include generating research reports on the stocks they trade, seeking buyers and sellers through retail networks and institutional sales representatives, and advising investors on initial and secondary public offerings and other investment transactions.

- *Liquidity.* By encouraging trading among a virtually unlimited number of market participants, Nasdaq's market structure offers an environment that facilitates greater *liquidity* —the ease with which stocks can be bought and sold without dramatic fluctuations in price. Market Makers enhance Nasdaq's liquidity by providing investors with ready access to capital and uninterrupted trading in their stock. ECNs add to the market's liquidity by bringing additional orders into Nasdaq.

- *Depth of market.* Knowing there are willing buyers and sellers in the marketplace can reassure investors of a stock's marketability, especially during periods of heavy trading volume. *Depth of market* refers to the total number of buyers and sellers within the market and is related to the amount of capital committed to a stock. By standing ready to commit capital to stocks in which they are registered, Market Makers provide great depth of market to Nasdaq-listed companies. ECNs strengthen Nasdaq's market depth by delivering additional buyers and sellers to the marketplace.

- *Transparency.* For investors and companies, *transparency*—the ability to view trade and quotation information—is crucial to the decision-making process. On Nasdaq, all Market Maker bids and ask quotations in a given security, plus orders from ECNs, are broadcast over the network for *all* market participants to see, making Nasdaq a "transparent" marketplace.

- *Price efficiency.* In securities trading, as in most industries, competition is one of the most important factors in creating price efficiencies. The aggressive competition for orders fostered among Nasdaq's Market Makers and all market participants helps to ensure investors the best price for the stocks they trade.

Nasdaq Market Enhancements

In 1997, Nasdaq implemented new SEC order handling rules, which have enhanced price efficiency and have made the market even more responsive to the needs of investors. The *Limit Order Display Rule* requires Market Makers to represent customer limit orders in their quotes, meaning that investors' limit orders can now set the *inside spread*—the difference between a stock's buy price and its sell price—when priced better than the Market Maker quote.

The *Quote Rule* requires that any Market Maker orders that were previously shown only on private trading systems (ECNs), must now also be displayed in Nasdaq. This ensures that the best-priced orders can be viewed and accessed by all market participants. In combination with Nasdaq's move to quoting in sixteenths (rather than eighths), these rules have resulted in an average spread reduction of more than 40 percent.

Nasdaq Market Innovations

Optimark

In mid-1999, the NASD will offer the Optimark Trading System as a facility of the Nasdaq Stock Market. This highly advanced electronic trading system offers traders and investors a "third dimension" to their trading criteria, essentially providing a new way for them to trade. Using Optimark, investors can indicate their interest in trading within certain price and size parameters based on their trading strategies. As frequently as every two minutes, the sophisticated Optimark system matches large orders anonymously—a feature that is especially beneficial to institutional investors who want to trade large orders with reduced market exposure.

Nasdaq-100 Shares

In early 1999, The Nasdaq Stock Market expects to introduce an innovative new Index Share product based on the Nasdaq-100 Index, enabling investors to make a single investment in the Nasdaq-100 companies as a whole. The product will be similar to SPDRS, DIAMONDS, and WEBS in that it will act like a mutual fund, but trade like a stock on the Amex floor. Investors who purchase shares of Nasdaq-100 Shares[2] will actually be buying into a trust that holds a portfolio consisting of Nasdaq-100 securities. Building on this existing and planned portfolio of innovative financial products, Nasdaq-Amex will continue to develop new ways for investors to participate in the market.

Nasdaq Listing Requirements

The Nasdaq Stock Market stands for integrity and ethical business practices in order to enhance investor confidence, thereby contributing to the financial health of the economy and supporting the capital formation process. The companies that list on Nasdaq are recognized as sharing these important objectives.

Companies listed on the Nasdaq National Market and the Nasdaq SmallCap Market are subject to different financial requirements for initial and continued listing. Each Nasdaq issuer must also execute a listing agreement with Nasdaq. These requirements are intended to preserve and to strengthen the quality of the market and to promote investor protection. (Prior to listing, Nasdaq assigns to prospective National Market companies a Business Development Director, who serves as a direct liaison between your business and the Nasdaq Stock Market. If you have questions regarding the listing criteria, please contact Nasdaq Business Development.)

The Nasdaq National Market's stringent entry and maintenance standards for public companies—in terms of both financial guidelines and corporate governance standards—distinguish a company as a quality investment. (See Exhibit B.1 for a detailed listing of these requirements

---

[2]A registration statement relating to these securities has been filed with the SEC but has not yet become effective. These securities may not be sold nor may offers to buy be accepted prior to the time the registration statement becomes effective. This letter shall not constitute an offer to sell or the solicitation of an offer to buy nor shall there be a sale of these securities in any State in which such offer, solicitation, or sale would be unlawful prior to registration or qualification under the securities laws of any such state. Complete information about shares of Nasdaq-100, including charges and expenses, is contained in a prospectus that may be obtained by calling: 800-843-2639.

EXHIBIT B.1. Nasdaq National Market listing requirements.

Requirements	Initial Listing 1	Initial Listing 2	Initial Listing 3	Continued Listing 1	Continued Listing 2
Net tangible assets[a]	$6 million	$18 million	N/A	$4 million	N/A
Market capitalization[b] Total assets	N/A	N/A	$75 million or $75 million	N/A	$50 million or $50 million
Total revenue			and $75 million		and $50 million
Pretax income (in most recent fiscal year or 2 of past 3 fiscal years)	$1 million	N/A	N/A	N/A	N/A
Public float shares[c]	1.1 million	1.1 million	1.1 million	750,000	1.1 million
Operating history	N/A	2 years	N/A	N/A	N/A
Market value of public float	$8 million	$18 million	$20 million	$5 million	$15 million

Minimum bid price	$5	$5	$5	$1	$5
Shareholders (round lot holders)[d]	400	400	400	400	400
Market Makers	3	3	4	2	4
Corporate governance	Yes	Yes	Yes	Yes	Yes

[a]*Net tangible assets* means total assets (excluding goodwill) minus total liabilities.

[b]For initial listing under option 3, or continued listing under option 2, a company must satisfy one of the following to be in compliance: the market capitalization requirement or the total assets and the total revenue requirement.

[c]*Public float* is defined as shares that are not held directly or indirectly by any officer or director of the issuer or by any other person who is the beneficial owner of more than 10 percent of the total shares outstanding.

[d]Round lot holders are considered holders of 100 shares or more.

and Exhibit B.3 at the end of this appendix for a comparison of the Nasdaq National Market entry fees with other major U.S. markets.)

Nasdaq-Amex Products and Services

With the Nasdaq-Amex Market Group, both Nasdaq and Amex listed companies now have access to an extensive portfolio of products and services, including the following:

nasdaq-amex.com

The Nasdaq-Amex web site, nasdaq-amex.com, is one of the top sources of financial information on the Internet, averaging 14 million hits a day. Designed to increase a company's visibility among shareholders and investors, the site includes several features to give users a window on the market, and provides fundamental stock information on all publicly traded companies, including analyst and stock reports, SEC filings, web site links, and company logos.

Additionally, nasdaq-amex.com provides companies with the following information:

- A one-page, printable, company stock report featuring up to five years of sales, net income, and earnings-per-share information as well as summaries of income statements and balance sheets for the previous four quarters.
- Company stock quotes (15-minute delay).
- Company-specific news from PR NewsWire, BusinessWire, Reuters, and MSNBC.
- Intraday and historical charting of daily closing price and share volume for 3-, 6-, 12-, 24-, 36-, and 60-month intervals.
- Direct links to a company's online filings with the SEC's EDGAR database.
- Links to web sites for company and product information.
- A company LogoTicker that helps investors quickly identify a company's stock information.

Nasdaq-Amex Online

Available exclusively to Nasdaq-listed—and now Amex-listed—companies, Nasdaq-Amex Online provides real-time market intelligence on all publicly traded companies from a single, integrated source.

Companies can use Nasdaq-Amex Online to see how their stock is trading, to follow their competitors, and to track the market's activity at any given moment. Continually updated, Nasdaq-Amex Online also offers a report generator to assist in preparing presentation-quality materials for institutional investors and board members.

Personal Service

Prior to listing, the Nasdaq-Amex Market Group assigns prospective National Market companies with a Business Development Director, who:

- Serves as a direct liaison between the company and the Nasdaq Stock Market.
- Provides consultation on going public and listing on Nasdaq.
- Provides customized analyses of company peers on Nasdaq and other exchanges.
- Will present the benefits of the Nasdaq Stock Market to the company's executive management team and board of directors.

After listing on Nasdaq, each Nasdaq-listed company is provided with a Director of Nasdaq Company Services, a primary day-to-day contact who:

- Is knowledgeable on finance and market matters.
- Is qualified to answer questions on the performance of a company's stock.
- Can help companies develop customized investor-relations programs.
- Can keep companies abreast of industry-related issues and rule changes.

Informative Programs

Both Nasdaq and Amex company executives are invited to participate in Nasdaq-sponsored investor relations and financial management programs. These programs are designed for a company at every stage of its life cycle. Topics include:

- Understanding the Nasdaq Stock Market.
- Disclosure and Safe Harbor.
- Communication to Shareholders.
- Shareholder Litigation.
- Managing Expectations of "The Street."
- Corporate Governance.
- Reaching International Investors.

GOING PUBLIC ON THE NEW YORK STOCK EXCHANGE (NYSE)

The NYSE participates in the capital-formation process through IPOs for U.S. and non-U.S. companies. These companies are joining the world's largest market to gain access to a broad investor base, market depth and liquidity, high visibility, and fair pricing.

The NYSE Delivers Liquidity and Market Depth

The NYSE is a highly liquid, transparent, and efficient market. Its auction market allows direct interaction between orders, investor to investor, which maximizes liquidity and results in the best possible price execution.

The NYSE brings together the buying and selling interests of all market participants in one central market, allowing them to trade directly with one another. The trading takes place through bids and offers by members acting as agents for institutions or individuals. Buy orders and sell orders meet directly on the trading floor, and prices are determined by the interplay of supply and demand. Central to this process are NYSE members known as specialists. The specialist is:

- A catalyst who brings together buyers and sellers.
- A provider of stability to assigned stocks by using his or her own capital when needed.
- A conduit for information.
- An agent executing orders on behalf of brokers representing their customers.

In 90 percent of trading on the NYSE, public order meets public order directly, without the intervention of the specialist. In the other 10 percent, specialists buy or sell for their own account to provide additional liquidity to the market. Specialists are required to make a fair and orderly market in assigned stocks, and this includes buying and selling against the trend of the market in the absence of public buyers or sellers.

Each listed stock is assigned to a single trading location where the specialist manages the auction process. As a result, the flow of orders for each stock is centralized, maximizing their direct interaction. When an investor's transaction is completed, the order will have been exposed to a wide range of prospective buyers and sellers. The combined interaction of all these market participants provides a very high level of liquidity and efficiency.

The specialist also provides listed companies with top-caliber information, including market information and assessments that are only available within a centralized market, trading-floor perspectives, and timely communication with management.

In highly unusual situations, the NYSE, in conjunction with the listed company, may halt trading of the listed company's stock under special circumstances or for news pending that could have a material impact on the stock's trading price. This is to ensure that all investors have equal access to the information so they can make educated investment decisions.

NYSE Market Performance

The competitiveness of the NYSE auction market can be measured in terms of average spreads (the differences between the best bids and offers), price continuity (the price movement from one trade to the next), market depth (the price movement within share sequences), and price volatility (the frequency of price movements over time).

- *Tighter spreads.* The NYSE auction market allows investors to determine the spreads and to trade directly with each other through the price-discovery process. This offers the opportunity for trades to be executed between bid and offers, with investors capturing the spread. The NYSE's trade-weighted average spread in 1997 was $0.17, and the volume-weighted average spread was $0.16. These tighter, investor-driven spreads result in lower transaction costs.

• *Price continuity.*   Trade-to-trade price continuity is one way of measuring liquidity. At the NYSE, buyers and sellers benefit from knowing that their trade will be executed at a price established by the prior trade. Over multiple trades, price movements are smooth and continuous, instilling investor confidence. In 1997, for example, 97.7 percent of all transactions occurred with no change or just a $1/8$-point variation. The quotation spread between bid and offer prices was $1/4$ point or less in 93.5 percent of NYSE quotes.

• *Market depth.*   Measures of market depth further define liquidity. Institutional and retail investors want to know that their orders can be filled with minimal price impact. Investment decisions can then be based on company performance, rather than on how that trade will impact the price. In 1997, the average stock price showed no change or a $1/8$ point-change in 3,000 shares of volume 86.9 percent of the time.

• *Volatility.*   NYSE-listed companies also benefit from lower price volatility. The narrower spreads, stable price continuity, and deeper markets of NYSE-listed companies result in lower price volatility. In general, low volatility is an indicator of an orderly, liquid market for a company's stock and will promote investor confidence in a company's securities.

The stability, liquidity and depth of the NYSE auction market also provide a critical foundation for companies to tap into their capital bases through secondary offerings. The auction process and last-sale reporting provide natural stability in pricing secondary transactions. In acquisitions, NYSE companies enjoy the added value of their securities being associated with the prestige of the world's largest market.

Offering Access to Investors across the Globe

The NYSE immediately offers IPOs not only access to the world's largest pool of capital—the U.S. market consisting of nearly 70 million individual and 10,000 institutional investors—but also the ability to tap investors from around the world. When companies list on the NYSE, they experience a significant increase in institutional holdings, both domestically and internationally. Many institutional investors have a preference or a charter requirement to invest only in NYSE-listed shares. Analyst coverage also is more extensive for NYSE-listed companies than for those on other markets.

Building Strong Relationships through Personal and Online Customer Service

Another benefit for new publicly traded companies listing on the NYSE is its customer service. The NYSE's Client Service team aims to build strong customer relations by understanding its customers, by promoting sound corporate policies, and by providing value-added services.

Each listing company is assigned to a team of professionals who aim to support companies in every possible way, from their original listing through their life on the NYSE. In addition to the New York headquarters, NYSE offices are located in London, Tokyo, Washington, D.C., and Palo Alto, California, to better serve the needs of its listed companies.

Listed companies also take advantage of opportunities to help their employees understand the securities marketplace, to track and analyze the trading of their stock, and to heighten awareness of their companies among investors, analysts and institutions. One of these opportunities is NYSEnet, a password-protected web site that provides daily information on proprietary trading data, price history, and market-quality statistics. NYSEnet delivers:

- Quotes and stock prices.
- Newswire services.
- Peer stock data.
- Graphing and analytical tools.
- Earnings and financial fundamentals.
- Options and commodities pricing.
- Foreign exchange rates.

Futhermore, on-site educational programs enable listed-company executives to learn firsthand how the NYSE benefits their company and investors and to keep abreast of current issues.

The NYSE Partnership

The strong relationship between the NYSE and its listed companies is evidenced by NYSE's Partnership Program. This program is designed to heighten the awareness of a company's NYSE-listed status, to raise visibility among investors and customers, and to provide listed-company management with a stage for communicating and celebrating corporate achievements before an increasingly diverse and global audience. The program puts the NYSE's brand assets to work, strengthening listed companies' positions in the marketplace.

The cornerstone of the program is the use of the "NYSE-listed" emblem, which communicates a clear, positive message to investors. When a company links its trading symbol or logo to the NYSE logo, it establishes a highly visible mark and a strategic business tool to leverage the globally recognized NYSE brand among investors worldwide.

The Partnership Program also provides opportunities to use the NYSE's facilities and support services to raise visibility among targeted constituents and the general public. A growing number of NYSE-listed companies are holding special events and promotions, analyst meetings, regional conferences, satellite broadcasts, board meetings, and seminars at the NYSE.

Delivering Peak Systems Performance on Demand

The NYSE offers its listed companies a technological plant that is designed to provide smooth, efficient, and continuous access for all investors. This state-of-the-art technology and advanced systems capacity allow the NYSE to handle trading volume in excess of 3 billion shares a day. On September 1, 1998, the NYSE handled more than 1.2 billion shares, running at only a 56 percent utilization rate during the day's peak five-minute period. By the end of 1999, the NYSE will have expanded capacity to handle peaks of 5 billion shares per day.

The NYSE has invested more than $2 billion in the past 10 years to further strengthen the speed, service, reliability, capacity, flexibility, and competitiveness of its market. This initiative has already introduced processing capability of 600 messages per second, soon to be about 1,000 messages; reliability in excess of 99.99 percent uptime; flat-panel, high-definition screens; and an advanced wireless network with mobile order-management devices and communications. The NYSE's technologically advanced site includes 2,700 flat-panel screens and 200 miles of fiber-optic cable carrying 100 megabits per second into 5,000 electronic devices on the trading floor.

Technological innovations continually improve the efficiency and quality of the NYSE. A sophisticated network takes a market order from anywhere in the world and delivers it to the trading floor, where it is introduced to the market, executed, and returned to its point of origin in an average of 22 seconds. Part of this process is the order's exposure to all other orders, ensuring its best execution.

Member firms can send orders directly to the specialist through the NYSE's SuperDot order-delivery system or to a floor broker through its order-management system, Broker Booth Support System (BBSS). More than 80 percent of all orders are delivered to the point of sale electronically, accounting for 45 percent of total share volume. The remaining 20 percent of orders, or 55 percent of share volume, are transmitted to floor brokers through electronic systems or via telephone. Floor brokers are supported by BBSS, an advanced wireless network and hand-held computers to communicate information and manage these orders. These systems bring the NYSE closer than ever to straight-through processing, or a seamless link from the customer to the point of execution and back again.

Protecting the Integrity of the Market

As a self-regulatory organization, the NYSE is responsible for ensuring an equitable market for all investors. This responsibility includes the real-time surveillance of trading and the monitoring of all members and member firms to see that they comply with federal securities law and NYSE rules and requirements.

The NYSE's regulatory standards are the toughest in the world and are designed to protect the interests of the least sophisticated market participants. The market's integrity helps generate the confidence on which the market ultimately depends.

To maintain this integrity, the NYSE dedicates more than one-third of its workforce and more than $80 million annually to fulfilling its vital regulatory function. The NYSE has an unmatched record in examining each year every one of its member firms that deal with the public.

Listing Requirements and Procedures

To go public on the NYSE, a company must meet the world's most stringent standards of size, earnings, share ownership, share distribution, and corporate governance. Other factors are considered, such as certain criteria with respect to outside directors, audit committee composition, voting rights, and related-party transactions. IPOs that qualify for an NYSE listing have the necessary size and shareholder base that warrant an auction market and do not need to rely on a dealer market for liquidity.

For companies organized outside the United States that meet the normal size and earnings yardsticks for NYSE listings, the NYSE provides an alternative set of listing standards and will consider the acceptability of such companies' shares and shareholders on a worldwide basis. (As of October 1998, the NYSE had filed with the SEC to revise its criteria governing U.S. and non-U.S. listings, copies of which can be obtained by contacting the NYSE.)

Companies seeking to list concurrent with their IPOs must meet all listing standards. However, with respect to the number of shares, the market value of shares, and the number of shareholders, the NYSE will accept an undertaking from the company's underwriter that the offering will meet or exceed NYSE standards.

The first step toward listing (see Exhibit B.2) is the confidential review

EXHIBIT B.2.   New York Stock Exchange listing timetable.

The following serves as an outline of steps to be taken and as a guideline for determining the time involved in effecting an original listing on the New York Stock Exchange. The NYSE will work closely with the corporation throughout the process to ensure that the listing is accomplished in a timely and efficient fashion.

Step 1. Confidential eligibility review is requested by listing candidate. The process begins on receipt of a complete eligibility package.

Step 2. The company receives verbal and written communication from the NYSE as to its eligibility clearance and any conditions of listing that might exist. The company may file its application on receipt of clearance or at any time within six months of clearance.

Step 3. The listing candidate files an original listing application at any time within the six month period following eligibility clearance. Acknowledgment of such will appear in the NYSE Weekly Bulletin the first Friday following receipt of the application.

Step 4. NYSE authorization of listing (recognizing receipt of all critical documentation) and certification to the SEC of such authorization takes place.

Step 5. The company's securities are admitted to trading. The original listing date is established at the company's convenience and can be set for a day any time after effectiveness of registration under the Securities Exchange Act of 1934.

---

of eligibility performed at the request of the listing candidate. This review is without cost and does not reflect a commitment to list. To facilitate a confidential review of eligibility, companies should submit their corporate charter and bylaws and a draft prospectus or registration statement, including financial statements. The NYSE recognizes that each IPO has its specific individual timing requirements and will work closely with listing candidates and their advisors to meet their needs. (See Exhibit B.3.)

On completion of the review, the NYSE will provide the company with both verbal and written communications relating its official listing status and itemizing conditions, if any, that would need to be satisfied in order to list. Assuming no significant change in the status of the company, clearance is effective for six months.

EXHIBIT B.3. Fee comparison: major U.S. stock markets.

Number of Shares	Nasdaq National Market	NYSE	Amex
<1 million	$34,525	$ 51,550	$10,000
1+ to 2 million	38,750	51,550 to 66,300	15,000
2+ to 3 million	48,750	66,300 to 73,700	20,000
3+ to 4 million	53,750	73,700 to 81,100	22,500
4+ to 5 million	60,000	81,100 to 84,600	25,000
5+ to 6 million	63,725	84,600 to 88,100	27,500
6+ to 7 million	66,875	88,100 to 91,600	30,000
7+ to 8 million	69,375	91,600 to 95,100	32,500
8+ to 9 million	72,875	95,100 to 98,600	35,000
9+ to 10 million	75,625	98,600 to 102,100	37,500
10+ to 11 million	78,875	102,100 to 105,600	42,500
11+ to 12 million	81,625	105,600 to 109,100	42,500
12+ to 13 million	84,875	109,100 to 112,600	42,500
13+ to 14 million	87,000	112,600 to 116,100	42,500
14+ to 15 million	88,500	116,100 to 119,600	42,500
15+ to 16 million	90,500	119,600 to 123,100	50,000
16+ to 20 million	95,000	123,100 to 137,100	50,000
20+ to 25 million	95,000	137,100 to 154,600	50,000
25+ to 50 million	95,000	154,600 to 242,100	50,000
50+ to 75 million	95,000	242,100 to 329,600	50,000
75+ to 100 million	95,000	329,600 to 417,100	50,000
100+ to 125 million	95,000	417,100 to 504,600	50,000
> 125 million	95,000	504,600+	50,000

CHOOSING A MARKET

For a company considering an IPO, selecting a securities market is as important as selecting the right investment banker, law firm, or accounting firm. This decision should be given much thought, taking into account the company's responsibilities to its future shareholders and the board of directors' and management's potential ability to fulfill them. Each of the following securities markets may be contacted for additional information:

The American Stock Exchange, Inc.
c/o The Nasdaq-Amex Market Group
86 Trinity Place
New York, NY 10006
(212) 306-1290

Boston Stock Exchange
One Boston Place
Boston, MA 02108
(617) 723-9500

Chicago Stock Exchange, Inc.
440 S. LaSalle Street
Chicago, IL 60605
(312) 663-2618

The Cincinnati Stock Exchange
49 E. Fourth Street, Suite 205
Cincinnati, OH 45202
(513) 786-8803

The Nasdaq Stock Market, Inc.
c/o The Nasdaq-Amex Market Group
1735 K Street, NW
Washington, DC 20006-1506
(202) 496-2500

New York Stock Exchange
11 Wall Street
New York, NY 10005
(212) 656-2017

Pacific Stock Exchange, Inc.
301 Pine Street
San Francisco, CA 94104
(415) 393-4198

Philadelphia Stock Exchange, Inc.
Philadelphia Stock Exchange Building
1900 Market Street
Philadelphia, PA 19103
(215) 496-5200

REGISTRATION EXEMPTIONS AND RESALE RESTRICTIONS

Securities laws require that an offering of securities be registered unless a specific exemption from registration is available for a particular offering. If no exemptions are available, a company seeking to offer its securities must register them under the Securities Act of 1933 (the 1933 Act) by filing a registration statement and obtaining clearance from the Securities and Exchange Commission (SEC) before selling those securities. A company also must satisfy the securities laws of any state in which securities are offered (for example, state Blue Sky laws are discussed under State Security Laws in Chapter 8).

The most commonly used exemptions from federal registration requirements are the "private placements" and "limited offering" exemptions provided for by the 1933 Act. Regulations A and D of the 1933 Act set forth the SEC's rules governing eligibility and the conditions attached to those exemptions. Other federal registration exemptions include private placements under 1933 Act Section 4(6) and intrastate offerings (Rule 147, "safe harbor").[1] These exemptions and Regulation A have not been as commonly used as Regulation D. The rules and restrictions applicable to each these federal exemptions are summarized in this appendix. Your attorneys will advise you on which registration exemption(s) may be available to your company.

---

[1]There are other exemptions under the federal securities laws (e.g., Regulation S, Section 4(2), Rule 701) that are not covered in this appendix. Check with your securities counsel on the possible availability of other exemptions.

Generally, when a company sells securities in a private placement transaction, the securities are *restricted securities*. The purchasers generally cannot publicly resell them unless they are subsequently registered *or* unless the purchaser holds them for a period of time. The length of the "holding periods" varies depending on several factors. For certain types of transactions, the holding periods are specified in Rule 144. Many companies take advantage of a special safe harbor exemption for *resales* of restricted securities to "qualified institutional buyers." This appendix describes the Rule 144 holding period restrictions and the special exemption for resales under Rule 144A. Exhibit C.1 highlights the significant provisions and restrictions that apply to the principal federal registration exemptions discussed in this appendix. It should be read in conjunction with the discussion in this appendix.

REGULATION A

Regulation A provides an exemption from registration for certain offerings of up to $5 million in a 12-month period. Regulation A imposes no restrictions on the number or the qualification of investors or on resale of the securities if the issuer has had net income from continuing operations in at least one of its past two fiscal years. The use of the Regulation A exemption does not in itself trigger periodic reporting obligations under the 1934 Act.

Why Regulation A?

In general, the SEC does not permit a company to solicit an offer of any kind until it files a registration statement. But, as we discussed in Chapter 8, a public offering is expensive. And even though a significant part of the costs (underwriting discounts and commissions) is not paid unless the offering is successful, the part of the costs that is incurred well before the closing is substantial. A company that starts a public offering but then finds insufficient investor interests will have incurred many costs and will have put a great deal of work into a losing effort.

Regulation A reduces the downside risks of a public offering by allowing a company to make offers to sell securities before filing a registration statement with the SEC. Under the Regulation A exemption, the SEC permits companies to "test the waters" for potential public interest

EXHIBIT C.1. Registration exemptions and resale restrictions.

	Private and Limited Offerings under Regulation D			Private Placements Section 4(6)	Intrastate Offerings Rule 147	Unregistered Public Offerings Regulation A
	Rule 504	Rule 505	Rule 506			
Dollar limit	$1 million in any 12-month period.	$5 million in any 12-month period.	None	$5 million	None	$5 million in any 12-month period.[a]
Limit on number of purchasers	No	35 nonaccredited, unlimited accredited.	35 nonaccredited, unlimited accredited.	No	No	No
Qualification for purchasers	No	No	Nonaccredited must be sophisticated.	All must be accredited.	All must be registrants of a single state.	No
Qualifications of issuers	Not available for investment companies, blank check companies, or public companies.	Not available for investment companies or those disqualified by bad-boy provisions.	No	No	Must be resident in and do business in same state as purchasers.	U.S. and Canadian companies. Not available for public companies, blank check companies, investment companies,

						sale of oil and gas or mineral rights, or those companies disqualified by bad-boy provisions.
Disclosure requirements	Not specified	Only if one or more nonaccredited purchasers.	Only if one or more nonaccredited purchasers.	Not specified	Not specified	Yes
Financial statement requirements	Not specified	Period varies for audited statements.	Period varies for audited statements.	Not specified	Not specified	Two years of unaudited statements.
General solicitation and advertising prohibited	No	Yes	Yes	Yes	No	No
Resale restrictions	No	Yes	Yes	Yes	Yes	Yes[b]

[a] The $5 million limit includes up to $1.5 million for resale of securities by selling shareholders.
[b] No affiliate resales are permitted unless the issuer has had net income from continuing operations in at least one of its past two fiscal years.

in the company before they incur the costs and spend the time to prepare and file an offering statement with the SEC. Companies are allowed to test the market through oral presentations, as well as through newspaper and media advertisements. All test-the-waters documents and broadcast scripts are required to be submitted to the SEC at the time of their first use. In the case of oral presentations, a copy of the speech or an outline of the presentation should be submitted.

The rules generally do not specify the content of the preoffering materials; thus small business issuers are allowed to include whatever factual information they deem useful to inform potential investors about the company and its business. However, the preoffering is subject to all of the SEC's antifraud provisions.[2] The regulations provide that certain minimum information be included in the preoffering materials, including a brief description of the issuer's business, products, and chief executive officer (CEO). Further, these materials must include language to make it clear that no money is being solicited by the presentation, that no sales can be made nor money accepted until delivery and qualification of the offering statement, and that indications of interest involve no obligation or commitment of any kind.

If, after testing the waters, the company decides not to offer securities for sale, then no further filings or notifications to the SEC are required. However, if there is apparent interest, the company may file a Form 1-A offering statement with the SEC. Once the offering statement is filed with the SEC, the company may no longer distribute or present the test-the-waters materials. In addition, at least 20 calendar days must elapse between the last use of the solicitation of interest document or broadcast and any sale of securities in the Regulation A offering. In the case of a company that determined, based on its testing the waters, that a potential market exists for an amount in excess of the Regulation A limit, the SEC will permit the test-the-waters material to be deemed exempt under certain conditions[3] if the issuer then files a registration statement.

---

[2]Section 10(b) of the Securities and Exchange Act of 1934 (the 1934 Act) and Rule 10b-5 thereunder and Section 17(a) of the Securities Act of 1933 (the 1933 Act) are commonly referred to as the *antifraud provisions*. These provisions make fraudulent activities in connection with the offer or the sale of securities illegal. For example, making false or misleading statements or omitting material facts would be a violation of these laws.

[3]These conditions include allowing 30 calendar days to elapse between the last solicitation of interest (all of which must have been filed with the SEC) and the filing of a registration statement.

Form 1-A

Offering statements under Regulation A are prepared on Form 1-A. The Form 1-A offering circular must be provided to investors at least 48 hours prior to mailing a confirmation of sale. Issuers can choose to provide narrative disclosure required by Part I of Form SB-2 in the offering statement or in the traditional registration disclosure format. Corporate issuers have the option of using a question-and-answer format (the "SCOR form") used in many states, in addition to the aforementioned choices. The circular is similar to a prospectus and must be filed as part of the offering statement. The SEC staff reviews Form 1-A filings and issues comment letters similar to those issued for 1933 Act registration statements. Amendments to the Form 1-A responding to SEC staff comments are filed with the SEC. The offering statement must be "qualified" (as opposed to "effective") prior to the issuer selling securities.

Two years of financial statements must be included in Form 1-A, although no audit requirements are imposed. However, many underwriters and state laws may nevertheless require audited financial statements. If audited financial statements are otherwise required, they are included in the offering circular.

PRIVATE AND LIMITED OFFERINGS UNDER REGULATION D

The SEC adopted Regulation D in 1982. The intent of Regulation D was to make capital markets more easily accessible to small businesses. (Even large public companies can take advantage of Regulation D.) Like other exemptions, Regulation D allows companies to avoid the costly registration requirements applicable to public offerings of securities.

Exemption Rules

The exemptions under Regulation D are commonly referred to by their rule number, as follows:

- *Rule 504—for offerings up to $1 million over a 12-month period.* This exemption is the least restrictive of the exemptions with respect to everything but the amount, which is limited to $1 million during a 12-month period. No restrictions are placed on the number or qualification of investors, and no information requirements are imposed. The exemption is directed at, and is well suited to, a small business seeking to raise a reasonably small amount of capital. It may not be used by investment companies, blank check companies, or reporting companies.

Unlike Rules 505 and 506, an exempt offering under Rule 504 is allowed general advertising and solicitation of investors. In addition, Rule 504 provides for free transferability (no resale restrictions) of securities acquired under Rule 504.

The $1 million offering price limitation is reduced by the amount of any sales of securities sold within the past 12 months in violation of the registration provisions of the 1933 Act or exempt from registration by this rule, Rule 505, or Regulation A.

• *Rule 505—for offerings up to $5 million over a 12-month period.* This exemption increases the amount that may be offered and also imposes some additional restrictions. The exemption is available to all issuers except investment companies and those issuers disqualified because of specified acts of misconduct with respect to the securities laws. These so-called "bad-boy" provisions apply not only to the issuer and its officers, directors, general partners, and major shareholders, but also to the underwriters and their partners, directors, and officers. Whether or not the issuer is aware of a prior disqualifying act of misconduct by one of the aforementioned, the exemption would be unavailable. Therefore, you must exercise extreme care and consult your attorneys to guard against such an event.

The exemption also limits the number of purchasers to 35 nonaccredited investors. However, no limit is placed on the number of accredited investors.[4] Certain related persons may be excluded, and certain other

[4]Accredited investors are defined as those who are or who the issuer reasonably believes are: (1) institutional investors, including banks; (2) savings and loan associations; (3) registered brokers and dealers; (4) insurance companies; (5) registered investment companies; (6) business development companies; (7) investment companies; (8) small business investment companies licensed by the Small Business Administration (SBA); (9) employee benefit plans subject to the Employee Retirement Income Security Act that have either a specified institutional fiduciary, total assets in excess of $5 million, or accredited people making investment decisions; (10) employee benefit plans established by a state or an agency of the state, if such plan's total assets are greater than $5 million; (11) any corporation, business trust, partnership, or certain tax-exempt organizations with total assets in excess of $5 million (not formed to acquire the securities offered); (12) any director, executive officer, or general partner of the issuer; (13) any individual whose net worth or joint net worth with spouse exceeds $1 million at the time

entities may be counted as one purchaser in calculating the number of purchasers.[5]

Unless the securities are sold exclusively to accredited investors, the SEC imposes certain disclosure requirements (see "Information Disclosure Requirements" later in this section). And, as with the Rule 504 exemption, the $5 million offering price limitation for this exemption is reduced by the amount of any sales of securities sold within the past 12 months in violation of the registration provisions of the 1933 Act or exempt from registration by this rule, Rule 504, or Regulation A.

- *Rule 506—for unlimited private placements.* This registration exemption is available to any issuer, including investment companies and reporting companies, and is not subject to bad-boy provisions. It may be used for offerings of any amount.

The number of purchasers is limited to 35 nonaccredited investors, but no limit is placed on the number of accredited investors. However, certain "sophistication" requirements are imposed for nonaccredited investors (in contrast to Rules 504 and 505). Specifically, the issuer must reasonably believe that each nonaccredited investor, either alone or with his purchaser representative, has enough knowledge and experience in financial and business matters to be able to evaluate the merits and risks of the prospective investment. The provision on sophistication relates to purchasers, not necessarily to offerees. Accredited investors are presumed to be sophisticated.

Unless the securities are sold exclusively to accredited investors, companies that make offers under Rule 506 must provide certain infor-

---

of the purchase; (14) any individual who has had income in excess of $200,000 or joint income with spouse in excess of $300,000 in each of the past two years and who reasonably expects such income in the current year; (15) any trust with total assets in excess of $5 million (not formed to acquire the securities offered) directed by a sophisticated investor; and (16) any entity owned entirely by accredited investors. Seek advice from your attorneys on what steps should be taken to support a "reasonable belief" that a prospective investor qualifies as an accredited investor.

[5]For the purposes of the specific exemptions in Rules 505 and 506, accredited investors and certain closely related parties need not be included in calculating the number of purchasers. In other words, an issuer may sell to an unlimited number of accredited investors in addition to the specified number of other purchasers. Also, certain corporations, partnerships, noncontributory employee benefit plans, and other entities may be counted as a single purchaser for this purpose.

mation about the company and the offering to prospective investors (see "Information Disclosure Requirements" later in this section).

General Conditions Applicable to Regulation D Offerings

The availability of Regulation D exemptions does not depend on the size of the company, and the exemptions under Rules 505 and 506 are available only to the issuer of securities and not to its affiliates or others for resale of the issuer's securities. The exemptions are also available for the issuance of securities in connection with a business combination.

The rules provide that certain offerings of the same securities may be considered as a single offering (i.e., "integrated"). Thus, they may be combined in determining whether the amount and numbers of purchasers comply with the exemptive provisions if those offerings are made within six months of the start or the termination of the Regulation D offering.

Other general conditions for the use of Regulation D exemptions under Rules 505 and 506 are that there may be no general solicitation or general advertising in connection with the offering and that the issuer must follow certain procedures to ensure that the securities are not being acquired for public resale. These procedures include exercising reasonable care that a purchaser is not an underwriter or an agent for an underwriter, providing written disclosure of the resale limitations, and including a legend to that effect on the certificate itself.

Finally, any company relying on a Regulation D exemption must file a notice of sales of securities on a Form D. This notice must be filed with the SEC within 15 days of the first sale of securities. Companies must also be prepared to give the SEC, on written request, copies of all information provided to purchasers of the securities. All such information would then become part of the public record.

Information Disclosure Requirements

The disclosure requirements applicable to private placements under Regulation D vary considerably, depending on the size of the offering and whether the company is already a public company.

Generally, unless the securities are sold exclusively to accredited investors, the offering document must include certain financial and nonfinancial information. The information requirements are described in

Rule 502 of Regulation D. All companies using a Rule 505 or Rule 506 exemption are subject to provisions dealing with the rights of nonaccredited investors to receive information furnished to accredited investors and with the right of all purchasers to ask the issuer questions about the offering.

If the securities are sold only to accredited investors under any of the exemptions or if the offering is $1 million or less, the SEC does not require any information to be furnished to investors. State laws and the investors themselves may nevertheless require certain information to be furnished.

Although the SEC does not impose informational disclosure requirements in some registration-exempt circumstances (such as those just noted), companies often decide to issue an offering circular or memorandum. This decision, which should be made in consultation with your attorneys, depends on a variety of factors, including the number of offerees or purchasers, their existing relationship with the issuer, and their degree of investment sophistication. The SEC's antifraud provisions apply equally to registration-exempt offerings and lead many issuers to voluntarily make relevant disclosures as insurance against later charges by disgruntled investors who complain that they were not informed of all material facts.

The information requirements for public companies are the same regardless of the size of the offering or the particular exemption claimed. The rules provide options as to information that must be provided, but such information generally includes publicly available reports and filings (e.g., Forms 10-K, 10-KSB, 10-Q, 10-QSB).

All other companies—including those selling securities for the first time, those selling to one or more nonaccredited investors, and those offering more than $1 million—are subject to specified information requirements based on the size of the offering, as follows:

- **Offerings up to $2 million**—Essentially, the financial information required in Item 310 of Regulation S-B must be provided. However, only the issuer's balance sheet (which must be dated within 120 days of the start of the offering) must be audited.
- **Offerings up to $7.5 million**—The issuer must provide the same financial statement information that would be required if a Form SB-2 were being used, subject to certain exceptions.
- **Offerings over $7.5 million**—In offerings of this size, the issuer must provide the same financial statements as would be required in a registered 1933 Act offering, based upon the registration form the issuer would be eligible to use, subject to certain exceptions.

ACCREDITED-INVESTOR OFFERINGS UP TO $5 MILLION UNDER SECTION 4(6)

Section 4(6) of the 1933 Act exempts from registration any offers and sales of up to $5 million by an issuer if they are made exclusively to accredited investors. This exemption is similar to the Regulation D, Rule 505, limited-offering exemption, and compliance with Rule 505 normally would constitute compliance with Section 4(6).

However, some important differences might make a Section 4(6) accredited-investor offering available to an issuer not able to use a Rule 505 limited-offering exemption. Specifically, Section 4(6) does not contain the bad-boy provisions that could block some issuers' use of Rule 505. And Section 4(6) is available to investment companies, whereas Rule 505 is not. Furthermore, subject to the general integration rules discussed earlier, the $5 million limit on Section 4(6) offerings is not reduced by sales in the previous 12 months under Rules 504 or 505, Regulation A.

Apart from these differences, the provisions of Section 4(6) are similar to those of Rule 505 with respect to accredited-investor offerings. The definition of *accredited investors* is the same, no advertising or general solicitation is allowed, no information requirements are mandated, and similar SEC notification requirements are imposed.

INTRASTATE OFFERINGS—RULE 147

The 1933 Act exempts from registration any security that is offered and sold only to residents of a single state by an issuer that is resident and doing business in such state (the "intrastate exemption"). Through the years, judicial and administrative interpretations of this section have resulted in various ambiguities and abuses of the exemption.

The intrastate exemption is available to all issuers, regardless of size, and without limitations on the amount of the offering or the number or the financial sophistication of purchasers. However, restrictions are imposed to ensure that the exemption is used only for genuinely local offerings. Rule 147 sets forth objective standards for determining whether an issuer is resident in and doing business within the state and whether offerees and purchasers are resident in the state.

An issuer is considered *resident in a state* if it is incorporated or organized in that state or, in the case of general partnerships and other such organizations not organized under any state law, if the principal office is located in that state.

An issuer is deemed to be *doing business in a state* if it derives at least 80 percent of its consolidated gross revenue from that state, has at least 80 percent of its consolidated assets in the state, intends to use (and does use) 80 percent of the net proceeds of the offering in the state, and has its principal office in the state.

Offerees and purchasers are deemed to be *resident in a state* if the company or other business organization has its principal office in that state and if the individuals have their principal residence in the state.

To ensure that the securities "come to rest in the hands of resident investors," the rule also imposes a limitation on resale of the securities. For nine months after the issuer's last sale of the securities, any resale may be made only to other residents of the state. As a precaution against sales and resales made to out-of-state investors, the issuer is required to disclose in writing the limitations on resale and must obtain written representation from each purchaser as to residence. In addition, a legend must be printed on the securities stating that the securities have not been registered and noting the resale limitations.

One of the primary drawbacks of this exemption is the potential exposure to the issuer if even one share is sold, either initially or resold within nine months, to a nonresident of the state. This risk can be substantial, particularly if the offering is anticipated to be widely distributed. Although various precautions are prescribed and other precautions can be taken, the rules of this exemption are absolute: A disqualifying sale can subject the entire offering to potential rescission, regardless of any precautions taken by the issuer.

Rule 147 does not prescribe any informational disclosures. However, the offering is not exempt from the antifraud provisions or applicable state securities laws.

PRIVATE PLACEMENTS AS AN INITIAL STEP TO REGISTRATION

An increasing number of securities (primarily debt) are being issued in private placements in reliance on the Regulation D exemption. Often, the primary purpose for selling the securities in a private placement is to avoid possible delays that can be caused by the SEC review process. In many cases, the issuing company plans to register similar securities with the SEC shortly after the sale, and a provision to that effect is included in the trust indenture or other agreement with the purchasers (i.e., the securities are sold with registration rights). The registered securities are then exchanged for the unregistered securities originally sold. This technique is referred to as a "registered exchange offer" or "*Exxon Capital Exchange Offer*," the later named after a series of no-action letters issued to Exxon Capital Corporation, which enabled the registered exchange technique. In the case of debt securities, the company often faces an interest-rate penalty if it fails to successfully register the securities within the time period specified.

Sometimes, the subsequent registration of securities in the registered exchange offer represents the issuer's initial public offering. The original private placement is sometimes referred to as a "Rule 144A" offering because all of the initial purchasers are "qualified institutional buyers (QIB)."[6] Rule 144A is a registration safe harbor for resales, not an exemption on primary sales of securities by the issuer.

These Rule 144A offerings combined with registration rights have become a very popular way to access institutional markets, particularly for high-yield debt offerings. According to data published by the SEC, 76 percent of the high-yield debt issued in 1997 was issued in Rule 144A transactions. Because of the registration rights (which usually result in the initial unregistered securities being exchanged for registered securities within 150 to 180 days of the initial sale), the liquidity premium associated with these securities is largely non-existent. The institutional markets have come to rely on the control and the flexibility to time the offering using this technique. (However, in Release 33-7606A [November 1998], the SEC proposed to repeal the *Exxon Capital* series of no-action letters that allow companies, both private and public, foreign and domestic, to use this technique. That proposal was a part of a very large and complicated package of reforms to the regulation of securities offerings dubbed the "Aircraft Carrier.")

Special Considerations for Rule 144A Exchange Offers

Even though the private placement offering document used in connection with the initial sale of unregistered securities to QIBs is not a registration statement and is not filed with the SEC, if the issuing company has agreed to a registered exchange offer shortly after the sale, the offering document is ordinarily prepared to substantially comply with SEC rules and regulations. This avoids problems (which could include the rescission of the earlier sale of securities) that could arise if the financial statements or

---

[6]See the Glossary for a definition of *qualified institutional buyers* or QIBs.

other information in the private placement offering document are revised in a subsequent registration statement (typically an exchange offer registration statement).

Companies that use the *Exxon Capital* exchange offer technique carefully consider whether they will be able to comply with all of the applicable disclosure obligations under Regulations S-X and S-K or S-B (as applicable) to ensure that they can consummate the registered exchange offer and to ensure that the QIBs are provided information consistent with the ultimate registration statement. Among the possible pitfalls are the SEC's disclosure requirements applicable to recently completed and probable business acquisitions. These rules, described in Appendix D, may require you to file audited financial statements of the acquired businesses in registration statements, as well as pro forma financial information.

Resale Restrictions for Restricted Securities

The registration exemptions in Regulations A and D apply to the primary offering of securities, that is, to the initial offer and sale of the securities. Privately placed securities (e.g., those offered under a Regulation D exemption) are not registered under the federal securities laws; therefore, they are considered to be "restricted securities" and are subject to resale restrictions. Under the Rule 144 resale restrictions, the subsequent resale of restricted securities generally must be registered unless the seller is *not* deemed to be an underwriter[7] as defined in the 1933 Act and unless the purchaser complies with the holding period restrictions set forth in the rule.

In general, in order to publicly resell unregistered securities without registering them under the 1933 Act, purchasers are required to hold the securities at least two years. However, under Rule 144, purchasers of restricted securities (that are not affiliates of the issuer) may resell *limited* amounts of a particular class of securities after only a one-year holding period. Similar holding-period restrictions apply to securities that are received as consideration in connection with business combinations under Rule 145.

These resale restrictions and holding periods are designed to ensure

---

[7]For this purpose, the term *underwriter* applies broadly to people who participate in the sale or distribution of securities, not just to an investment banker or other party who acts as an underwriter in a registered securities offering.

that the purchaser did not purchase the securities with a view to conducting an unregistered public distribution, which would be a violation of the federal securities laws. Because of these restrictions, privately placed restricted securities are typically sold at a discount to their comparable freely tradable (registered) counterparts.[8]

Rule 144A

Rule 144A is intended to promote a more liquid and efficient institutional resale market for the unregistered securities of U.S. public and private companies, as well as foreign private issuers and foreign governments. Under Rule 144A, securities offerings that are exempt from registration under the Securities Act of 1933 may be sold to purchasers who can immediately resell the restricted securities in a Rule 144A exempt transaction. Accordingly, private placement issues may be originated with the intent that they will trade in the Rule 144A institutional secondary markets. The development of an institutional secondary market for restricted securities is important because it provides a reduction in the liquidity premium in private placements and offers an attractive alternative to public offerings for smaller public and private companies.

Rule 144A provides a safe harbor exemption from the registration requirements of the 1933 Act for resales of restricted securities to qualified institutional buyers. In essence, Rule 144A allows holders of eligible securities to resell the securities to certain large institutional investors who generally are regarded as able to perform their own due diligence and assess investments without the investor protection afforded by the public registration process.

ADVANTAGES AND DISADVANTAGES OF EXEMPT SECURITIES

Many companies that qualify for an exemption from registration choose to proceed with a registered public offering anyway; but for others, an exempt offering may be an attractive alternative, in particular when a

---

[8]As mentioned earlier, Rule 144A effectively created a secondary market for privately placed restricted securities held by QIBs. This secondary market has resulted in substantial reductions in the liquidity premium associated with restricted securities sold into that market.

company is uncertain as to the extent of public investment interest in that company. In fact, some companies may conclude that, in their circumstances, an exempt offering is the only viable way to raise equity capital. Before a decision is made, a company should weigh the advantages and the disadvantages.

Among the many *advantages* of private placements are the following:

- Exempt transactions save time and money as compared to registered offerings. The risk of incurring the costs and the expenses of a registered securities offering and then not being able to complete the offering is a significant deterrent.
- Raising capital in the private markets can enable you to maintain the control and most of the confidentiality you enjoy as the owner/manager of a private company.
- Private placements offer increased flexibility because they can be designed to meet the specific needs of your company.
- Private placements can be used as a stepping stone to going public—they provide an entry to the doorways of institutional investors.
- Disclosure and audit requirements for exempt offerings vary but may be less extensive than for a registered public offering.
- Prior to a registered public offering, some companies use the exemptions to issue shares to employees, friends, and business associates before the public offering price is determined.

Among the *disadvantages* to raising debt or equity through private placements are the following:

- Under some exemptions, restrictions on the subsequent resale of the securities limit the purchasers' ability to resell them.
- Because the securities lack marketability, they do not command the same price as do registered securities. Be prepared to accept a lower price for unregistered equity securities or to pay a higher interest rate for unregistered debt. For debt, you may have to add "kickers" to the mix to attract investors (e.g., warrants, conversion features, and other forms of participations).
- Federal securities laws limit the number and type/qualifications of investors who may purchase the securities and, in some cases, the dollar amount of the offering.
- Generally, you will not achieve the level of publicity that results from a public offering and the enhanced image and credibility that emanates from a public offering.

APPENDIX D

OVERVIEW OF THE SEC AND SEC RULES AND REGULATIONS

THE SECURITIES AND EXCHANGE COMMISSION

The 1929 stock market crash drove investor confidence to never-before-seen-lows. In the wake of the crash, it became apparent that the Blue Sky laws enacted by various states were inadequate in policing interstate investment transactions. To restore investor confidence, Congress enacted the federal securities laws and created the Securities and Exchange Commission (SEC). Those laws are designed to protect investors by requiring public companies to disclose certain financial and nonfinancial information and by prohibiting fraudulent and manipulative practices in the public distribution of securities. The two most important of these laws, the Securities Act of 1933 (the 1933 Act) and the Securities Exchange Act of 1934 (the 1934 Act) are discussed in Chapter 7.

Organization of the SEC

The SEC is an independent federal regulatory agency. Its primary responsibility is to administer the federal securities laws. In addition to regulating the issuers of publicly registered securities, the SEC also regulates firms engaged in the purchase or the sale of securities (broker dealers), people who provide investment advice (investment advisers) and public investment companies. The SEC also functions in an oversight capacity with respect to self-regulated organizations (SROs) such as the National Association of Securities Dealers (NASD) and the stock exchanges. These functions are performed by various offices and divisions within the SEC.

The Commission

The overall responsibility for performing the work of the SEC rests with the commissioners. The Commission is composed of five commissioners who serve staggered five-year terms, with one commissioner designated as the chairman. All of the commissioners are appointed by the President, with the advice and consent of the Senate, for a five-year term. Not more than three commissioners may be members of the same political party. The Commission is headquartered at 450 5th Street, N.W., Washington, D.C. 20549. The Commission interprets the federal securities laws, amends existing rules under the laws, proposes and approves new rules, enforces the laws, disciplines those subject to direct regulation, and oversees other matters related to the administration of the Commission and its staff.

SEC Divisions and Offices

The SEC is assisted by a professional staff of lawyers, accountants, engineers, securities analysts, and examiners who are organized into divisions and offices that report to the commissioners. The divisions and offices of the SEC are as follows:

Divisions

Corporation Finance
Enforcement
Investment Management
Market Regulation

Offices

Administrative and Personnel
  Management
Compliance Inspections and
  Examinations
Equal Employment Opportunity
Executive Director
General Counsel
Operations
Inspector General
Investor Education and
  Assistance
Public Affairs, Policy
  Evaluation and Research
Administrative Law Judges
Chief Accountant
Comptroller
Economic Analysis
Freedom of Information and
  Privacy Act
Information Technology
International Affairs
Legislative Affairs
Municipal Securities
Regional Offices
Secretary

Accounting and auditing matters are addressed primarily by the Office of the Chief Accountant of the SEC and the Division of Corporation Finance.

Office of the Chief Accountant

The Office of the Chief Accountant (OCA) is the Commission's principal adviser on accounting and auditing matters. OCA oversees the accounting standards setting and the profession's self-regulatory organizations. In its oversight function, OCA monitors the Financial Accounting Standards Board (FASB), the Accounting Standards Executive Committee (AcSEC), the Emerging Issues Task Force (EITF), the Auditing Standards Board (ASB), the AICPA's SEC Practice Section (SECPS) Peer Review Committee and the Public Oversight Board.

OCA also advises the Commission on the establishment, expression, and coordination of SEC policy and enforcement concerning auditing standards and accounting principles or practices. OCA is responsible for the preparation of regulations, financial reporting releases, and staff accounting bulletins.

The Chief Accountant is appointed by the Chairman of the SEC. OCA includes permanent staff (a Deputy Chief Accountant, Associate Chief Accountants, and Assistant Chief Accountants), Professional Accounting Fellows (PAFs), and an Academic Fellow.

Division of Corporation Finance

The Division of Corporation Finance (DCF) serves the function of maintaining disclosure standards in connection with the public offering of securities under the 1933 Act. Companies going public work with the staff of this division to get their initial public offering (IPO) registration statements reviewed and cleared before they can be declared effective. DCF also administers the periodic reporting requirements of the 1934 Act (e.g., Forms 10-K, 10-Q, and 8-K and proxy statements) of companies whose securities are traded on exchanges or in the over-the-counter market. The solicitation of proxies is another area of jurisdiction for DCF. One of the principal functions of DCF is to review and to comment on filings made under the 1933 and 1934 acts. Registrants will inherently have greater interaction with DCF because DCF, through the review and comment on filings, affects the accounting and disclosure practices of public companies.

DCF is organized as follows:

Offices of the Division of Corporate Finance

Office of the Director	Office of the Assistant Directors
Office of the Chief Accountant	Office of Chief Counsel
Office of Mergers and Acquisitions	Office of Information and Analysis
Office of EDGAR Policy	Office of International Corporate Finance

The *Office of the Director* is responsible for the overall administration of the Division. Companies making an IPO will interact primarily with the Office of the Assistant Directors and the Office of the Chief Accountant of the Division, and therefore those offices are described here in greater detail:

The *Office of the Assistant Directors* is responsible for the review of the registration statements and periodic reports of corporations filed with the SEC and for the issuance of comment letters (i.e., deficiency letters). Companies are assigned to one of the assistant director offices along industry lines (based on their primary Standard Industrial Classification [SIC] code).

If a company is a new small business issuer, it will generally be assigned to the Office of Small Business. The Office of Small Business serves as the focal point for rule making regarding small business issues and as the SEC's liaison with government and private sector organizations regarding small business issues.

The industries handled by the Assistant Director offices are as follows:

- Health care and insurance.
- Consumer products.
- Computers and office equpment.
- Natural resources.
- Transportation and leisure.
- Manufacturing and construction.
- Financial services.
- Real estate and business services.
- Small business.
- Electronics and machinery.
- Telecommunications.
- Structured finance and new products.

Each Assistant Director is assigned a Special Counsel, who assists with interpretations of legal issues, and two Assistant Chief Accountants, who are responsible for the supervision and review of the staff accountants assigned to the office. Each of the Assistant Director's offices includes six or seven examiners (who are either attorneys or financial analysts) and six or seven staff accountants (sometimes referred to as "Review Accountants").

The *Office of the Chief Accountant of the Division of Corporation Finance* (DCAO, not to be confused with the Office of the Chief Accountant of the SEC previously discussed) is responsible for supervising the accounting activities of the division. On request, DCAO will review the proposed accounting and disclosure of companies that have registered securities with the SEC or that are considering such a registration. DCAO will advise these companies whether their proposed accounting and/or disclosure is consistent with the SEC's rules as well as with the division's interpretations of generally accepted accounting principles (GAAP). DCAO works closely with OCA regarding accounting and disclosure issues. As a general rule, matters relating to specific filings by registrants are handled by the accounting staff of DCF. Questions on accounting issues and auditing matters that involve basic policies of the SEC, questions that relate to auditors' independence or qualifications, or questions that concern new, unusual or controversial accounting issues relating to a registrant's financial statements are referred to OCA.

DCAO is headed by the Chief Accountant of DCF. Reporting to the Chief Accountant are a Deputy Chief Accountant and Associate Accountants (who primarily are responsible for prefiling and other consultations with registrants), Assistant Chief Accountants and Staff Accountants.

Also within the DCF, the Office of the Chief Counsel is responsible for interpretations of the securities laws and regulations. On request, the Office of the Chief Counsel will review the proposed interpretation of the securities laws and regulations by registrants or their legal counsel. The Office of Mergers and Acquisitions is responsible for the processing of tender offers. The Office of International Corporate Finance administers offerings and reporting by foreign private issuers, although it is not directly involved in the review of documents filed by foreign private issuers.

Division of Market Regulation

Market Regulation is responsible for the registration and regulation of broker/dealers and for the oversight of the stock exchanges, national securities associations (SROs) and other participants in the secondary markets (transfer agents). Its work includes the monitoring of the financial responsibility of these entities, of trading and sales practices, and of the policies affecting the operation of the securities markets. In addition, Market Regulation oversees the Securities Investor Protection Corporation and the Municipal Securities Rulemaking Board.

Division of Investment Management

Investment Management monitors and ensures the compliance with regulations regarding the registration, sales practices, and advertising of mutual funds and investment advisers. Its work includes the review of investment company registration statements, proxy statements, and periodic reports.

Division of Enforcement

Enforcement is responsible for the supervision and conduct of all enforcement activities under the federal securities laws. If the Division of Enforcement believes that potential securities violations warrant further investigation, the Commission is consulted before proceeding. The Commission determines whether additional investigation should take place and may issue a formal order of investigation. In situations where an investigation reveals possible criminal action, Enforcement works with the Office of the General Counsel to refer the case to the U.S. Department of Justice with a recommendation for criminal prosecution. Enforcement is composed primarily of attorneys but also includes a group of accountants, headed by the Chief Accountant of the Division of Enforcement. These accountants work with the attorneys in the division to help pursue enforcement cases involving accounting and auditing matters and coordinate with OCA on these matters.

OVERVIEW OF SEC RULES, REGULATIONS, AND OTHER GUIDANCE

The SEC's financial reporting and disclosure requirements are set forth in numerous rules, regulations, and interpretations. The following discussion provides an overview of some of the key rules and regulations.

Regulation S-X

Most of the SEC's financial statement requirements and the rules that govern their form and content are contained in Regulation S-X. Regulation S-X applies to all filings under the 1933 Act, the 1934 Act, the Public Utility Holding Company Act of 1935, and the Investment Company Act of 1940, except for registrants that are eligible to file as small business issuers under Regulation S-B. Small business companies may comply with less onerous requirements set forth in Item 310 of Regulation S-B.

Regulation S-X requires financial statement disclosures beyond those required by GAAP. These additional disclosures may be required in footnotes, schedules, separate financial statements, or summarized financial information. The SEC considers these disclosures necessary for investors' protection.

Regulation S-X Rule 4-01(a) states: "The information required with respect to any statement shall be furnished as a minimum requirement to which shall be added such further material information as is necessary to make the required statements, in the light of the circumstances under which they are made, not misleading." Thus, the SEC regards Regulation S-X as being only a minimum standard.

Regulation S-X is comprised of 12 articles (see Exhibit D.1). Each article is organized into rules that contain the specific S-X disclosure requirements.

Regulation S-K

Regulation S-K sets forth disclosure requirements for the nonfinancial statement portions of (1) registration statements under the 1933 Act; (2) registration statements under Section 12 or other reports under Sections 13 and 15(d) of the 1934 Act; (3) annual reports and proxy and information statements under Section 14 of the 1934 Act; and (4) any other documents required to be filed under the 1934 Act.

Regulation S-K is comprised of nine subparts (see Exhibit D.2). Each subpart is organized into items that contain the specific S-K disclosure requirements.

Regulation S-B

Regulation S-B was adopted in 1992 in an effort to reduce the reporting burden on small business issuers. Regulation S-B rules simplify the initial

EXHIBIT D.1. Regulation S-X articles.

Article	Description of Content
1	**Application of Regulation S-X**—Includes information concerning the application of Regulation S-X and definitions of terms used.
2	**Qualifications of Accountants**—Includes accountant qualifications, such as independence, and contents of accountant's opinion.
3	**General Instructions as to Financial Statements**—Includes general instructions for the presentation of audited balance sheets, statements of income, and statements of cash flows. Further instructions for the form and content of these financial statements are located in another portion of Regulation S-X.
3A	**Consolidated and Combined Financial Statements**—Includes rules for consolidating or combining financial statements, such as majority ownership considerations and the use of different fiscal periods.
4	**Rules of General Application**—Includes requirements for the specific contents of the financial statements and footnotes.
5	**Commercial and Industrial Companies**—Sets forth the specific line items to be included in the balance sheet and income statement, and requires certain financial statement schedules to be filed.
6	**Registered Investment Companies**—Includes financial statement and schedule requirements for registered investment companies (RICs).
6A	**Employee Stock Purchase, Savings, and Similar Plans**—Includes financial statement and schedule requirements for employee stock plans.
7	**Insurance Companies**—Includes financial and schedule requirements for insurance companies.
9	**Bank Holding Companies**—Includes financial statement and schedule requirements for bank holding companies.
10	**Interim Financial Statements**—Includes presentation requirements for interim financial statements. Also indicates when interim data is required, and indicates that interim data does not need to be reviewed by an independent public accountant.
11	**Pro Forma Financial Information**—Includes presentation and preparation requirements. Also includes requirements for the presentation of financial forecasts.
12	**Form and Content of Schedules**—Includes sample schedule formats and instructions for completing each schedule required by Articles 5 through 9.

EXHIBIT D.2. Regulation S-K.

Subpart	Description of Content
100	**Business**—Includes a description of business, property owned, and any legal proceedings involving the registrant.
200	**Securities of the Registrant**—Includes the market price of and dividends on the registrant's common equity and related stockholder matters and a description of registrant's securities.
300	**Financial Information**—Includes selected financial data, supplementary financial information, management's discussion and analysis of financial condition, and results of operations and changes in and disagreements with accountants on accounting and financial disclosure.
400	**Management and Certain Security Holders**—Includes information about directors and executive officers and their compensation, security ownership of management, certain related party transactions, and compliance with Section 16(a) of the Exchange Act (the 1934 Act).
500	**Registration Statement and Prospectus Provisions**—Includes information to be included on the front and the back covers of the prospectus, summary information, risk factors, ratio of earnings to fixed charges, use of proceeds, determination of offering price, dilution, selling security holders, plan of distribution, interest of named experts and counsel, and other expenses of issuance and distribution.
600	**Exhibits**—Includes exhibits to be filed with the various forms in accordance with the Securities Act (the 1933 Act) and Exchange Act (the 1934 Act).
700	**Miscellaneous**—Includes recent sales of unregistered securities and indemnification of directors and officers
800	**List of Industry Guides**—Includes Securities Act and Exchange Act Industry Guides.
900	**Roll-Up Transactions**—Includes disclosure and reporting guidance for roll-up transactions.

and ongoing disclosure and filing requirements for qualifying small businesses. (Regulation S-B is described in more detail in Appendix E.)

Regulation S-T

Regulation S-T, along with the *EDGAR (Electronic Data Gathering and Retrieval) Filer Manual,* governs the electronic submission of documents filed or otherwise submitted to the SEC. Regulation S-T provides guidance on the electronic format of a document and the provisions for filing such electronic document. Virtually all documents processed by the SEC, including correspondence and supplemental information, are required to be submitted electronically.

Financial Reporting Releases (FRRs)

Financial reporting releases (FRRs) contain rules or amendments of existing SEC rules pertaining to accounting, financial reporting, and auditing matters. FRRs have the same authority as Regulation S-X. The *Codification of Financial Reporting Policies* (referred to as "FRC") contains excerpts and commentary from SEC rule-making actions that were originally published in Accounting Series Releases (ASRs), as well as in the FRRs. The FRC is organized into six topics:

- 100—General.
- 200—Annual Financial Statements.
- 300—Interim Reporting.
- 400—Specialized Industries.
- 500—Information Outside the Financial Statements.
- 600—Matters Relating to Independent Accountants.

Staff Accounting Bulletins and Staff Legal Bulletins

Staff accounting bulletins (SABs) and staff legal bulletins (SLBs) are administrative interpretations and practices followed by the SEC staff. They are distinguishable from FRRs in that they are not rules or interpretations of the SEC, nor do they bear official SEC approval. SABs do not have the same authority as FRRs and other SEC rules, but they are considered "Category A" GAAP—so public companies must follow them. SLBs typically address legal and nonfinancial topics such as procedures to be followed when a company requests confidential treatment or must make a certain type of filing.

SEC Guides

From time to time, the SEC has issued industry guides that also must be considered in the preparation of registration statements and periodic reports. The guides that are presently effective for registration statements under the 1933 Act are:

- Guide 2—Disclosure of Oil and Gas Operations.
- Guide 3—Statistical Disclosure by Bank Holding Companies.
- Guide 4—Prospectuses Relating to Interests in Oil and Gas Programs.
- Guide 5—Preparation of Registration Statements Relating to Interests in Real Estate Limited Partnerships.
- Guide 6—Disclosures Concerning Unpaid Claims and Claim Adjustment Expenses of Property-Casualty Insurance Underwriters.
- Guide 7—Description of Property by Issuers Engaged or to Be Engaged in Significant Mining Operations.

Guides 2, 3, 6, and 7 are also applicable to periodic reports filed under the 1934 Act; (Guide 6 under the 1933 Act is the same as Guide 4 under the 1934 Act). Guides are not rules of the SEC, nor are they published as having the SEC's official approval. Like SABs, they represent policies and practices followed by the SEC staff in administering the disclosure requirements of the federal securities laws.

Less Formal SEC Staff Guidance

In addition to SABs and SEC guides, the SEC staff follows numerous, less formalized positions on accounting and disclosure issues that do not carry the same authoritative stature as rules or regulations or even SABs. SEC staff positions are communicated to registrants and their auditors through various sources including: speeches given by SEC Commissioners or staff; no-action letters in response to registrant inquiries; informal discussions; SEC staff training materials (e.g., the *SEC Staff Training Manual*); and SEC staff comment letters on registrant filings.

Some of these materials can be found on the SEC's Internet web site (www.sec.gov). For example, the Division of Corporation Finance periodically publishes a *Manual of Publicly Available Telephone Interpretations*, which contains answers to frequently asked questions about filing requirements and other disclosure requirements. In addition, the SEC staff periodically updates its publication *Current Financial Reporting and Disclosure Issues and Rule-Making Projects* on the web site. You also may find the text of speeches made by SEC Commissioners and staff members at www.sec.gov.

Like SABs, SEC staff positions are not rules or interpretations of the SEC, nor do they bear the SEC's official approval. They represent interpretations and practices followed by the Division of Corporation Finance and the Office of the Chief Accountant in administering the accounting and disclosure requirements of the federal securities laws.

ADDITIONAL FINANCIAL STATEMENT REQUIREMENTS IN IPO REGISTRATION STATEMENTS

As discussed in Chapter 7, in addition to providing the requisite audited and unaudited financial statements of your company in your IPO registration statement, Regulation S-X may require you to provide audited and unaudited financial statements of other companies in the registration statement. Following is an expanded discussion of the important requirements for providing financial statements of predecessors, equity method investees, subsidiaries that guarantee publicly registered debt, acquired businesses (whether recently acquired or probable at the time of the IPO), and recently acquired operating real estate properties.

Predecessor Company Financial Statements

As discussed in Chapter 7, if your present company structure has been in existence for less than two or three years, you may need audited financial statements of your "predecessor"[1] company or companies. This requirement frequently comes into play when your company was recently organized to make an acquisition of one or more established operating companies. One or more of those companies could be considered a predecessor under the SEC's rules.

The determination of whether an acquisition is a predecessor is a matter of judgment—based on whether the acquired business will constitute the main thrust of your business or operations. Although the definition of *predecessor* is very broad, the SEC staff generally does not require you

---

[1]The term *predecessor* is broadly defined in Rule 405 of Regulation C as "a person the major portion of the business and assets of which another person acquired in a single succession, or in a series of related successions in each of which the acquiring person acquired the major portion of the business and the assets of the acquired person."

to designate an acquired business as a predecessor unless your company has succeeded to "substantially all the business or separately identifiable line of business of another entity or group of entities" and your company's own operations prior to the succession are "insignificant relative to the acquired business." Each situation must be evaluated based on its specific facts and circumstances to make this determination.

In addition to audited financial statements, you will need to provide other disclosures about predecessors in your IPO registration statement (e.g., selected financial data, management's discussion and analysis). These disclosures provide information to investors about a significant part of your past operating performance—thereby enabling them to evaluate your historical operating results and to put those results in perspective with your present business.

Financial information about any predecessors may be required for up to five years prior to the date of succession; however, not all of those periods must be audited. Selected financial data for the registrant (or any predecessor) may be unaudited for the two earliest years shown in the table of selected financial data (assuming this is acceptable to your underwriters). In general, only those periods prior to the succession within the past three years (two years for small business issuers) must be audited, but there can be no gaps in audited information. Any interim periods of the predecessor company prior to its acquisition should be audited if the registration statement includes audited financial statements of your company for one or more periods after the acquisition.

Equity Method Investees

The SEC requires that separate financial statements be presented for unconsolidated subsidiaries and equity method investees that individually represent more than 20 percent of consolidated assets or of income for the most recent year (S-X Rule 3-09). Also, if the 20 percent threshold is not met for any single investee, but unconsolidated subsidiaries and equity method investees on a combined basis account for more than 10 percent of consolidated assets or income, summarized financial information or separate financial statements must be presented (S-X Rule 4-08). Small business issuers filing under Regulation S-B need only provide summarized financial information for individual unconsolidated subsidiaries or for equity method investees that exceed 20 percent of consolidated assets or income.

Affiliates—Guarantors and Collateral Pledges

Separate audited financial statements may also be required in registration statements for (1) a guarantor of any class of the registered securities of the registrant and/or (2) any affiliate whose securities constitute a "substantial portion of the collateral" for a class of securities registered. In either of these situations, the facts and circumstances will dictate whether full financial statements, summarized financial information, or only narrative disclosure is required.

Recent and Probable Business Acquisitions

Separate audited financial statements are required for certain businesses that recently have been or probably will be acquired. Depending on how "significant" the acquired "business" is to the consolidated statements, the number of preacquisition periods for which audited financial statements of the target company are required to be presented varies from one to three years. Rule 3-05 of Regulation S-X describes the SEC's requirements for registrants to provide audited financial statements of a business acquired or to be acquired, including acquisition of an interest in a business accounted for under the equity method. Item 310 of Regulation S-B sets forth the requirements for small business issuers. Rule 1-02(w) of Regulation S-X provides guidance in determining the level of significance of a particular acquisition.

These rules, however, do not require you to provide audited financial statements for a significant "acquisition of assets" that does not constitute a "business." Thus, it is important to determine whether a particular acquisition is an acquisition of assets (no audited financial statements required) or a business (preacquisition financial statements required, subject to materiality tests). Following is a summary of some of the key aspects of the rules for acquired business financial statements.

Definition of *Business*.   The SEC staff's interpretation of what is a *business* is very broad. In several cases, the SEC has overruled registrants who believed that separate financial statements were not required because the purchase of a portion of another company's assets did not constitute the acquisition of a business. In one instance, the SEC staff considered the assets constituting a particular production process to be a business because the acquiring company continued to produce the predecessor's product, even though production was moved to a different location and most prior employees and management were not retained.

Rule 11-01(d) of Regulation S-X describes the SEC's interpretation of what constitutes a business. According to the SEC, each situation must "be evaluated in light of the facts and circumstances involved and whether there is sufficient continuity of the acquired entity's operations prior to and after the transactions so that disclosure of prior financial information is material to an understanding of future operations." Although a separate company, subsidiary, or division is usually a business, a lesser component of an entity may also be a business. The SEC believes the following should be considered in making the evaluation:

1. Whether the nature of the revenue-producing activity of the component will remain generally the same after the transaction as before the transaction; *or*
2. Whether any of the following attributes remain with the component after the transaction:
   - Physical facilities.
   - Market distribution system.
   - Customer base.
   - Production techniques.
   - Employee base.
   - Sales force.
   - Operating rights.
   - Trade names.

These guidelines are not all-inclusive, so management must use judgment in this area.

Types of Transactions. The SEC's acquired-business financial statement rules apply to *probable* acquisitions (e.g., a letter of intent has been signed, but the transaction has not closed or conditions precedent to closing have not been satisfied) and to *recently completed* (i.e., within the past three years) acquisitions, and to any group *of related businesses*[2], as follows:

- *Probable acquisitions.* Audited financial statements for businesses that are likely to be acquired (i.e., "probable acquisitions") are required in most registration statements, including IPO registration statements, when the significance of the probable acquisition (or any group of "related" probable acquisitions) exceeds 50 percent. (See information on how to compute "significance" later in this section.) Management

---

[2]*Related businesses* are defined as "businesses under common ownership or common management or whose acquisitions are conditioned on each other or on a single common condition."

must use judgment in identifying probable transactions. The SEC's guidelines are general and are based principally on individual facts and circumstances.

• *Recently completed acquisitions.* For recently completed acquisitions (including any group of "related" businesses) that are significant at the 20 percent level (or higher), audited financial statements of the acquired business or businesses are required in the IPO registration statement, unless the registration statement is declared effective within 74 days of the acquisition date (in which case the financial statements may be omitted).

• *Individually insignificant acquisitions.* Audited financial statements for a majority of individually insignificant (i.e., less than 20 percent) acquisitions consummated since the date of the most recent, year-end balance sheet may be required to be included in the filing if the individually insignificant acquisitions reach 50 percent or more on an aggregate basis. When required, audited financial statements for a majority of the individually insignificant acquisitions must be presented for the most recently completed fiscal year of each acquiree.

In addition, unaudited statements for any interim "stub" periods also must be included in the filing for any probable, recently completed, or individually insignificant acquisition for which audited financial statements are required.

Content of Audited Financial Statements of Acquired Businesses. The accounting and disclosure rules applicable to the separate financial statements of acquired businesses generally are the same as those that apply to the registrant's financial statements, except that the number of years of audited statements of operations and balance sheets (if any) that are required in the IPO registration statement is determined by the level of significance. Also, certain financial statement disclosures (e.g., segment disclosures, earnings per share) and financial statement schedules (as required by Article 12 of Regulation S-X) are not required for acquired businesses if the acquired business is not a public company.

Number of Periods Required. The number of periods of audited financial statements required for acquired businesses (and the acquiree's predecessors, if any) varies depending on the significance of the acquired business or businesses to the registrant. For purposes of this test, acquisitions of "related businesses," as defined, must be treated as a single

EXHIBIT D.3. Audited financial statements required for acquired businesses.

Highest Significance Percentage	Number of Years of Audited Financial Statements Required	
	Regulation S-X Filers	**Regulation S-B Filers**
Less than 20%	None	None
Over 20%, but less than 40%	One year	One year
Over 40%, but less than 50%	Two years	Two years
Over 50%	Statements of income and cash flows for three years and balance sheets for two years*	Two years

*If the acquired business's revenues for its most recently completed fiscal year are less than $25 million, audited statements of income and cash flows for, at most, the two most recently completed fiscal years are required for both S-X and S-B filers.

business combination (i.e., computed on a combined basis). Exhibit D.3 summarizes the number of periods required, based on the level of significance of the target company to the registrant.

The required financial statements include a balance sheet, a statement of income, and a statement of cash flows for the number of periods shown in Exhibit D.3 plus interim periods ended before the date of the acquisition. However, if the registrant's audited balance sheet in the filing reflects the acquisition (i.e., it is as of a date after the acquisition was consummated), the balance sheet of the acquired business can be omitted. Comparable prior interim-period statements of operations and cash flows also are required.

Calculating *Significance*.　Significance is based on the "significant subsidiary" tests in Rule 1-02(w) of Regulation S-X.

1. Asset test.　The percentage of the registrant's proportionate share of the total (historical) assets of the business acquired (or to be acquired) to total consolidated assets as of the end of the most recently completed fiscal year.

2. Investment and advance test.　The percentage of the registrant's investments in and advances to the business acquired (or to be acquired) to total consolidated assets as of the end of the most recently completed fiscal year.

3. *Pooling of interests test.* If the acquisition or proposed acquisition is to be accounted for as a pooling-of-interest, the percentage of common shares exchanged (or to be exchanged) by the registrant to its total common shares outstanding at the date the pooling is initiated.

4. *Income test.* The percentage of the registrant's equity in the income from continuing operations before income taxes, extraordinary items, and the cumulative effect of an accounting change of the business acquired (or to be acquired) to such consolidated income of the registrant. However, if consolidated income for the most recent year is 10 percent less than the average of the past five fiscal years (computed excluding any loss years) and if the registrant did not have a loss in its most recent year, the registrant's five-year average may be used in the test.

The significance test calculations are based on the most recent annual (preacquisition) financial statements of both the registrant and the acquired business.

Alternative Significance Tests for IPOs under SAB 80. In certain circumstances, registrants may elect to comply with the acquired-business financial statement rules by filing audited financial statements of a sufficient number of completed or probable business acquisitions such that the significance (measured by reference to the pro forma registrant at the initial filing date) of businesses for which audited statements are omitted does not exceed 10 percent in the most recent year, 20 percent in the preceding year, and 40 percent in the second preceding year. SAB 80 (Topic 1.J), *Application of Rule 3-05 in Initial Public Offerings,* allows first-time registrants to use pro forma information in their calculations if the company was built through the aggregation of discrete businesses that remain substantially intact after the acquisition.

By allowing registrants to use pro forma information in measuring significance, in some cases, these rules can reduce the number of acquisitions for which audited financial statements are required, the number of audited periods, or both.

Registrants Unable to Comply. Registrants often have difficulty complying with these rules. It often is difficult or impossible to retroactively audit an acquired business, such as when physical inventories were not observed by independent auditors. Also, the SEC's broad interpretation of what constitutes a "business" may necessitate audited financial statements of a component of another company's operations that may not have been accounted for by the former owner as a separate business. Despite the difficulties, the SEC staff rarely will waive the requirements for audited financial statements of significant acquired businesses.

The SEC's rules and administrative positions related to financial statements of acquired businesses can be quite complex. They also are subject to frequent interpretation by the SEC staff. Because disagreements with the SEC staff about whether registrants need audited financial statements (or for how many periods) for a particular acquisition can significantly delay (or stop) an IPO, if a registrant's particular circumstances are complex or otherwise not clearly addressed in the SEC's rules, the registrant should consider consulting with the SEC staff on a prefiling basis.

Operating Real Estate Properties

If your company has acquired one or more operating real estate properties, a special SEC rule (S-X Rule 3-14) may require you to file audited income statements of the acquired properties for one or more periods prior to their acquisition. To determine whether the rule applies, compare the purchase price of the properties acquired (individually and in the aggregate for each reporting period) to your company's consolidated total assets. Then,

• If the purchase price of any individual property exceeds 10 percent of consolidated total assets, you will need an audited income statement of the property for one year (if purchased from an unrelated party and certain specified disclosures are included in the registration statement) or three years (if purchased from a related party).

• If no single acquired property's purchase price exceeds 10%, but the aggregate of all operating properties acquired during the most recent fiscal year exceeds 10 percent, you'll need to file audited income statements of a mathematical majority of the acquired properties for the most recent fiscal year (plus any interim periods ended before the acquisition date).

The income statements required under S-X Rule 3-14 should exclude items that are not comparable to the proposed future operations of the properties (e.g., mortgage interest, depreciation, corporate expenses, income taxes). These statements are sometimes captioned "Statements of Direct Revenues and Direct Expenses."

SIMPLIFIED REGISTRATION UNDER THE SMALL BUSINESS DISCLOSURE SYSTEM

The Securities and Exchange Commission (SEC) has been continually challenged to reduce the regulatory burden placed on smaller businesses and to provide smaller businesses the same access to capital markets as larger enterprises, such as Fortune 500 companies. The goal is to reduce the initial cost of registration and the ongoing expenses of being a public company. In August 1992, the SEC adopted Regulation S-B for small business issuers, which included rules that make it easier for small businesses to raise money in the capital markets. The rules simplify both the initial and the ongoing disclosure and filing requirements for qualifying small businesses (see "Regulation S-B—Eligibility").

Regulation S-B sets forth the financial statement and nonfinancial statement disclosure requirements for small business issuer filings under the 1933 and 1934 Acts. Regulation S-B is intended to simplify the registration and the reporting processes by reducing financial and nonfinancial disclosure requirements and by publishing these requirements in an all-inclusive regulation.

REGULATION S-B—ELIGIBILITY

Under the current rules, to qualify as a "small business issuer" under Regulation S-B, your company must be a U.S. or a Canadian company with annual revenues of less than $25 million for the past fiscal year and public float[1] of less than $25 million.[2] Investment companies are not permitted to use Regulation S-B. Further, if the small business issuer is a majority-owned subsidiary of another company, its parent must also meet the definition of a small business issuer in order for the subsidiary to use Regulation S-B.

Once eligible, a company may continue reporting under the small business integrated disclosure system until it exceeds $25 million in revenue for two consecutive fiscal years or $25 million in public float for two consecutive years. However, if a company exceeds the revenue limit in one year but not the public float limit, and the next year exceeds the public float limit but not the revenue limit, it will still qualify as a small business issuer. If a company exceeded the limits and was not eligible to file under Regulation S-B, the company must meet the definition of a small business issuer for two consecutive fiscal years before it will be eligible to file under Regulation S-B. The SEC adopted this two-year test to avoid the possibility that temporary changes in the level of revenue or public float would force a small business issuer to prematurely enter or exit the small business disclosure system. Continued eligibility to use the small business reporting system will be determined at the beginning of each fiscal year.

SIMPLIFIED REGISTRATION PROCESS

Chapter 8 discusses the registration of initial public offerings (IPOs). Large and medium-sized companies (i.e., those with more than $25 million in revenues or public float) must provide financial and nonfinancial disclosures in their IPO registration statements and in subsequent periodic 1934 Act reports in compliance with Regulations S-X and S-K. Regulation S-B simplifies these registration and reporting rules by cre-

---

[1]*Public float* for purposes of Regulation S-B is defined as "the aggregate market value of the issuer's voting and nonvoting common stock held by nonaffiliates." The public float of a company making an initial public offering of securities is determined based on the number of shares held by nonaffiliates prior to the offering and the estimated public offering price of the securities.

[2]In Release No. 33-7606A (November 1998), the SEC proposed to expand the availability of Regulation S-B by changing the eligibility criteria. If adopted, the proposal would eliminate the public float test and would raise the revenue test from $25 million to $50 million.

ating a level of required disclosure that is somewhat less than that required for larger registrants. Some of the requirements under Regulation S-B differ from the requirements under Regulations S-X and S-K. Following is a summary of the some of the key differences.

Financial Statements

Regulation S-B requires an audited balance sheet as of the end of the most recent fiscal year and audited statements of income, cash flows, and changes in shareholders' equity for each of the two years preceding such audited balance sheet, all prepared in accordance with generally accepted accounting principles (GAAP). Small business issuers need not comply with the more extensive disclosures required by Regulations S-X and S-K (other than those specifically referenced in Regulation S-B).

Financial Statement Schedules

Under Regulation S-B, the registrant is not required to include the financial statement schedules required under Regulation S-X. The elimination of the schedules reduces record keeping and annual report preparation time.

Significant Acquisitions

Regulation S-B, like Regulation S-X, requires audited financial statements for significant acquisitions. *Significance* is defined in terms of the relationship of the target's income and total assets to the registrant's income and total assets, as well as the relationship of the acquisition price to the registrant's total assets. If the highest level of significance exceeds 20 percent but does not exceed 40 percent, one year of audited financial statements is required. If significance exceeds 40 percent, two years of audited financial statements are required. However, unlike Regulation S-X, where up to three years of preacquisition audited financial statements could be required in an IPO registration statement, or in a Form 8-K, small business issuers never need to provide more than two years of audited financial statements for an acquired business.

Nonfinancial Statement Disclosure Requirements

Certain nonfinancial statement disclosure requirements under Regulation S-K, such as executive compensation and description of business, are simplified for small business issuers. Other disclosures, such as selected financial data (S-K Item 301), supplementary financial information (S-K Item 302), and market risk disclosures (S-K Item 305) are not required. Management's discussion and analysis (MD&A) disclosure is required for small business issuers that have had revenue in each of their past two fiscal years; those that have earned no revenues are required to include a description of their business plan (referred to as "plan of operations" in Regulation S-B) in their registration statement. In addition, the disclosure requirements for executive compensation are somewhat streamlined for small business issuers. Small business issuers can choose between two registration forms to register their securities offerings: (1) Form SB-1, for offerings up to $10 million, and (2) Form SB-2, for offerings in unlimited dollar amounts.

1. Form SB-1.   Using this registration statement form, small business issuers may offer up to $10 million worth of securities in any 12-month period. This form allows them to provide information in a question-and-answer format, similar to that used in Form 1-A for Regulation A offerings (see Appendix C). Unlike Regulation A filings, however, Form SB-1 requires audited financial statements.

2. Form SB-2.   Most small business issuers use Form SB-2 instead of Form SB-1 because Form SB-2 allows them to register an unlimited dollar amount of securities. (As a practical matter, however, if a small business issuer sells more than $25 million in common equity securities, its public float will exceed the current eligibility thresholds, and it will no longer be eligible under the small business disclosure system.)

Companies have used both of the small business forms in dramatically increasing numbers since the SEC revised the forms in 1992. The small business rules allow a small business issuer to register debt, preferred stock, common stock, and other securities on one registration statement without specifying the dollar amount of each class of security to be offered.

Regulation S-B does not preclude small business issuers from registering securities on forms intended for use by larger companies, provided they otherwise meet the requirements for use of those forms. If a small business issuer chooses to register securities on one of the forms applicable to larger companies, it may satisfy the narrative and financial disclosure requirements of those forms by complying with the disclosure requirements of Regulation S-B rather than those of Regulations S-X and S-K.

Exhibit E.1 compares the registration statement disclosures applicable to a small issuer (under Regulation S-B) with those applicable to larger companies, which must comply with Regulations S-X and S-K.

AFTER THE CLOSING—PERIODIC REPORTING UNDER REGULATION S-B

Small business issuers file annual reports on Form 10-KSB (instead of Form 10-K) and use Form 10-QSB (instead of Form 10-Q) for quarterly reports. As with small business issuer registration statements, Form 10-KSB requires somewhat less extensive disclosures than those required in Form 10-K. For example, financial statement schedules, market risk disclosures, selected and supplementary financial data, and some executive compensation disclosures applicable to larger companies are not required in Form 10-KSB. Form 10-QSB, on the other hand, requires essentially the same disclosures and financial information as Form 10-Q.

EXHIBIT E.1. IPO registration statement disclosures.

Content	IPO Registration Statement Disclosures	
	Larger Companies	Small Business Issuers
Nonfinancial statement disclosures	Summary information, risk factors, and ratio of earnings to fixed charges (S-K Item 503).	Same, except the ratio of earnings to fixed charges need not be presented (S-B Item 503).
	Use of proceeds; determination of offering price; dilution; selling security holders; plan of distribution; description of securities; interests of named experts and counsel (S-K Items 504-509 and Item 202).	Same (S-B Items 504-509 and Item 202).
	Description of the business (S-K Item 101).	Less extensive (S-B Item 101).
	Description of property (S-K Item 102).	Less extensive (S-B Item 102).
	Legal proceedings (S-K Item 103).	Same (S-B Item 103).
	Market and dividend data (S-K Item 201).	Less extensive (S-B Item 201).
	Market risk disclosures (S-K Item 305).	Not required.
	Management's discussion and analysis (MD&A) of financial condition and results of operations (S-K Item 303 and FRR 36).	Less extensive discussion of operations or plan of operations (S-B Item 303).
	Five-year table of selected financial data and supplementary financial	Not required.

	information (S-K Item 302).	
	Disagreements with auditors on financial and disclosure matters (S-K Item 304).	Same (S-B Item 304).
	Directors and executive officers (S-K Item 401).	Generally the same (S-B Item 401).
	Executive compensation and transactions with management (S-K Items 402 and 404).	Less extensive disclosures (S-B Items 402 and 404).
	Ownership of securities by certain beneficial owners and management (S-K Item 403).	Generally the same (S-B Item 403).
Financial statement requirements	Financial statements must comply with Regulation S-X and GAAP; additional financial statements are required for investees and for significant acquired or to-be-acquired companies.	Financial statements prepared in accordance with Regulation S-B and GAAP; additional financial statements are required for significant acquired or to-be-acquired companies.
Balance sheets	Two years' audited balance sheets, updated by a condensed interim balance sheet as required.	One year's audited balance sheet, updated by a condensed interim balance sheet as required.
Statements of income and cash flows	Three years' audited statements of income and cash flows and reconciliations of other shareholders' equity accounts, updated by comparative condensed interim statements as required.	Two years' audited statements of income and cash flows and reconciliations of other shareholders' equity accounts, updated by comparative condensed interim statements as required.
Financial statement schedules	Financial statements and schedules required by S-X (Article 12).	No schedules.

GLOSSARY

ACCREDITED INVESTORS—Individual or institutional investors who meet the qualifying SEC criteria with respect to financial sophistication or financial assets.

AFTERMARKET—Trading in an issuer's securities once the company has gone public. Aftermarket trading is between third parties and does not involve the issuer.

ALL-HANDS MEETING—A meeting of all the parties involved in preparing the registration statement, including company management, the company's attorneys, auditors, underwriters, and the underwriters' attorneys.

AMERICAN DEPOSITORY RECEIPTS (ADRs)/AMERICAN DEPOSITORY SHARES (ADSs)—Non-U.S. companies that wish to list on a U.S. exchange must abide by the regulatory and reporting standards of the SEC. These securities are called *receipts* because they represent a certain amount of the company's actual shares.

ANALYST—A specialist, often employed by an investment banking firm, who follows certain companies and analyzes their financial statements for the purpose of providing investment advice.

ANNUAL REPORT TO SHAREHOLDERS (ARS)—A report prepared annually by public companies to communicate important financial and nonfinancial information to shareholders and others. The ARS includes audited financial statements, selected and supplementary financial data, Management's Discussion and Analysis (MD&A) of Financial Condition and Results of Operations, a description of the company's business and segments, and information about its common stock and stock price, among other things. The ARS must be delivered to shareholders before the annual meeting of shareholders at which directors are elected.

BAD-BOY PROVISIONS—Provisions that disqualify issuers from using certain registration exemptions if certain individuals involved in the offering have engaged in specified acts of misconduct with respect to the securities laws.

BECOMING EFFECTIVE—The date and the time the SEC declares that the IPO offering is effective and that sales of stock can begin.

BEST-EFFORTS UNDERWRITING—A type of underwriting agreement in which the underwriters only agree to use their best efforts to sell the shares on the issuer's behalf. The underwriters do not commit to purchase any unsold shares. *(See, in contrast, Firm-Commitment Underwriting.)*

BLANK CHECK COMPANY—A company that raises capital to invest in a business opportunity that has not been identified at the time of the offering.

BLUE SKY LAWS—A common term for state securities laws. Blue Sky laws are not uniform across the states and must be complied with in any state in which shares will be offered, not just sold.

BLUE SKY MEMORANDUM—A memorandum, usually prepared by the underwriters' attorneys, that sets forth the various securities law provisions and restrictions applicable to each of the states in which the offering may be made.

BRIDGE FINANCING—Financing obtained by a company expecting to secure permanent financing (e.g., through an initial public offering) within a short time, such as two years.

BRING-DOWN LETTER—The update to the comfort letter issued as a condition of closing an IPO offering. The bring-down letter reaffirms the detailed comfort issued when the offering becomes effective.

BUSINESS—For purposes of determining whether an acquisition constitutes a "business" under Article 11 of Regulation S-X (rather than an acquisition of "assets"), the entity, assets, or operations acquired must be evaluated to determine whether there is sufficient continuity of the acquired entity's operations before and after the acquisition so that disclosure of prior financial information is material to an understanding of future operations. A separate entity, a subsidiary, or a division is ordinarily considered a "business" for SEC reporting and disclosure.

CAPITAL RESOURCES—Generally refers to equity, debt, or off-balance-sheet financing arrangements. One of the requirements of Regulation S-K Item 303, Management's Discussion and Analysis of Financial Condition and Results of Operations, is to discuss the company's material commitments for capital expenditures and the anticipated sources of funds (i.e., capital resources) that are expected to be available to fulfill those needs.

CAPITALIZATION—The company's debt and equity structure.

CERTIFIED PUBLIC ACCOUNTANT—An accountant who has met the requirements of a state law and has been granted a certificate.

CHEAP STOCK—Common stock issued to selected persons (e.g., company insiders and promoters) within one year of a public offering at a price less than the public offering price. (Also applies to stock options, warrants, or other potentially dilutive instruments.)

CLOSING MEETING—The final meeting for the purpose of exchanging company securities for the proceeds of the offering. The closing meeting generally will occur five business days after the commencement of the offering to allow the underwriter sufficient time to collect the proceeds from its customers.

COMFORT LETTER—A letter provided by a company's independent auditors detailing procedures performed at the request of the underwriters. The letter supplements the underwriters' due diligence review.

COMMENT LETTER—A letter from the staff of the SEC describing deficiencies noted in its review of a registration statement. Comment letters request additional information or changes that must be made before the offering can become effective and the shares offered to investors.

COMMON EQUITY SECURITIES—Any class of common stock, or an equity interest, including but not limited to a unit of beneficial interest in a trust or a limited partnership interest.

COMMON STOCK—A certificate that evidences an undivided share of ownership in the equity of a company.

CONSENT—In a securities offering, usually refers to the company's auditors giving their approval for the use of their audit report on prior year's financial statements in a registration statement. Such financial statements cannot be used in a registration statement without the accountant's consent. Thus, the CPAs will update their work to confirm the continuing validity of their audit report.

CONVERTIBLE SECURITIES—Securities that are exchangeable into other securities of a different type or class of the issuer (e.g., convertible debt may be exchanged for shares of the issuer's common stock).

CPA—Certified public accountants.

DEFICIENCY LETTER—*See* Comment Letter.

DILUTION—The effect on prospective purchasers' equity interest caused by a disparity between the public offering price per share and the tangible book value per share immediately preceding the offering.

DIRECT PUBLIC OFFERING—To avoid the expense of lawyers and investment bankers, some companies try to sell their shares directly to the public. These offerings are usually extremely small and highly illiquid.

DISCLOSURE—The conveyance of information about a company, its business, and specific transactions in a document intended to protect the interest of potential investors. One of the underlying premises of the federal securities laws is that investors must have adequate disclosure if they are to make informed investment decisions.

DUE DILIGENCE—The responsibility of those preparing and signing the registration statement to conduct an investigation in order to provide a reasonable basis for their belief that statements made in the registration statement are true and do not omit any material facts. Proper due diligence can help protect these parties from liability in the event they are sued for a faulty offering. The company, on the other hand, has strict liability for errors or omissions in the registration statement.

EDGAR—Electronic data gathering and retrieval.

EFFECTIVE DATE—The date on which the registration statement becomes effective and actual sales of the securities can begin.

EMPLOYEE STOCK OWNERSHIP PLAN (ESOP)—A tax-favored type of employee benefit plan providing a vehicle for employee ownership of a company.

EQUITY SECURITY—Any stock or similar security, certificate of interest or participation in any profit sharing agreement, pre-organization certificate or subscription, transferable share, voting trust certificate or certificate of deposit for an equity security, limited partnership interest, interest in a joint venture, or certificate of interest in a business trust; or any security convertible, with or without consideration into such a security, or carrying any warrant or right to subscribe to purchase such a security; or any such warrant or right; or any put, call, straddle, or other option or privilege of buying such a security from or selling such a security to another without being bound to do so.

EXEMPT OFFERING—An offering that does not need to comply with most of the detailed and time-consuming SEC registration requirements.

Financial Accounting Standards Board (FASB)—The primary private-sector body responsible for establishing accounting standards.

Financial Reporting Releases (FRR)—Releases from the SEC announcing new or revised rules (e.g., amendments to Regulation S-X or S-K and to the various forms) and matters of general accounting and auditing interest.

Firm-Commitment Underwriting—A type of underwriting agreement in which the underwriters agree to purchase all the shares in the offering and to then resell them to the public. Any shares not sold to the public are paid for and held by the underwriters for their own account. (*See,* in contrast, Best-Efforts Underwriting.)

Float—The total number of a public company's outstanding shares held by the general public. For example, if a company offers 10 million shares to the public in an IPO and has 20 million shares outstanding, its float (or public float) is 10 million shares.

Foreign Corrupt Practices Act (FCPA)—Enacted in 1977, the FCPA requires all public companies to maintain adequate accounting records and an adequate system of internal controls, and prohibits certain payments from being made to specified foreign officials and politicians.

Foreign Issuer—Any issuer that is a foreign government, a national of any foreign country, or a corporation or other organization incorporated or organized under the laws of any foreign country. (Not the same as a "foreign private issuer").

Foreign Private Issuer—A foreign company (not a foreign government) that is more than 50 percent owned by persons who are not residents of the United States and that meets other criteria pertaining to the participation by U.S. residents in the management and the location of operating assets.

Form 8-A—An abbreviated form for registration of a class of securities under the 1934 Act.

Form 8-K—A report required to be filed with the SEC when certain material events have occurred.

Form 10-K—The annual report required to be filed with the SEC.

Form **10-KSB**—The annual report to be filed with the SEC by small business issuers electing to file under Regulation S-B.

Form **10-Q**—The quarterly report required to be filed with the SEC.

Form **10-QSB**—The quarterly report required to be filed with the SEC by small business issuers electing to file under Regulation S-B.

Form **S-1**—The most comprehensive registration statement, used by issuers who are not eligible to use any of the abbreviated registration forms.

Form **S-2**—A registration statement used by certain seasoned companies that permits incorporation by reference of the annual report (and other periodic reports, as applicable) and requires delivery of the latest annual report to investors.

Form **S-3**—A registration statement used by certain seasoned companies, which also permits incorporation by reference of the annual report (and other periodic reports as applicable) but which does not require delivery of the latest annual report to investors.

Form **S-4**—An abbreviated registration statement typically used to register securities to be issued in connection with Rule 145 transactions involving certain reclassifications, mergers, consolidations, and transfers of assets; exchange offers for securities of the issuer or another entity; and reoffers or resales of securities registered on the form.

Form **SB-1**—A short-form registration statement that may be utilized by small business issuers for both initial and repeat offerings and for both primary and secondary offerings. May be used to register securities offerings of up to $10 million in any continuous 12-month period, excluding securities registered on Form S-8.

Form **SB-2**—A short-form registration statement that may be utilized by small business issuers for both initial and repeat offerings and for both primary and secondary offerings. It differs from Form SB-1 in that it may be used to register an unlimited dollar amount of securities.

Form **SR**—A report required to be filed periodically with the SEC, during and after an offering, describing the amount of proceeds from the offering to date and the use of the proceeds.

GAAP—Generally accepted accounting principles.

Generally Accepted Accounting Principles (GAAP)—Accounting practices established by recognized standard-setting bodies or through practice.

Green Shoe Option—An overallotment option granted to underwriters that allows them to purchase up to a specified number of additional shares from the company in the event that they sell more shares than allocated to them in the underwriting agreement. The Green Shoe Corporation was the first company to use this technique.

Indication of Interest—An order for a specific amount of stock given to the lead underwriter by an investor interested in buying an IPO. Because most IPOs are oversubscribed, indications of interest are often for more shares than the investor really wants.

Initial Public Offering—A corporation's first offering of stock to the public.

Insiders—Management, directors, and significant stockholders who are privy to information about the operations of a company not known to the general public. Insiders are restricted in the timing and the manner in which they can dispose of shares.

Insider Trading—Trading in a company's securities by company insiders or others with access to nonpublic information about the company.

Intrastate Offerings—An SEC-registration exempt offering made only to residents of the state in which the issuer resides and carries on its business.

Investment Bankers—Specialists who advise companies on available sources of financing and on the optimal time for a public offering of securities, and who often also act as underwriters for a public offering.

IPO—Initial public offering.

Lead Underwriter—The underwriter who manages a securities offering and who acts on behalf of the underwriting syndicate. Traditionally listed on the left on the cover of a prospectus. Also known as *managing underwriter*.

Letter of Intent—A preliminary agreement between the underwriters and a company specifying the terms that will be contained in the actual underwriting agreement. This usually precludes a company's hiring another underwriter and authorizes the underwriters to incur expenses in connection with the proposed offering.

LEVERAGE—The extent to which debt, rather than equity, is used to fund a business. Increasing leverage can increase return on equity, but it also increases the need for cash flow to cover debt amortization.

LEVERAGED BUYOUT—An acquisition of an existing company using a high proportion of debt.

LIMITED OFFERING—Sales of securities exempt from registration pursuant to certain exemptions that limit the size of the offering and the number of purchasers.

LOCK-UP PERIOD—A period of time—usually 180 days—for which insiders are restricted from selling their shares.

MANAGEMENT'S DISCUSSION AND ANALYSIS (MD&A)—Section of an IPO prospectus that provides investors with management's assessment of historical financial information as well as forward-looking information about expectations for the future.

MANAGING UNDERWRITERS—Also known as *lead underwriters*, underwriters who organize the underwriting syndicate and are the primary contact with the company.

MARKET CAPITALIZATION—The total market value of a firm; defined as the product of the company's stock price per share and the total number of shares outstanding.

MARKET MAKERS— The managing underwriters and some or all of the syndicated underwriters who offer to buy shares from or to sell shares to the public at a firm price, helping to sustain financial community interest and providing aftermarket support for a company's shares.

MD&A—Management's discussion and analysis.

MEZZANINE FINANCING—A subordinated debt instrument with warrants to purchase an equity interest. Like venture capital, mezzanine financing generally provides the investor an opportunity to cash out the investment within several years.

NATIONAL ASSOCIATION OF SECURITIES DEALERS (NASD)—An association of U.S. securities brokers and dealers. Among other things, the NASD reviews underwriters' remuneration arrangements for all public offerings to challenge whether they are fair and reasonable.

NATIONAL ASSOCIATION OF SECURITIES DEALERS AND AUTOMATED QUOTATIONS (Nasdaq)—An automated information network that provides price quotations and volume information on securities traded over the counter.

OFFERING CIRCULAR—A disclosure document, similar in content to a registration statement, that is provided to investors for offerings exempt from SEC registration requirements.

OFFERING PRICE—The price at which the IPO is first sold to the public. It is set by the lead underwriter, usually after the close of stock market trading the night before the shares are distributed to IPO buyers.

OFFERING RANGE—An estimated price range for a stock, indicated on the front page of the preliminary prospectus. The range usually has a spread of $2, for example, $18 to $20. However, the ultimate price to the public may be above the range, below the range or within the range, depending on demand and market conditions.

OTC—Over the counter.

OVERSUBSCRIBED—Refers to an IPO in which the underwriter has the ability to sell more shares than it has agreed to buy from the issuer. Underwriters try to achieve this situation and, as a result, exercise the overallotment option to fill those orders, resulting in additional profit for it and additional funds for the company. An oversubscribed offering will usually jump in price once the offering commences trading in the aftermarket.

OVER-THE-COUNTER MARKET—The market for securities not listed on a stock exchange.

PRICE-EARNINGS RATIO—The price of a share of common stock divided by earnings per share.

PRIMARY OFFERING—An offering by a company of previously unissued securities.

PRIVATE PLACEMENT—Sales of securities not involving a public offering and exempt from registration pursuant to certain exemptions.

PROSPECTUS—Part I of the registration statement, used as a selling document by the underwriting syndicate. The prospectus discloses information about the company and the offering and is distributed as a separate document or booklet to prospective investors.

PROXY—A shareholder's written authorization for some other person to represent him or her and to vote at a shareholders' meeting.

PROXY STATEMENT—The information required by the SEC to be given to shareholders by those soliciting shareholder proxies.

PUBLIC FLOAT—The aggregate market value of voting and nonvoting common stock held by nonaffiliates. *See also* Float.

QUALIFIED INSTITUTIONAL BUYER (QIB)—Any of the following entities acting for its own account, or for the accounts of other QIBs, that in the aggregate owns and invests on a discretionary basis at least $100 mixllion in securities of issuers that are not affiliated with the entity: certain insurance companies; any investment company; small business investment company; employee benefit plan; trust fund whose trustee is a bank or trust company; business development company; any organization described in 501(c)(3) of the Internal Revenue Code other than a bank or savings and loan, partnership, Massachusetts or similar business trust; and investment advisor.

RED HERRING—The preliminary prospectus that is distributed to the underwriting syndicate for further distribution to prospective investors. It includes a legend in red ink on the cover stating that the registration statement has not yet become effective.

REGISTRAR AND TRANSFER AGENT—As an agent for the company, issues the securities sold to investors, maintains current records of all shareholders and their addresses, and maintains the records for subsequent transfers of securities on resale.

REGISTRATION STATEMENT—The disclosure document filed with the SEC pursuant to the registration requirements of federal securities laws. The registration statement includes the prospectus and other information required by the SEC.

REGULATION A—SEC rules governing the exemption from registration of certain public offerings of up to $5 million.

REGULATION C—SEC rule prescribing the procedures to be followed in preparing and filing a registration statement (e.g., paper size, numbers of copies).

REGULATION D—SEC rules governing the exemptions from registration for private placements and limited offerings.

REGULATION S-B—SEC rules governing financial- and nonfinancial-statement-related disclosures in both registration statements and periodic reports filed by small business issuers.

REGULATION S-K—SEC rules governing nonfinancial-statement-related disclosures in both registration statements and periodic reports (other than small business issuers).

REGULATION S-X—SEC rules governing the form, content, and periods to be covered in financial statements included in registration statements and periodic reports (other than small business issuers).

RESTRICTED STOCK—Certain shares acquired in a private placement that are subject to resale limitations.

ROAD SHOW—A series of meetings in different cities to allow members of the underwriting syndicate and prospective investors to view presentations usually by a company's CEO and CFO and to ask company management questions relating to the company and the offering.

RULE 144—The rule governing sales of shares by controlling shareholders and holders of restricted stock.

RULE 144A—A non-exclusive safe harbor exemption from the registration requirements of the Securities Act of 1933 (the 1933 Act) for specified resale of restricted securities to QIBs. Securities that are eligible for resale under Rule 144A are generally initially sold by issuers in offerings that are not required to be registered under the 1933 Act.

SAFE HARBOR RULE—Commonly used to describe SEC provisions that protect issuers from possible legal actions if they have made a good faith effort to comply with certain specified requirements.

SEC—Securities and Exchange Commission.

SECONDARY OFFERING—Public offerings subsequent to the IPO of previously issued shares usually held by large investors.

SECURITIES ACT OF 1933 (1933 ACT)—Generally requires that public offerings of securities be registered with the SEC before they may be sold.

SECURITIES AND EXCHANGE COMMISSION (SEC)—The government agency responsible for administration of U.S. federal securities laws, including the 1933 Act and the 1934 Act.

SECURITIES EXCHANGE ACT OF 1934 (1934 ACT)—Regulates securities exchanges and over-the-counter markets. Also, generally requires publicly held companies to file periodic reports with the SEC.

SHORT-SWING PROFITS—Profits realized by specified company insiders on transactions in the company's securities completed within a six-month period, whether or not based on insider information.

SMALL BUSINESS ISSUER—A company incorporated in the United States or Canada that has less than $25 million of revenue and public float (as defined) in the two most recent fiscal years.

STAFF ACCOUNTING BULLETINS (SABs)—Published interpretations and practices followed by the staff of the SEC.

STRATEGIC PARTNERSHIP—A collaboration of a company with a larger, financially stronger company that can provide resources to meet economic and strategic goals. Also known as a *strategic alliance* or a *corporate venture*.

SYNDICATE—The group of underwriters formed to underwrite an IPO. A syndicate might include underwriters who specialize in institutional business as well as retail-oriented firms. The lead underwriter and co-underwriters usually do most of the selling. The syndicate members share in the risk of underwriting the IPO.

TENDER OFFER—An offer, usually in an attempt to gain control of another company, to purchase existing shareholders' securities.

TOMBSTONE AD—A published notice of an offering, generally disclosing only the amount of the offering, the name of the company, a description of the security, the offering price, and the names of the underwriters.

TRANCHE—A French word used to describe segments of the IPO being sold in different countries. A multi-*tranche* distribution is commonly used for large U.S. and foreign IPOs for which there is demand both in the United States and in the foreign country.

TRANSFER AGENT—*See* Registrar and Transfer Agent.

TRANSMITTAL LETTER—Document used to file the registration statement with the SEC. The transmittal letter should call attention to matters of importance or uncertainty to facilitate the SEC's review of the documents. It should also confirm the results or resolutions of any informal conversations held with the SEC staff.

UNDERWRITERS—Firms whose primary function is to purchase securities from a company and sell securities to the investing public includes the managing underwriter and the underwriting syndicate. *See also* Investment Bankers.

UNDERWRITING AGREEMENT—Document that contains the details of the company's arrangements with the underwriters, including the type of underwriting (i.e., best-efforts or firm-commitment), the underwriters' compensation, the offering price, and the number of shares.

VENTURE CAPITAL—High-risk financing, generally in the form of common stock, preferred stock convertible into common stock, or debentures convertible into common stock, often provided to companies not qualifying for other forms of financing. The venture capital investor requires a potential for exceptionally high returns and will structure the investment so that it can be liquidated through an IPO or otherwise, generally within three to seven years.

ABOUT THE AUTHORS

Ernst & Young's **National SEC Practice Group** provides technical support and guidance on current SEC developments to E&Y clients and professionals in the U.S. and abroad. The firm currently serves more than 2,500 SEC registrants and has helped more than 600 companies complete their IPOs in the past five years.

Within Ernst & Young LLP, **The Center for Strategic Transactions®** is a unique, confidential business environment where we help CEOs and upper management look objectively at their business and its growth, ask the tough questions that public and private investors ask, and explore the risks and opportunities of transactions, operational improvements, and strategic enhancements.

Ernst & Young's CST is a convergence of strategy and objective transaction advice. It connects you to the firm's top resources and knowledge leaders—experts in *every aspect* of operations and transactions. It convenes teams of world-class professionals in a candid, high-energy arena to help you execute the right transaction or enhancements at the right time, in the right way, with the right team—and with the follow-through to sustain gains over the long term.

Stephen C. Blowers is a Professional Practice Partner in Ernst & Young's National Professional Practice Group. He served as a Professional Accounting Fellow in the Office of the Chief Accountant at the Securities and Exchange Commission.

Peter H. Griffith is Ernst & Young's National Director of The Center for Strategic Transactions. He is a former Managing Director and Head of the Investment Banking Division at Wedbush Morgan Securities. He served as a member of the Advisory Board to the University of Southern California Entrepreneur Program, and is a past president of both the Los Angeles Venture Capital Association and the Southern California Entrepreneurship Academy.

Thomas L. Milan is the National Director of Accounting and SEC Matters for Ernst & Young's Professional Practice Group. He served as Chairman of the American Institute of Certified Public Accountants' Securities and Exchange Commission Liaison Committee.

INDEX